AF512177

The Writings of
Amitav Ghosh
Exploration of Multiple Worlds

Edited by
P.V. Laxmiprasad

ATLANTIC
PUBLISHERS & DISTRIBUTORS (P) LTD

Published by
ATLANTIC
PUBLISHERS & DISTRIBUTORS (P) LTD
7/22, Ansari Road, Darya Ganj, New Delhi-110002
Phones : +91-11-40775252, 40775214, 23273880, 23275880
Fax : +91-11-23285873
Web : www.atlanticbooks.com
E-mail : orders@atlanticbooks.com

Branch Office
5, Nallathambi Street, Wallajah Road, Chennai-600002
Phones : +91-44-48531784, 28411383
E-mail : chennai@atlanticbooks.com

© 2019 P.V. Laxmiprasad for selection and editorial matter;
the contributors for individual chapters

All rights reserved. No part of this publication may be reproduced, stored in a retrieval system, transmitted or utilized in any form or by any means, electronic, mechanical, photocopying, recording or otherwise, without the prior permission of the copyright owner. Application for such permission should be addressed to the publisher.

Disclaimer

The author and the publisher have taken every effort to the maximum of their skill, expertise and knowledge to provide correct material in the book. Even then if some mistakes persist in the content of the book, the publisher does not take responsibility for the same. The publisher shall have no liability to any person or entity with respect to any loss or damage caused, or alleged to have been caused directly or indirectly, by the information contained in this book.

The publisher has fully tried to follow the copyright law. However, if any work is found to be similar, it is unintentional and the same should not be used as defamatory or to file legal suit against the author/publisher.

If the readers find any mistakes we shall be grateful to them for pointing out those to us so that these can be corrected in the next edition.

All disputes are subject to the jurisdiction of Delhi courts only.

Printed in India at Nice Printing Press, A-33/3A, Site-IV,
Industrial Area, Sahibabad, Ghaziabad, U.P.

Preface

Indian English Literature originated as a necessary outcome of the introduction of English education in India under colonial rule. In recent decades, it has attracted interest and attention, both in India and abroad. It is now recognized that Indian English Literature is not only a part of the commonwealth literature but also occupies a great significance in the world literature. Fiction, being the most powerful form of literary expression today, has acquired a decent position in the Indian English Literature. It is generally agreed that the novel is the most suitable literary form for the exploration of experiences and ideas in the context of our time, and Indian English fiction occupies its proper place in the field of literature. M.K. Naik observes that "One of the most notable gifts of English education to India is prose fiction, though India was probably a fountain head of story-telling, the novel as we know today was an importation from the West".

Indisputably, the Indian English novel has gained a unique viability, vibrancy, and vitality, attracting a remarkably wide readership and universal acclaim to which the new novelists have made a positive contribution. A survey on the beginnings of the Indian novel in English shows that the novelists largely wrote either romances or sociological novels. It is after the nationalistic stirrings gained momentum during the independence movement that the novel changed its direction and attention from romances, history, sociology, and culture to politics, revealing a new kind and pattern of awareness and relationship of the individual with the specific of the milieu.

Each age has its own compulsions, tensions, fears, aspirations, and logic, and accordingly finds a genre suitable to it. Even a cursory glance at the history of English Literature would approve it. The sensibility conditioned by the industrial progress had altogether different hopes, wishes, fears, anxieties, feelings, and emotions, and so it found itself authentically reflected in the novel genre. Of all forms of literature, novel perhaps, is driven by the sense of past in the context of political present. The strong traits of the past are reflected in the writings of R.K. Narayan, Mulk Raj Anand, and Raja Rao. The post-independence scenario, more so, feels uprooted and searches for the base to have strong foothold in the Indian origins. For instance, the expatriate writers like Salman Rushdie, Rohinton Mistry, Vikram Seth among others, present a strong case of alienation in their fictional works, and whatever they present is the sense of their past with the country. It was Bengal that led the Indian reception of the novel form and its use for creative endeavours with its writers like Bankim Chandra Chatterjee, Rabindranath Tagore, Sarat Chandra Chatterjee, Bibhutibhushan Bandyopadhyay and others. Writers from other Indian regions—Nirad C. Chaudhuri, K.S. Venkataramani, Romesh Chunder Dutt, Jogendra Singh and the trio—R.K. Narayan, Mulk Raj Anand, and Raja Rao, to name only a few, soon joined the league. All these writers engaged themselves in the art of novel writing, followed the model of English type, for it was easily accessible and practiced by the master colonizers. With colonial complex in operation, the English novel came to be known as the Western novel for us and became the guiding novel for Indian writers, though there were the few like Bankim Chandra and Govardhanram Tripathi, who resisted colonial influence in the ways as different as they themselves were. The novel, primarily, dealt with the middle class or masses. In that sequence, the early Indian fiction in English by Mulk Raj Anand, Manohar Malgonkar, G.V. Desani, and others depict the world, which is ruled, not by individuals or kings, but by masses. The masses in these works—identifiable with certain groups, cities, towns, slums, or colonies—assume the role of the hero or the protagonist. For instance, in Khushwant Singh's *Train to Pakistan*, Juggat

Singh, the protagonist becomes a convincing figure only in the background of the village, Mano Majra, and the community to which he belongs. Place of action and action of protagonist go side by side in the work.

The Indian novel in English thematically before independence preoccupied itself with the subject matters like Indian freedom movement, patriotism, evils of feudalism, and the matters of national concern and social reforms after independence. Then, the writers with socialistic concerns emerged on the scene—Premchand, K. Shivaram Karanth, Yashpal, Ismat Chughtai, Rajinder Singh Bedi, and Qurratulain Hyder. The voice of women novelists urging emancipation in forceful terms has been heard after independence, particularly in the novels of Kamala Markandaya, Kamala Das, Anita Desai, Nayantara Sahgal and Uma Vasudev.

Consequently, a shift from traditionally accepted standards and forms of life to the popular and marginalized forms of life, and fixed literary norms of presentation to altogether new, striking, and wonderful, has resulted in the writings of contemporary Indian writers as well as the writers of Indian diaspora such as V.S. Naipaul, Salman Rushdie, Rohinton Mistry, Arundhati Roy, Kiran Desai, Vikram Seth, Amitav Ghosh, Shashi Tharoor, Jhumpa Lahiri, Aravind Adiga, and others.

However, the Indian novels in English during the recent years, especially in 1980s and 1990s and after, revealed new heights with sudden spurt in creative activities rich in quality and quantity as well. Amazingly, many of these novels have either been awarded or shortlisted for one prize or the other of international repute. Rushdie's *Midnight's Children* showed the way for a new direction to Indian fiction in English with its publication in 1981 and got the Booker Prize of the year, and subsequently, it also won The Best of the Booker. The experimentation and innovation at the levels of language, theme, and style in this novel have been consolidated and extended by many other Indian English novelists in their works.

The Indian writings in English, especially of eighties and nineties, worked to overcome the so-called "colonial hangover", and "Raj syndrome", and the fiction of this period is marked by the experimentation at various levels of language, theme, and technique. For instance, *The Golden Gate* by Vikram Seth explores new avenues of craftsmanship and technical excellence, and Shobhaa De and Firdaus Kanga experiment with the unexplored and even prohibited themes. Other contemporary writers like Salman Rushdie, Amitav Ghosh, Bharati Mukherjee, and Shashi Deshpande, to name only a few, have also captivated the literary scene around the world with their experimental yet gripping creative endeavours of fiction. The mind and milieu projected in the works of these writers are prominently urban and cosmopolitan. Simultaneously, they have added new meanings to their novels in their postmodernist garbs, for instance, a master stroke like that delivered by Rushdie's *The Satanic Verses* became the spotlight of criticism around the world. The works of other authors in English, especially minority writers, have worked hard to lend voice to similar feelings occurring out of similar angst. In fact, their rootlessness or their so-called minority status and threats related to it are vociferated in the expatriate writers like Rohinton Mistry, Meenakshi Mukherjee, Salman Rushdie, Farrukh Dhondy, and other native writers. With the intentions of perennial rule over the Indian Sub-continent's colonies, the British had indigenous plans. One of them, as our history states and though it did not see its heyday, was their game-plan to divide and rule. India was divided into two independent nations. As a result, Partition Literature emerged on the literary scene with writers resorting to these narratives in the form of fiction. It attracted worldwide attention. However, the idea succeeded at the cost of their reign. The Indian subject was almost perennially divided among the majorities and minorities. Artists and writers were very worried to reflect these bitter experiences in their respective genres. Such fiction spoke of the dissection of the country. Selfish designs of individuals and parties were the major focus of writings. Post 1980, Indian English Fiction has become variegated, complex, and thematically diverse and rich. However, the country, which emerges from these works, is quintessentially a tangible, perceptible India, with all its follies and foibles, virtues and wisdom intact as represented by its authors.

Amitav Ghosh has now established himself as one of the significant Indian writers in English. As a prolific writer, Ghosh has not only dealt with a number of issues but also experimented with different styles and conventions. He has been consistently writing novels and non-fictional prose, which have won him acclaim and honors throughout the world. Despite the panoramic scope of his novels, both in terms of the issues and settings, Ghosh has been persistently exploring the issues of identity and its formation in his works. He has combined history with a contemporary vision of a world free from divisions of all sorts. Travel motif has been used to create a neutral space where barriers dissolve, and borders are blurred. Further, Ghosh has made a unique experiment to amalgamate Literature, Science, Philosophy, History, Psychology, Anthropology, and Sociology. As a fiction-historian, he celebrates and explores diversity and hybridity, i.e., both physical and psychological. Major issues that dealt with in his essays range from nuclearization, political crisis in Burma and Cambodia, pre-colonial commerce and trade between India and Africa to religious fundamentalism and anthropology and economics in local communities. His concern is largely with historical movements and events, which are beyond the control of individuals, at the same time concentrating upon the predicament of the individual under such circumstances. *The Writings of Amitav Ghosh: Exploration of Multiple Worlds* is a critical volume consisting of twenty-three essays on the fictional and non-fictional works of Amitav Ghosh, an internationally acclaimed novelist in English. The contributors have explored different dimensions of his works. To begin with, Dr. D. Gnanasekaran has evaluated Amitav Ghosh's *Sea of Poppies* for a brilliant analysis. His paper entitled "Amitav Ghosh's *Sea of Poppies*: A Fictional Metaphor for the Process of Change" traces that the climax of the novel shows the ship in mid sea, fighting a tempest. The real storm, however, is in the minds of those aboard the Ibis, as they watch their dear ones—the convicts and the condemned—move away in search of safer shores. *Sea of Poppies* is, thus, imbued with a deep commitment to human values. Dr. C.A. Assif, through his scholarly paper "Narrativizing History and Historicizing the Narrative: Reading of Amitav Ghosh's *The Hungry Tide*" observes that it unfolded the history of a whole region and its people along with the animals and nature there. Ghosh is innovative is proved by the fact that he has attempted to disclose the hitherto unravelled stories of the people and places. S. Malathy traces out certain elements of post-colonialism and post-modernism in Amitav Ghosh's *The Glass Palace*. The novel *The Glass Palace*, as a masterpiece, represents the recurrent themes of post-colonial and post-modernist novels like absurdity of wars, colonization, quest, dislocation, fragmentation or disintegration of identity process of growing, exile, etc. combined with a fascinating story of a family saga. Prasaja VP has worked on *In an Antique Land* for ethnographic study. Ghosh transports his readers to fresh pastures and new locales, and gives them a plethora of ideas regarding the new land. He portrays the people and culture of the place in minute details through vivid descriptions. He familiarizes the readers with the new foreign culture. With his narrative, he invites the readers to the land of Sphinx. The text acts as the carrier of culture. Dr. P. Premchander is another critic to focus on subaltern voices in the select novels of Amitav Ghosh. According to Dr. Premchander, a close analysis of the novels of Amitav Ghosh is an intellectual experience, because they discuss social, cultural, and subaltern issues, and try to voice them. They provide the readers with many ideas and valuable inputs. They help the readers in understanding history in the right way.

Voicing the subaltern by Amitav Ghosh gives confidence to the underlings of the contemporary society and boosts up their morale. S. Mohan Raj, a research scholar, has studied characterization in the novels of Amitav Ghosh. Through the characterisation, Amitav Ghosh makes touching comments on the lives of people of old generation of the subcontinent, who have lost their spaces—literal, emotional, and spiritual—because of the partition. Dr. R. Karthika Devi has studied the colonial impact from the novel *Sea of Poppies*. She writes that the whole novel moves fast with the movement of the characters from one country to another above the sea waves on the ship, *Ibis*. This transfer from place to place or migration causes not only agony, sense of alienation, and identity crisis but also leads to the emergence of a multicultural society in which new diaspora blooms in a new world in the multicultural society; not only the natives adopted and assimilated the western culture or became uncultured but also the westerners accepted Indian way of living and learnt the Indian language. They suffered, struggled, and survived, and whether they gain or lose would be discussed in *River of Smoke* and *Flood of Fire*. Dr. S. Barathi deals with food as metaphor in Ghosh's *In an Antique Land*. Throughout the book, Ghosh discusses the cultural issues and food, right from the beginning. Like the Indians, he mentions that the Egyptians too offer tea and biscuits to their guests. Though there are differences in the method of cooking and spices used, the writer has relished all the dishes, which are reflected in this work. Further, food shows the acceptance of one's culture, where the writer gets adapted to the Egyptian foods while in Egypt. Dr. Charles Joseph has studied *The Shadow Lines* for Inclusion and Exclusion. He observes that post-colonialism is an academic discipline that analyzes, explains, and responds to the cultural legacy of colonialism and imperialism. Post-colonialism speaks about the human consequences of external control and economic exploitation of the native people and its lands. Drawing from postmodern schools of thought, postcolonial studies analyse the politics of knowledge (creation, control, and distribution) by examining the functional relations of social and political power that sustain colonialism and neo-colonialism. The depiction of imperial regime demarks the social, political, and cultural ambit of the colonizer with reference to the colonized. As a genre of contemporary history, post-colonialism questions and reinvents the manner in which a culture is being viewed and challenges the narratives expounded during the colonial era. Dr. N. Asharudeen is another critic to study the history and influence in the select novels of Amitav Ghosh. He evaluates that Amitav Ghosh's novels *The Circle of Reason*, *The Shadow Lines*, and *The Glass Palace* deal with the experience of displacement; trauma and nostalgia play a vital role in determining and shaping the characters to different intolerable situations. Dr. X. Anita Arul highlighted the element of marginalization in Amitav Ghosh's *Sea of Poppies*. According to her, marginalisation and uncertainty are quite unavoidable in a place of colonial set up. Those marginalised people are in an unimportant position. Their identity is crushed to the core. They are pushed to the least floor. They are away from the benefits provided to the other groups. They cannot climb up easily the socially-upward ladder. All these deprived sections joined hands to create a feel of oneness under the sky in 'Ibis' and they come out with their multiple aspects including intolerance and acceptance. Prasaja VP has dealt with post-modern historiography in *The Glass Palace*. She concludes that Ghosh proves his mettle as a postmodern historian by re-reading and re-interpreting history, and giving subalterns a prime place in the pages of his books and thereby in the annals of history. Gobinda Sahoo is another critic to study the novel *The Shadow Lines*. He evaluates that in spite of being separated by national borders, the people of Calcutta and Dhaka follow and observe the same culture. Though, both these cities are geographically separated as parts of different countries, they are bound in the narrator's consciousness through common suffering. *The Shadow Lines* becomes one of the notable creations of postcolonial literature and finds its place along with the novels *Train to Pakistan* by Khushwant Singh and *Final Solutions* by Mahesh Dattani. Palakurthy Dinakar through his paper on *The Hungry Tide* finds that Amitav Ghosh provides enough material to read subaltern history as a counter discourse to national identity. He challenges the social stigma and hegemonic society, and fights for the rights of the subaltern people. His ideas try to dethrone the considerations of the canonised opinion foisted by colonial rules. He considers that migration and dislocation are the results of the colonials and a curse to the oppressed people, who can be named as subalterns. Amitav asks the validity of borders on the earth, which divide the people into two groups—native and subalterns, through his works. He raises his voice in support of the subalterns, who are often pushed forcibly to the margin and are made marginalized sections of the society. His concern for the subalterns is noteworthy in the novel. He represented the plight of Sundarbans' refugees as the representative for the dislocated people across the globe. He described the native and the police as 'the hungry tide' who are ready to devour the small creatures on the shore. Anju S. Nair has evaluated *Sea of Poppies* for introspective narrative. She writes that Amitav Ghosh leaves the readers speculating about the fate of those left in the ship and those who had left in the boat. It is a deliberate and ambiguous ending. In fact, the novel does not have an end. On the other hand, the ending of the novel/writing begins the events. In metafiction, it is precisely the fulfillment as well as the non-fulfillment of generic expectations that provide both familiarity and the starting point for innovation. Metafictional writers assert that although literary fiction is only a verbal reality, it constructs through language an imaginative world that has, within its own terms, a full referential status as an alternative to the world we live in. Lingaraj Patra has dealt with transcultural travel. He writes that travelling is a predominant theme in the novels of Amitav Ghosh. His characters keep on moving and crossing the boundaries in order to explore new possibilities of truth and fulfillment in an alien land. In the novel *In an Antique Land*, Ben Yiju and Bomma travel during the medieval period. Nabeel and Ismail travel from Egypt to other Arab countries to seek better financial stability in the modern times. The writer himself is a traveller in the novel and travels to Egypt in 1980, 1988 and 1990 for his field work of doctoral research. Travel in the novel is a symbol of quest and discovery and the narrator having an extraordinary sense of history and place, has shown his deep interest in exploring the transcultural diversities in a socio-cultural backdrop of the societies of two centuries, separated from one another by eight hundred years. S. Jayalakshmi has studied transcultural communication in *The Hungry Tide*. The novel touches upon the conservation issues of dolphins and tigers along with its interest in the history of human settlement in the Sundarbans. Amitav Ghosh indicates that with some amount of will and planning, both the tigers and human beings can be protected. This vision also indicates that the boundaries of lives between species have to be overlooked to develop healthy ecosystem. Dr. S. Karthik Kumar has taken up the eco-critical study in *The Hungry Tide*. According to Dr. Karthik, the novel is under the realm of ecocide, deep ecology, social ecology, environmental, racism, and environmental justice issues. Ghosh portrays the pathetic condition of both the land and its people in the Sundarbans. It is a location where locals and outsiders meet together, share and feel that the ecological degradation is the global concern. The objective of Ghosh is to bring to light the environmental decline in the Sundarbans and to create an awareness to help prepare action plans for the safety of the settlers. *The Hungry Tide* can be considered as a survey on an endangered ecosystem—the Sundarbans in the Bay of Bengal. D. Geraldin has dealt with the concept of "Maximalism" in *The Glass Palace*. Ghosh gets out of the main stream of the story to tell about things that seem to divert the readers from the plot. On one hand, it is interesting to know about many things, authentic or inauthentic, and on the other, it takes time to return to the string of the story and characters. It is well known that the postmodern text, unlike other texts, takes the readers mind, heart, and soul to understand the story in a three dimensional aspect. Thus, the postmodern text gives a holistic stature to the fiction, which is not a mere fiction. Vidya Merlin Varghese has located marring boundaries in *Sea of Poppies*. Cultural differences or cultural divides have augmented the disparity among mankind. Cultural diversity is the salient feature of the Indian subcontinent. Regions are divided or differentiated by the variant cultural patterns. Pre-independent India was known for its distinct cultural divide. Amitav Ghosh's *Sea of Poppies* narrates the historical events of the nineteenth century Calcutta, in the form of an entertaining story mixed with ample ingredients of love, intrigue, colonialism, violence, murder, and adventure. The bulk of events occur upon the ship, *Ibis*, that is en route to Mauritius. The novel is the first amongst the *Ibis* trilogy penned by the author. What makes the novel enthralling is that the writer has artfully charted out the cultural divide and differences of the inmates aboard the ship. The opium trade of the late nineteenth century also provides the backdrop of the tale. The paper entitled "Shifting Contours / Marring Boundaries: A Cultural Reading of Amitav Ghosh's *Sea of Poppies*" has traced out the cultural elements within the text. The cultural reading is an attempt to portray, in the light of Cultural Studies, how boundaries that lead to cultural distinction and distances on land tend to be marred or shifted while on sea. G. Srilatha is another critic to deal with a paradoxical reading of *The Shadow Lines* with special reference to Tha'mma. She has studied the life of Tha'mma. The writer has illustrated how a generation was affected during partition and had led a nostalgic life of the past. Most of the grandmother's vision is nostalgic. Her ancestral home in Dhaka has been occupied by Muslims after the partition. Therefore, when she visits Dhaka after partition she tries to see her birth place, which has changed completely. Paradoxically, she becomes a foreigner in her own birth place. Candy D' Cunha has studied *The Great Derangement* for a brilliant analysis. In "Ecological Degradation in Amitav Ghosh's *The Great Derangement*", Candy observes that Ghosh's work, *The Great Derangement* is an enlightening work as it captivates the minds of the readers to understand the destiny of human if he doesn't change for the better. He tries to draw the minds of the readers to heed to the cry of the earth. Ghosh has mastered the technique of storytelling by making use of his own insights and experiences, which are thought provoking for the human to understand the state of the environmental disaster. Dr. K.V. Raghupathi is an eminent critic who has dealt with Ghosh's travel writings from the study of *In an Antique Land*. He finds the collection having anthropological comparisons which are really integration and thought-provoking. Ghosh has a strong affinity for the places and people he writes about.

In conclusion, I firmly hold that Amitav Ghosh is a faithful chronicler of the contemporary world and has substantially enhanced and enriched our knowledge of buried histories. Language, culture, and society go side by side in Amitav Ghosh's fiction. The tendency of Ghosh to blend the various genres to produce unparalleled works of literature is a literary innovation of which Ghosh is undoubtedly the supreme master. One finds global concerns towards the end of his novels. His novels have opened the universal gates of knowledge and wisdom. That is how he became successful as a writer.

Dr. P.V. Laxmiprasad

Bio-note of Amitav Ghosh

Amitav Ghosh was born in Calcutta on 11 July 1956, and studied at Dehradun, New Delhi, Alexandria, and Oxford. He was awarded a doctorate from Oxford University. He has written for many publications including *The Hindu*, *The New Yorker,* and *Granta,* and taught in universities in both India and the United States.

His first novel, *The Circle of Reason*, set in India and Africa and winner of the 1990 Prix Médicis étranger, was published in 1986. Further novels are *The Shadow Lines* (1988); *The Calcutta Chromosome* (1996), about the search for a genetic strain, which guarantees immortality and winner of the 1997 Arthur C. Clarke Award for the Best Science Fiction; *The Glass Palace* (2000) and *The Hungry Tide* (2004), a saga set in Calcutta and the Bay of Bengal.

His books of non-fiction include three collections of essays: *Dancing in Cambodia, At Large in Burma* (1998); *The Imam and the Indian* (2002), around his experience in Egypt in the early 1980s; and *Incendiary Circumstances: A Chronicle of the Turmoil of Our Times* (2005).

His recent novels form a trilogy: *Sea of Poppies* (2008), an epic saga set just before the Opium Wars, shortlisted for the 2008 Man Booker Prize for Fiction; *River of Smoke* (2011), shortlisted for the 2011 Man Asian Literary Prize; and *Flood of Fire* (2015), which concludes the story. He has also published *The Great Derangement* (2016), a non-fiction book on climate change.

In 2007, Amitav Ghosh was awarded the Padma Shri by the Indian Government, for his distinguished contribution to literature.

Amitav Ghosh's writing deals in the epic themes of travel and diaspora, history and memory, political struggle and communal violence, love and loss, while all the time crossing the generic boundaries between anthropology and art work.

Both his fictional and non-fictional narratives tend to be transnational in sweep, moving restlessly across countries, continents, and oceans. Formidably learned and meticulously researched, there is something equally epic about the scale of scholarship that sits behind each of his books. However, Ghosh never loses sight of the intimate human dimension of things. It is no coincidence that his writing ritually returns to Calcutta (the author's birth place), and for all its global ambition, is thickly accented by the registers and referents of Bengali and South Asian culture.

Ghosh's first novel is typical in this sense. At the centre of *The Circle of Reason* (1986) is Alu, an eight-year-old Bengali boy with a huge head, "curiously uneven, bulging all over with knots and bumps". These bodily deformities, along with the series of coincidences and connections that emerge between Alu's personal life and the political world around him, have led to obvious comparisons with Rushdie's Booker of Bookers, *Midnight's Children*. However, this is in some ways unfortunate as the novel has its own integrity and ambition, from its philosophical exploration of reason to its peripatetic wanderings across South Asia, North Africa, and the Middle East. Ghosh's beautifully written second novel, *The Shadow Lines* (1988), is also reminiscent of Rushdie in terms of its formal experimentations with geography and chronology. However, unlike Rushdie, it is written in an understated, condensed prose that comes close to poetry. The novel deals with the invention of the past and the arbitrariness of partition as it moves between India and the UK, Calcutta and London, the Second World War and present. The title is an allusion to Joseph Conrad's novella, *Heart of Darkness*, and while its precise relationship to Conrad's text is oblique and shadowy, both share a preoccupation with the threshold between East and West, and with the ghostly hauntings of imperial memory. More generally, Ghosh's second novel draws inspiration from diverse modern European and Indian texts from Proust to Tagore, Ford Madox Ford to Satyajit Ray.

Even this sort of promiscuous intertextuality comes to appear tame and provincial within the context of Amitav Ghosh's next work, *In an Antique Land* (1992). Ostensibly a work of non-fiction, the book draws heavily on the author's training in anthropology, but ultimately defies generic pigeon holes. Combining autobiography, fiction, travel writing, and history, *In an Antique Land* is a delicate, vivid, and deeply moving evocation of Egypt since the twelfth century.

The strong emphasis on history, memory, and the past that has by this stage become a trademark of Ghosh's writing is given a fresh twist in his next book, *The Calcutta Chromosome* (1996), a work of science fiction set in the near future. Ghosh's flirtation with the popular genre of the thriller in *The Calcutta Chromosome* marks a radical departure from the various sorts of archive fever and scholarly self-consciousness that readers typically associate with the author. When Antar, an office worker in New York, discovers a discarded ID card, it leads him on an investigative journey to Calcutta at the close of the nineteenth century. However, beneath this thin veneer of pulp, is a novel with as intricate a plot line as anything in Ghosh.

After the pleasurable melodrama of *The Calcutta Chromosome*, *The Glass Palace* (2000) strikes the reader as one of the Ghosh's most subtle and elusive works. Sprawling across three generations of the same family and moving from Burma and Malaya to India and the United States, if this novel has a centre, it is Rajkumar Raha, a shipwrecked sailor boy whose rags to riches story is counterpointed with that of the Burmese royal family. Built on the same sort of formidable research that made *In an Antique Land* a classic, Minna Proctor's review of the novel captures something of the book's vicarious pleasures:

"When you have your final sigh and turn the last page of Amitav Ghosh's new novel, *The Glass Palace*, you feel as if you've travelled for 100 years on foot, through the most distant and lush lands on the globe. *The Glass Palace* is as close as a person tucked cozily into an armchair on a rainy day can get to the rubber plantations of Malaysia, the teak forests of Burma, and the bustling city streets of Rangoon and Singapore, bearing witness to the demise of the Burmese monarchy and the rise and fall of the British Empire. A stately and vibrantly detailed family saga set in south-central Asia against the tumultuous backdrop of the 20th century."

In his next work of fiction, *The Hungry Tide* (2004), Ghosh evokes a shadow line that in certain respects overshadows even that of his second novel. The Sundarbans is a vast area of mangrove forest on the Eastern coast of India, much of it submerged and spreading with little respect for human geography across India and Bangladesh. A borderless, hostile, transitional zone, that is neither land nor water; this enveloped and treacherous landscape forms an unlikely backdrop to this hypnotic tale of adventure and love.

Sea of Poppies (2008) marks the opening of an epic trilogy that combines and extends Ghosh's established interests in the global histories of diaspora, movement, and migration. The novel is set aboard the 'Ibis', an old slaving ship whose crew combines a series of shady figures, mariners, renegades, and castaways in a voyage across the Indian Ocean. Comparing *Sea of Poppies* favourably with both Herman Melville and Joseph Conrad, John Thieme has said that "...if Amitav Ghosh can sustain its brilliance in the two remaining parts, his 'Ibis' trilogy will surely come to be regarded as one of the masterpieces of twenty-first century fiction".

Bibliography

Books

2016 *The Great Derangement: Climate Change and the Unthinkable*

2005 *Incendiary Circumstances: A Chronicle of the Turmoil of Our Times*

2002 *The Imam and the Indian*

1999 *Countdown*

1998 *Dancing in Cambodia, At Large in Burma*

1992 *In an Antique Land*

Novels

2015 *Flood of Fire*

2011 *River of Smoke*

2008 *Sea of Poppies*

2004 *The Hungry Tide*

2000 *The Glass Palace*

1996 *The Calcutta Chromosome*

1988 *The Shadow Lines*

1986 *The Circle of Reason*

Awards

2018 Utah Award in the Environmental Humanities

2014 Honorary Doctorate, University of Puget Sound

2012 Myanmar National Literature Award (*The Glass Palace*, Burmese translation by U Nay Win Myint)

2012 Tagore Literature Award, Sahitya Akademi (*Sea of Poppies*)

2012 Shortlisted Man Booker Asian Prize (*River of Smoke*)

2011 Blue Metropolis International Literary Grand Prix

2010 Doctorate, Honoris Causa, Sorbonne

2010 Dan David Prize

2010 Honorary degree, Queens College, City University of New York

2009 Indiaplaza Golden Quill Popular Vote Award, (*Sea of Poppies*)

2009 Indiaplaza Golden Quill Award for best novel, (*Sea of Poppies*)

2009 Crossword Book Award, for best novel of the year, (*Sea of Poppies*)

2008 Shortlisted, Man Booker Prize, (*Sea of Poppies*)

2007 Asian-American Literary Award for non-fiction (for Incendiary Circumstances)

2007 Grinzane Cavour Prize for lifetime achievement, Turin, Italy

2007 Awarded the Padma Shri by the Government of India

2006 Finalist, Kiriyama Prize, San Francisco (*The Hungry Tide*)

2005 Crossword Book Award, for best novel of the year (*The Hungry Tide*), Mumbai

2001 Grand Prize for Fiction, Frankfurt eBook Award (*The Glass Palace*)

1999 The Pushcart Prize, for ('The March of the Novel through History: The Testimony of my Grandfather's Bookcase')

1999 Nomination for American Society of Magazine Editors Award, for reporting (Countdown)

1996 The Arthur C. Clark Award, (*The Calcutta Chromosome*)

Contents

Preface iii

Bio-note of Amitav Ghosh xiv

Bibliography xviii

Contributors xxiii

1. Amitav Ghosh's *Sea of Poppies:* A Fictional Metaphor for the Process of Change 1
   D. Gnanasekaran
2. Narrativizing History and Historicizing the Narrative: Reading Amitav Ghosh's *The Hungry Tide* 12
   C.A. Assif
3. Impacts of Post-colonialism and Post-modernism in Amitav Ghosh's *The Glass Palace* 23
   S. Malathy
4. Culture Speaks: An Ethnographic Study of Amitav Ghosh's *In an Antique Land* 36
   Prasaja VP
5. Giving Voice to Subaltern in the Select Novels of Amitav Ghosh 45
   P. Premchandar
6. The Art of Characterization in the Select Novels of Amitav Ghosh 55
   S. Mohan Raj

7. The Colonial Impact on the Individual and the Social Lives: A Postcolonial Reading of Amitav Ghosh's *Sea of Poppies* 71
R. Karthika Devi

8. Food as a Metaphor in Amitav Ghosh's *In an Antique Land* 84
S. Barathi

9. Inclusion and Exclusion: A Postcolonial Reading of *The Shadow Lines* 93
Charles Joseph

10. Significance of History and Human Influence in the Select Novels of Amitav Ghosh: A Critical Overview 109
N. Asharudeen

11. Marginalisation and Uncertainty in Amitav Ghosh's *Sea of Poppies* 116
X. Anita Arul

12. Postmodern Historiography: A Study on Amitav Ghosh's *The Glass Palace* 125
Prasaja VP

13. *The Shadow Lines*: A Futuristic Post-colonial Voyage 133
Gobinda Sahoo

14. Amitav Ghosh's *The Hungry Tide:* A Subaltern Narrative 145
Palakurthy Dinakar

15. *Sea of Poppies*: Introspective Narrative 152
Anju S. Nair

16. *In an Antique Land*: A Transcultural Travel Narrative 159
Lingaraj Patra

17. Trans-cultural Communication in Amitav Ghosh's *The Hungry Tide* 167
S. Jayalakshmi

18. Nature vs. Nurture: An Eco Critical Reading of Amitav Ghosh's *The Hungry Tide* 172
S. Karthik Kumar

19. Maximalism in Amitav Ghosh's *The Glass Palace* 181
D. Geraldin

20. Shifting Contours/Marring Boundaries: A Cultural Reading of Amitav Ghosh's *Sea of Poppies* 187
Vidya Merlin Varghese

21. A Paradoxical Reading of *The Shadow Lines* with Reference To Tha'mma 198
G. Srilatha

22. Ecological Degradation in Amitav Ghosh's *The Great Derangement: Climate Change and the Unthinkable* 211
Candy D'Cunha

23. Multiple Narratives in Amitav Ghosh's Travel Writings: A Reading of *In an Antique Land*.......... 221
K.V. Raghupathi

Contributors

D. Gnanasekaran, Professor (Rtd.), PG Dept of English & Research, Kanchi Mamuniwar Government College, Pondicherry. A versatile scholar, he is a master critic on all genres of literature. His outstanding publications are considered to be authoritative contributions to different areas. He is a research supervisor and an adjudicator of theses. Recently, he has published his maiden short story collection in English.

C.A. Assif, Associate Professor and Head, Department of English, MGGAC College, Mahe, UT, Pondicherry. A distinguished teacher and an eminent literary critic, he has scholarly papers to his credit.

S. Malathy, Assistant Professor, Department of English, Tagore Arts College, Pondicherry. She is a regular contributor to journals and anthologies. A master critic, she has written wonderful papers to books.

Prasaja VP, Assistant Professor, Department of English, Sree Ayyappa College for Women, Chunkankadai, Nagercoil, Tamil Nadu. She is an expert critic on Indian Writing in English.

P. Premchander, Assistant Professor, Department of English, Annamalai University, Annamalai Nagar, Chdambaram, Tamil Nadu. He has contributed immensely to journals and books.

S. Mohan Raj, Research Scholar, Department of English, VIT University, Vellore, Tamil Nadu. He is an active scholar and seminarian.

R. Karthika Devi, Assistant Professor, MVM Government Arts College for Women, Dindigul, Tamil Nadu. An eminent critic, she regularly contributes her research papers to different journals and books.

S. Barathi, Assistant Professor, Department of English, Srinivasa Ramanuja Centre, SASTRA Deemed University, Kumbakonam, Tamil Nadu. A serious researcher, she reviews and contributes to books and anthologies She is a bilingual poet, translator and also a reviewer for the journals *Writers Editors Critics* (*WEC*) and *International Journal of Multicultural Literature* (*IJML*). She has co-edited a book with Dr KV Dominic titled *Diasporas and Dilemmas: The Voice of an Exile*, besides she has published numerous research papers in UGC indexed, refereed and SCOPUS journals. At present, she is guiding Ph.D. students and her areas of interest include Indian Writing in English, Diaspora Literature, Religion, Culture and Peace studies, Literary Theory and Translation Studies.

Charles Joseph, Assistant Professor, P.G. Department, Teresian College, Mysore, Karnataka. He has innumerable publications to his credit. He is a regular contributor to journals and anthologies.

N. Asharudeen, Assistant Professor, Department of English, Edayathangudi G.S. Pillay, Arts & Science College, Nagapattinam, Tamil Nadu.

X. Anita Arul, Assistant Professor, Department of English, PMT College, Sankarankovil, Tamil Nadu. A regular contributor, she has published innumerable papers in journals and books.

Gobinda Sahoo, Lecturer in English, Sarbamanagala Degree College, Golamunda, Kalahandi, Odisha. An eminent critic, he has published as many as 65 papers in journals and books. He is acting as the co-editor of *Rock Pebbles*.

Palakurthy Dinakar, Asst. Professor, Dept. of English, Government Degree and PG College, Koratla, Dist.: Jagtial of Telangana

State. He has more than two decades of teaching experience. He was a gold medallist in MA English, has Ph.D. from Kakatiya University and P.G.D.T.E. from EFLU, Hyderabad. He has authored 11 books, edited four books and translated 90 poems, 29 short stories and three booklets. His translated poems have appeared in Central Sahitya Akademi's Indian Literature. He has presented papers in six International and 29 National Seminars and published 45 research articles in edited anthologies and scholarly journals. He has also received best teacher awards from the state government, Lions Club International and teacher organizations.

Anju S. Nair, Assistant Professor, Department of English, Tagore Arts College, Pondicherry. An established critic, she has contributed her papers to journals and books.

Lingaraj Patra, [A bi-lingual poet, critic, editor and a translator, teaches English Language and Literature, Panchayat College, Dharmagarh, Kalahandi, Odisha.]

S. Jayalakshmi, Assistant Professor, Department of English, Sri Parasakthi College for Women, Courtallam, Tamil Nadu.

S. Karthik Kumar, Asst. Professor of English, Annamalai University, Chidambaram, Tamil Nadu. An academician and a serious researcher, he has several publications to his credit on diverse branches of literature. He has published books and presented papers in seminars and conferences.

D. Geraldin, Assistant Professor, Department of English, Idhaya Arts & Science College, Puducherry.

Vidya Merlin Varghese, Assistant Professor, Department of English, Baselius College, Kottayam, Kerala.

G. Srilatha, Reader in English, PB Siddhartha College of Arts and Sciences, Vijayawada. She is an established critic in all forms of literary appreciations. A successful academician, she organizes seminars every year. She writes on all genres of literature.

Candy D'Cunha, Assistant Professor, Department of English, Andhra Loyola Institute of Engineering and Technology, Vijayawada, A.P. She has contributed her research papers in the area of Eco-Literature. She regularly contributes her articles to journals and books. An active academician, she organizes seminars. She has passion for music and social service.

K.V. **Raghupathi,** Senior Asst. Professor, Department of English, School of Humanities and Social Sciences, Central University of Tamil Nadu, Thiruvarur. He is a poet, novelist, reviewer and short-story writer. He has 23 books to his credit. He has published innumerable papers in journals and books. He has successfully organized seminars and workshops at CUTN, Thiruvarur.

1

Amitav Ghosh's *Sea of Poppies*: A Fictional Metaphor for the Process of Change

D. Gnanasekaran

Abstract

Ghosh has an inherent fascination with the cyclical pattern of history and its dissemination in society and culture. In the process of change, there is tension between the process of de-territorialization and that of re-territorialization, the tension never quite dissipates, but is held in a constant delicate balance between a memory of the past and the desire for a change—basically a change in man's condition through an all-embracing exercise for a better and safer one. So, the process of change is inescapably linked with human life. Ghosh tries to overcome the ambivalent nature of complex and dialectical relationship between homelands and the adopted home by situating the characters in the course of a journey by which means they themselves hope to find some possibility of arriving at the transcendental. Ghosh prefers to locate an individual's drama in the general, often uncontrollable, sweep of humanity's destiny and actions. The people aboard the Ibis behave as individuals transcending all man-made barriers and so ultimately begin to realize instinctively that they are just human beings shorn of the unwanted trimmings by proving that fundamentally they are bundles of emotions and feelings, and by raising themselves above the divisions they unfortunately find themselves in at birth. A certain psychological and spiritual change floods over most of the characters on board and the process of change is a much-awaited one in this strife-torn human life, indulging in violence on the grounds of religion, race, nationality, caste, gender, economic status and so on. Life aboard the ship is as stratified and as subject to both cruelty and courage as the occupants have experienced on land, but as the ship heads for new ports in foreign lands revealing new horizons that symbolize new hopes, hopefully, the occupants see it as the only escape from their past and its problems.

Postmodern novelists help to forge and shape a new reality which has strains of the past and the present and looks towards a more satisfying future. They focus mainly on a vision of contradictory, fragmented and indeterminate world. These writers create an 'open' work in which the reader is expected to supply his own connections and provide his own interpretations. They tend to portray feelings of anxiety, the alienation of individuals and the meaninglessness human existence. In life, the only change is constant. The evolution of life on earth has been subject to perennial change. Humans struggle to survive everywhere and especially people on the margins that are weak and oppressed find themselves in predicaments for which they are generally not responsible. They are often led by forces beyond their physical power, cognitive comprehension and logical reasoning. However, they are optimistic and with their stoic attitude, look forward to a change of air in a congenial atmosphere.

We meet such people in Amitav Ghosh's sixth novel, *Sea of Poppies* (2008), the first in his *Ibis* trilogy, which bears the hallmarks of his fiction. He has postmodernist leanings in his outlook on life in general and presents in particular an evocative, scholarly recreation of a historical period that reflects his training as a social anthropologist, who sets his eyes on the cross-section of the society involved in the opium trade. It sees Ghosh painting upon a larger canvas than ever before, with a colourful array of individuals on a triple-masted schooner named the Ibis and epic vision. Ghosh has an inherent fascination with the cyclical pattern of history and its dissemination in society and culture. In the process of change, there is tension between the process of de-territorialization and that of re-territorialization, and the tension never quite dissipates, but is held in a constant delicate balance between a memory of the past and the desire for a change, that is, basically a change in man's condition through an all-embracing exercise for a better and safer one. So, the process of change is inescapably linked with human life.

Amitav Ghosh's novel *Sea of Poppies* is set during the period when the economy of Bengal and poppy fields along the banks of the Ganges were dominated by the East India Company's monopoly of trade in Indian-grown opium, and there are hints of wars of the South China seas to come. The novel takes place at the moment in the late 1830s when shortly after emancipation, the plantations of the Caribbean, Mauritius, and Fiji needed a new labour force, and the system of indentureship came into being, with 'coolies' signing 'girmits' (agreements) to cross the Black Waters. In doing so, they lost both caste and many of the certitudes of their former lives. But at the same time, they brought new diasporic communities into existence. By yoking the freedom of the Chinese people with the presence of the opium drug, Burnham unwittingly lays bare the empty rhetoric of the imperialists whose moral judgment is completely clouded by the vision of mercenary profits.

Ghosh shows these beginnings that take shape during the first part of their voyage to their new lives. The migratory movements animate the pages of Ghosh with his adventurous trip to the colonial past. Apart from all this, it is the panorama of characters whose diaspora encapsulates the vexed colonial history of the East itself that makes *Sea of Poppies* so breathtakingly alive. Ghosh tries to overcome the ambivalent nature of complex and dialectical relationship between homelands and the adopted home by situating the characters in the course of a journey, by which means they themselves hope to find some possibility of arriving at the transcendental.

In the Indian culture and tradition that believes in life as a pilgrimage and a sojourn on earth, diaspora, and by inference 'diasporic journey', becomes an appropriate metaphor for the human condition. Journey entails quest, exploration and suffering before the final process of inner experience of chastening, leading to maturity of vision. The Indian diasporic literature uses the journey of metaphor frequently with philosophic detachment to express the writers' existential angst and nostalgia for the lost home, which in the ultimate analysis becomes analogous to man's quest for eternal home (Bande, 7). With the help of a physical journey here in this novel, Ghosh re-inscribes the psycho-cartography and constructs a space away from the binaries of the centre and periphery.

Amitav Ghosh's novels implicitly suggest the need for coexistence and strong humanitarian ties across cultures, overlooking personal, regional and political considerations. Men and women in his novels begin to question their sense of themselves, conditioned by the events which take place around them, and embark on a journey of discovery of their new identities. His narrative method with his treatment of history weaves delicate connections between different phenomena so that no event becomes absolutely autonomous. This generates the mobility with which history traverses past and present creating an acceptable fluid pattern of time. The novel consists of three parts—"Land", "River" and "Sea". This is the story of the people aboard the Ibis that is bound for Mauritius from the Bay of Bengal. The novel's setting makes an apt symbol for the ebb and flow of history and the uprooting of populations, both of which have come to be seen as 'Ghosh-ian' themes. Furthermore, just as the natural tides of the sea tend to obliterate the sense of permanent divisions between land and sea, Ghosh's characters gradually undergo a transformation and in the process begin to recognize the transient nature of the divisions between individuals—of whatever social class. Ghosh prefers to locate an individual's drama in the general, often uncontrollable, sweep of humanity's destiny and actions.

The Ibis transports indentured labour to British colonies like Mauritius, its cargo men and women from Agrarian Eastern India and Bengal to work on the Caribbean sugar plantations. The indentured migrants will become the equivalent of slaves. When the ship, "a black birder" leaves Calcutta and sets out across the Bay of Bengal, the seas darken and become stormy. As the ship tosses and conditions deteriorate, the ship soon becomes a microcosm for life on land full of tumult and unexpected twists of fate and each person's heart is laid bare. Through Deeti's eyes we see the huge sheds with lofty ceiling and gigantic scales to weigh the raw opium and "bare-bodied men stuck waist-deep in tanks of opium, tramping round and round to soften the sludge. Their eyes were vacant, glazed, and yet somehow they managed to keep moving, as slow as ants in honey, tramping, treading" (*Sea of Poppies*, hereafter abbreviated as *SP*, 97).

The ship Ibis owned by Burnham brothers is a dual metaphor. Deeti, an Indian woman who grows poppies for her livelihood, describes the ship metaphorically: "the prow of the ship tapered into a figurehead with a long bill, like a stork or heron" (*SP*, 8). On the one hand, it is a metaphor for a journey, in this case an unfinished one since the novel ends in the middle of the ocean. On the other, it is a metaphor for fate, in so far as once they are on the ship, the direction in which the passengers move is determined by the movement of the ship and hence it becomes possible to discern who has greater agency and authority within the limits set by history. An intricate saga, *Sea of Poppies* brings together a motley multitude of sailors and stowaways, coolies and convicts, who have embarked on a tumultuous voyage across the Indian Ocean in the midst of opium wars between China and Britain. This panorama of characters, including a mulatto freedman from America, Zachary Reid; a bankrupt Raja, Neel; the erstwhile Raja of Raskhali; a free-spirited French orphan; Paulette Lambert; a widowed tribeswoman; Deeti and other desperate members of society, represents a period of upheaval that caused seismic cultural shifts throughout the world. Ghosh portrays his characters with integrity and dignity. For instance, they all come alive when they are represented by their distinctive voices in the conversation among Zachary, Mr. Doughty and Seran Ali at the unexpected dinner: "Demijohns of French loll-shrub and carboys of iced simkin. And the Kari bat! ... Pishpash and cobbily-mash at the Rascally table" (*SP*, 47).

Deeti is married to an opium addict, Hukam Singh, a crippled worker in the Ghazipur Opium Factory, who treats the drug as his first wife, "You should know, he said at last, that this is my first wife. She's kept me alive since I was wounded; if it weren't for her, I would not be here today. I would have died of pain long ago" (*SP*, 9). Ghosh feels very deeply indeed about emotional victims like Deeti who are forced to exile by events beyond their control. Deeti's family is one of the many that supply opium produce to the British-run opium factory in colonial India. Poppy farming is considered a perfectly legitimate line of agricultural work, especially by the businessmen who find it highly profitable. Forced to cultivate opium as part of the company's colonial policy, she and her rural folk have abandoned centuries-old agricultural traditions. Their land doesn't yield grains or fruits and they have no control over their opium production. As Hawley observes, "Ghosh is fascinated by the interaction of space and time, and his narrator is fascinated throughout the novel with the impact that a particular place—an alleyway, a darkened living room—can have on a particular individual, while others pass it unscathed" (qtd. in Khair, 132). Deeti would appear to be in the latter category, whereas the narrator is very much susceptible to the connotations of place.

Hukam Singh, an *afeemkhor* or opium addict, dies a few days later. Deeti possesses intuitive convictions and courage to declare when Chandan Singh makes advances: "Listen to my words. I will burn on my husband's pyre rather than give myself to you" (*SP*, 158). When she does so, Kalua rescues her from the funeral fire by placing "the platform against the fire, scrambled to the top, and snatched Deeti from the flames" (*SP*, 177). Ghosh portrays her feeling of joy mixed with resignation that "crept into heart, for it was as if she really had died and been delivered betimes in rebirth, to her next life; she had shed the body of the old Deeti, with the burden of its Karma" (*SP*, 178). Deeti having lost her husband and her fields to opium is now joining the migrant aboard the Ibis to escape her fate. She owes her survival to Kalua and sees his shoulder to lean on but he is a low-caste carter of colossal strength. However, fate decides otherwise and she flees downstream to the Ibis with him. Two like-minded souls facing a common human predicament get united here by throwing over board their caste affinities and seeking solace in each other's company. But it is short-lived. The imperial insensitivity is reinforced when the foreman Bhyro Singh seeks permission for sixty lashes of the whip to be inflicted on Kalua for the elopement with Deeti, and his wish is granted forthwith by the British captain of the Ibis, in the full knowledge that Kalua would certainly die before the flogging comes to an end. Now her future is bleak since it has led to another unusual human predicament and she feels like falling out of the frying-pan into the fire: "Is this what you saved me for? To feed me to the demons? Why it would have been better if you'd left me to die in that fire..." (*SP*, 205). Kalua becomes a victim of the combined hegemonies of British imperial force and native abhorrence for inter-caste unity. The professed superiority of the high caste people over the low caste people exposes the multiple layers of subjugation prevalent in the traditional Hindu society. Deeti's male relatives avenge themselves for the sake of their family honour and in the eyes of Zachary, it is much worse than the feudal judgment. To quote Brinda Bose's words, "Ghosh offers a compelling critique of nationalism and the failures of migration through the experiences of women as citizens and subjects" (37).

Neel, the erstwhile *Raja* but now a convict, is forced to confront his own personal convictions and finds that they are at odds with his professed ones, "the fact was that he did not believe in caste or so at least he had said, many times, to his friends and anyone else who would listen" (*SP*, 267). However, his superficial idealism gives way to "stomach-clenching revulsion" (*SP*, 268) even at the thought of eating a meal cooked by unknown hands. With enormous will and effort, he accepts the change thrust upon him and extends a helping hand to Ah Fatt, going as far as physically washing and cleaning him, and in the process forging a deep bond that will undergo many endurance tests ahead. Conquering the self-construct of Neel's 'I' as a separate and superior creature from the rest of his prison-mates and Ah Fatt in particular, Neel's journey is a difficult one, but one that he makes taking pains. Initially, almost afraid to change from an extremely fastidious and caste-conscious *raja,* Neel is reluctant to part with his old ways, "the risk involved seemed unimaginably great; for he knew he would cease to be the man he had been a short while before" (*SP*, 323).

Neel is shipped out in chains as a debtor who becomes the instrument of redemption of the pathetic Lei Leong Fatt. Neel's transformation from self indulgent aristocrat to a man who single-handedly converts a fellow convict, Ah Fatt alias Freddie, from an out-of-control addict to a sober and clean man, exemplifies the abundantly positive changes which an engagement with the other can produce within the 'I'. He ponders over his own transformation, "Was it possible that the mere fact of using one's hands and investing one's attention in someone other than oneself, created a pride and tenderness that had nothing to do whatever with the response of the object of one's care—just as a craftsman's love for his handiwork is in no way diminished by the fact of it being unreciprocated?" (*SP*, 326). Ghosh's post-humanist responses to such injustices and inequalities foreground his broad-minded, all-encompassing vision and also give his narrative much of the zest and interest that arises from clashes between forces of domination and subjugation.

Ghosh greatly draws our attention to Zachary Reid, a light-skinned young sailor from Baltimore who has left America because his status as an octoroon has led to constant harassment by other American sailors. Aboard the ship, he becomes the protégé of Serang Ali, the leader of lascars who perform the hard manual labour aboard ships. Paulette Lambert, a spirited French orphan, is raised by a Bengali Muslim woman with her son Jodu. She disguises herself as one of the migrant women and escapes to the sea because she could not get accustomed to the constraints of proper colonial life with her new guardians, the Burnham family. Paulette catches the fancy of Reid. With the support of the lascars and Serang Ali, Reid has the potential to progress to officer status. The Vaishnavite Baboo Nob Kissin Panda, Mr. Burnham's *gomusta*, is an agent responsible for the indentured labourers. He undergoes an inner transformation by his aunt Taramony and releases Neel by giving him the keys saying that it's your 'mukti'. He is convinced that he has found Lord Krishna in the second mate of the Ibis, Zachary Reid and begins to behave like Radha transfixed by divine love. He also whispered to Kalua that, "You too will find your freedom; 'moksha' is at hand for you too" (*SP,* 503). Ghosh creates a transnational space and links "communities across borders through its desires and discourses of material and emotional belonging" (Bose, 38).

The people aboard the Ibis behave as individuals transcending all man-made barriers and so ultimately begin to realize instinctively that they are just human beings shorn of the unwanted trimmings, by proving that fundamentally they are bundles of emotions and feelings, and by raising themselves above the divisions they unfortunately find themselves in at birth. A certain psychological and spiritual change floods over most of the characters on board and the process of change is a much-awaited one in this strife-torn human life, indulging in violence on the grounds of religion, race, nationality, caste, gender, economic status and so on. But individuals have to put up a long and brave battle against such regressive forces to free themselves from all such nasty identities imposed from outside. For instance, the romance between Jodu, the Muslim lascar and Munia, a Hindu indentured labourer on board the Ibis is gruesomely butchered by the rigidity of caste and religious structures. When their frequent flirting comes to light, Jodu is savagely beaten up for taking liberties with a Hindu girl, although she was a willing party to their light-hearted relationship. Crowle, the British first mate, who really had nothing to spur his anger except personal dislike, also joins forces with the outraged Hindu foreman in the savage beating. Ghosh emboldens himself to attack traditional religious dogmas and beliefs that continually drive wedges between people, preventing unity and reducing their power in the face of oppression. His response to colonialism is then not only a rejection of its dominant ideologies but also a powerful propagation of a post-humanist philosophy.

In the last part of the novel, almost everybody aboard the Ibis distances themselves from their identities imposed on them in their life on land. Literally and metaphorically, they are sailing in the same boat as they have begun to shed those erstwhile roles and transcend them through their common humanity. Everyone is so anxious to put their problems behind them that they see no choice but to submit initially to the atrocious living conditions and sometimes sadistic overseers aboard the Ibis. Life aboard the ship is as stratified and as subject to both cruelty and courage as the occupants have experienced on land, but as the ship heads for new ports in foreign lands revealing new horizons that symbolize new hopes, hopefully, the occupants see it as the only escape from their past and its problems. The climax of the novel shows the ship in mid sea, fighting a tempest. The real storm, however, is in the minds of those aboard the Ibis as they watch their dear ones—the convicts and the condemned—move away in search of safer shores. *Sea of Poppies* is thus imbued with a deep commitment to human values. It is a reclamation of all that is "valuable, possible, and indispensable in our heterogeneous culture" (Gopal, 1). It is sometimes elegant, sometimes obscene, and always illuminating. Blends of tragedy and compassion, of the bizarre and the familiar, surprise the reader into the glimpses of the self with the looking glass of the text, and sometimes make the ugliness that is there unbearable to behold, only because it can become a powerful incentive for change.

Works Cited

Bande, Usha. *Cultural Space and Diaspora: Journey Metaphor in Indian Women's Writing*. New Delhi: Print Perfect, 2003. Print.

Bhargave, Rajul, ed. *Indian Writing in English: The Last Decade.* Jaipur: Rawat Publications, 2002. Print.

Bose, Brinda. *Amitav Ghosh: Critical Perspectives*. New Delhi: Pencraft International, 2003. Print.

Clarke, Colin, Ceri Peach, and Steven Vertovec. *South Asians Overseas: Migration and Ethnicity*. Cambridge: CUP, 1990. Print.

Dhawan, R.K., ed. *The Novels of Amitav Ghosh*. New Delhi: Prestige Books, 1999. Print.

Ghosh, Amitav. *Sea of Poppies*. New Delhi: Penguin, 2008. Print.

Gopal, Priyamvada. "Histories of belonging and becoming." Literary Review. *The Hindu* Chennai ed. 5 October 2008: 1. Print.

Kandasamy, Meena. "Another World is Possible." *The New Sunday Express*. 12 October, 2008: 4-5. Print.

Khair, Tabish, ed. *Amitav Ghosh: A Critical Companion*. New Delhi: Permanent Black, 2003. Print.

Kumar, Divya. "Sea of Thoughts." MetroPlus. *The Hindu* Chennai ed. 12 July 2008: 1. Print.

Sinha, Aditya. "It's slow addiction, like Opium." *The New Sunday Express* 22 June 2008: 4-5. Print.

Sharma, Charu, ed. *Mapping Migrations: Perspectives on Diasporic Fiction*. New Delhi: Nagri Printers, 2006. Print.

http://www.vidyanidhi.org.com.

2

Narrativizing History and Historicizing the Narrative: Reading Amitav Ghosh's *The Hungry Tide*

C.A. Assif

Abstract

The paper attempts to look how Ghosh has been successful in probing into the depths of unrecorded history of people and places. What makes his writing significant is the sincere attempt to present the subaltern history of the hitherto marginalized sections. There is an unusual mingling of fictional and factual in his writings as he thinks history is a fuel for creativity. How the concept of home appears different to different people, also falls within the purview of the investigation.

Probing into the depths of unrecorded history of people and places is axiomatic of Ghosh's writing. Exploring the national and transnational histories and thereby narrativizing them is a visible feature of his writings. Novels like *In an Antique Land*, *The Shadow Lines* and *The Glass Palace* are examples. What makes *The Hungry Tide* interesting is its treatment of subaltern history. The attempt of the author is not to valorize the valorous deeds of the so-called elites but the simple acts of the marginalized and the poor. Voicing the concerns of the voiceless has been characteristic of writers with social consciousness. In Ghosh's hands, the novel becomes an equipment for not only conjuring up an imaginary world but presenting factual events as well. It becomes as D.H. Lawrence says, a bright book of life and at the same time a dark book also, as it envelops both comic as well as the tragic aspects of the vast panorama of human life. To Ghosh, writing is not merely a means to attain aesthetic fulfillment but to document the history of the underdogs. There is an unusual mingling of fictional and factual in his writings. Writing for him is life endearing process.

What is striking about the novel is the panoramic reach that it has surveyed. All the more effective is the peculiar way in which things are discussed here. Ghosh is a writer who has been able to distinctly defy the barriers of genres and thereby establish his own place in Indian English of Diasporic Indian fiction. Though the novel has a fictional frame work, it encompasses the very history of people and places in a slightly stylized manner. The paper attempts to highlight how history at various levels, whether it be the history of the land, people and personal histories, play a vital role in the unfurling of the narrative. Amitav Ghosh, being a writer of novels with themes sober and great like that of displacement and dislocation, has tried to delineate a meta-history with verve and vigour.

The setting is Sundarbans, which is often called a labyrinthine area of mangrove islands on the Bay of Bengal. It is an intermediate border zone between the land and sea where river water mixes with sea water producing peculiar environs. It is also called the tide country which forms the delta of the Irrawaddy River. Mixing of waters of sea and river provides the author with a significant of metaphor for inter- cultural connections among the characters of the novel. The settlement here was instituted by a Scotsman named Hamilton. The narrative unfurls at different levels. It explores the journey undertaken by Piya, the cetologist to the Sundarbans and its surroundings. Her endeavour is to explore the lives of different species of dolphins. Her journey from America to Calcutta and from there to Sundarbans is highly interesting.

The concept of home appears different to different characters in the novel, as it is not a homogenous concept for them. Each thinks in his/her own manner. The novel is infested with people who are on the move. Their movement away from their respective homes is due to various reasons. Piya, one of the central figures of the novel meets Kanai, another major character while travelling in a train and later only they realize that they have more or less the same destination but their missions are different. It is through their individual quests that the narration of the novel unfolds. Piya, the cytologist from America, whose parents are from Calcutta, has undertaken a journey to Sundarbans island, particularly Lusibari with a mission to survey a peculiar type of dolphins in that area and her ardent and devoted research makes her take risks that normally people are hesitant to take up. Kanai, the translator and professional has honoured the invitation of his aunt Nilima to come to her place and explore the writings of her late husband, Nirmal, the revolutionary thinker and teacher. He has to find out the circumstances that led to the mysterious death of his uncle. Equally significant is the role of Fokir who often acts as the link between the urban researcher and the villager guide. Caught between the two streams there are other characters who also amplify the action of the novel.

The novel has two parts: the Ebb : Bhata and Flood : Jahar. At the beginning, we see Piyali Roy and Kanai Dutt travelling together to Canning and from there they separate. Kanai understands that Piya has come with a mission of studying the Irrawaddy dolphins which are available in plenty in this particular part of the land. After reaching the island, she hires the services of a dubious guide and also that of an official. After realizing their fraud ways she sends them away and seeks the help of a fisherman named Fokir. It was he who saves her from a terrible mishap. As she was about to drown, he pulled her out of the water. This person is Fokir and he is a reticent character in the novel. A person who is always on the move and defies categories. Being a fisherman, he has water in his veins. He epitomizes everything indigenous and as opposed to Kanai, the man of words, he has been silently carrying out his duties not only to Piya but also to the general public. An unusual kind of bond is established between Piya and Fokir. There is a complementary kind of relationship in the sense that Piya's bookish knowledge is supplemented ably by Fokir's practical knowledge. Had Fokir not been there, things could have been very difficult for Piya. His timely interventions enable her to face challenges. Though an introvert and a sort of escapist, who wants to be away from the mainstream of the society, his guidance has been extremely helpful for Piya. As a husband to Moyna he has not been very successful but he has a very strong bond with his son Tutul and has often been accused of taking him away from the school. Ghosh makes this illiterate a central figure in the novel and thereby marking his presence in the novel conspicuous.

What Piya loved best about her work is being out on the water alert and on the watch. She was called by one of her professors at Scripps's Institute of Oceanography at California as "a minnow among the whale watchers" (*The Hungry Tide*, 74). She considers her profession very seriously and she is wedded to that so as to consider it her home. She says to Nilima once, "You know, Nilima, for me, home is where the Oracella are, so there's no reason why this couldn't be" (400). Her environmental concern is also deep rooted and she had disagreement with the general populace. When the issue of killing a tiger comes, she argues with Kanai and the other local fishermen. She even snatches the spear from a villager. Even Fokir is against her sort of environmental fundamentalism which places animals at the centre. Her affinity to biology gives meaning to her life. She had a disturbed childhood and she could overcome all her difficulties with her passion and profession. She is well equipped with all the modern gadgets for her study. She has with her a GPS, range finder and other scientific apparatuses. On the other hand, she has also stocked enough drinking water, food and all. Her journey was difficult. She was accompanied by Kanai and Horen, Fokir's step father. Horen was the one who saved Fokir's mother from the clutches of a pimp. However, when a terrible cyclone was about to begin, Kanai and Horen withdrew but they continued their quest. Unrelenting Piya was well supported by Fokir and it was he who saved her from perilous waters but for that he had to sacrifice his life. After the storm, Piya returned without Fokir. While trying to save Piya's life, he had to sacrifice himself. She went back to Calcutta and raised funds to help his family and there was tremendous response as all helped her to make it a success. As a tribute to the selfless services of Fokir, she even named her project after him.

The novel has another layer of narrative which is revealed through the journals by Nirmal. Actually Kanai reached the island to collect a parcel his late uncle Nirmal has left him. His letters and notes have been explored by his nephew Kanai Dutt, the successful translator and publisher, who is settled in Bombay. When invited several times by his aunty Nilima, who is called Mashima there, he has to come and help her. She is the founder of a trust which helps poor people there and her efforts made many local people get good education and consequently jobs. Fokir's wife Moyna received help from the trust to become a nurse. Even after her husband's death, she continues to run the activities of the trust and is well respected in Lusibari and adjoining areas.

Nirmal, her husband came to this place as a sort of exile as he had no other option but to settle here as a school master since he was haunted by the Bengali police for his alleged activism and maoist links. He was a professor in Ashutosh College and there he fell in love with Nilima, his own student. After an intense love affair, they got married to each other but Nilima's parents were against this marriage. But later, they were reconciled to this and it was them who suggested Nilima to take him to this island. This island has its stories to tell both colonial and post colonial. It was Britishers who named some of the places like Lusibari and Canning and others. At the same time, the locals have a rich history to unfold. Their huts, shacks and shanties were built with the usual materials of the tide country-mud, thatch and bamboo. After reaching here Nirmal engaged himself in reading and writing. When Kanai told Nilima that the diary was written in 1979, the year of his death, Nilima couldn't believe was it as the most restless period in his life. In those days he had a bout of instability and he used to disappear for days together. But they assumed that it might have been in one or two days. He was always seen quoting his favourite poet Rainar Maria Rilke. *Duino Elegies* was the book that he always carried with him. Among the bare minimum things he had taken while coming to this place were copies of Rilke's Duino Elegies, both in Bangla and English versions. His diary contained many quotations from this book. It works as an intertextual back up for the novel. After his successful teaching stint at Lusibari, he went to Marichjhapi, where there was an uprising of the people against the policies of the state, denying them space as well as means of substance. Marichjhapi is translated as Pepper Island and it is rich in resources in one way or the other. His going there against the wish of his wife Nilima, made him befriend Kusum, a poor woman who has lost her husband and is living alone with her son, Fokir. Kusum is determined to help the agitators and she stood with them till the end.

This island had been inhabited mostly by refugees. They had to face umpteen problems as they were forced to leave but they withstood all the pressures with the help from people like Nirmal. Police cordoned them off and even denied drinking water, as they destroyed their tube wells. In order to survive, they were forced to drink from the puddles and contaminated ponds and consequently epidemics broke out there. State power was used to demoralize and physically subdue a whole lot people. Citizen groups filed petitions and High court ruled against barricading the settlers. Much of the history of dislocation and displacement has been suggested by Ghosh. What makes matters terrible is the approach of the authorities in not realizing the reality of the situation. They were simply led by some draconian rules which deny the poor the opportunity to live with dignity "by fishing, by clearing the land and by planting the soil" (262). Just because they were not born there didn't disqualify them in settling in such a place as no land belongs to anybody.

Sense of history is something which has always fascinated Ghosh and his novels documented the lives of the underprivileged with verve and enthusiasm. Bangladeshi Independence of 1971 is at the background of the novel. Inhabitants of both sides of the Sundarbans belong to the lowest stratum of the society. The refugees here are not from Bangladesh but those who have managed to escape from the rehabilitation camps set in Dandakaranya, Madhya Pradesh. Doubly dispossessed, they receive inhuman treatment from authorities. "They called it resettlement", said Nilima, "but people say it was more like a concentration camp, or a prison. They were surrounded by security forces and forbidden to leave. Those who tried to get away were hunted down" (118). Even the so-called progressive left governments also tried to put people down.

Nilima had suspicion about the relationship between Nirmal Bose and Kusum and she even shared her concern with Horen, her father's friend and well wisher. But he dismissed such doubts as baseless and assured her of taking care of such things. Kusum also played a vital role in the uprising and she was killed in the massacre that took place and Fokir was left in the company of Horen. Villagers had their tales to tell. They depended upon the cult of Bon Bibi, the local deity who seems to protect everybody. People of the tide country turned to her when they are in danger. When Kusum found that Nirmal hasn't heard of Bon Bibi she asks "Then whom do you call on when you are afraid?" (101). Nirmal considers this folktale as false consciousness. People like Nirmal couldn't understand the idea behind these kinds of beliefs as they were bound by the rationale of the urban life and its settings. The villagers have their own logic and it can't simply be analyzed using the scientific philosophy of the so-called educated and civilized. But there is something significant about their belief in this as the ritual prayer to Bon Bibi is a curious mixture of Islamic and Hindu rituals. It is a kind of localized Islam which even questions the very tenets of this Semitic religion. This belief is characterized by its syncretism as it encompasses a wide variety of things.

The diary of Nirmal relates one part of the story which is essential in the sense that it throws light upon history, politics and geography of the locale of the novel. The scholar in him makes a point to record things in an objective manner while he narrates his own story after his retirement from the service. The school had been everything for him for three decades and he was actively engaged in teaching and administration. His days as a school master and then a head master, Marichjhapi uprising and a host other things are there in this diary. *The Shadow Lines* has a similar narrator like that of Nirmal, who doesn't want his memories to be erased and that compels him to put down things on paper. His memoir is well crafted and drafted as it is a compendium of history, biography, geography and even political philosophy. Though people look at him as a romantic who is not all bothered about the immediate realities, he has in him the spirit of a humanist par excellence who wants identify himself with the less privileged of the society. Those who have been thrown into the constituency of the dispossessed have always been a matter of concern and this is the reason why he went to Marichjhapi when an uprising was in the offing there. There he was ably assisted by Kusum, the village woman and her guardian Horen. He was even ready to part with his wife Nilima for some time.

The novel deals with the issue of immigration, exile and the question of home and homelessness. Some of the major characters in the undergo experiences of dislocation and displacement related with the issues mentioned above. World over migration has been a reality as people have to be on the move for various reasons whether it be for safety and security, means of living and better standards of living. Nirmal and Nilima had to flee from Calcutta because of familial as well as political reasons. Nirmal's marriage with Nilima was not approved by her parents initially but later they accepted them conditionally. The police accused him of having maoist links and he had to move towards a safer place after quitting his teaching position in a college and he reached Lusibari and took up the job of a school master. While teaching at school, the revolutionary in him played a vital role. As far as he is concerned, this leaving home has brought about miseries to him but has a brighter side also as it nurtured the creative urge in him and made him do services to the most deserving of people. Same is the case with Nilima as the stint in Lusibari had brought about radical changes in her life. Though she had lost the comforts of an upper middle class family after getting married to Nirmal and had been thrown out of the comfort zone of city life after reaching the island, it has made her a person who could do something very meaningful and beneficial to the women of the place. She established a trust which took care of the poor girl children and destitute women and could make many face challenges in life. Moyna, Fokir's wife has become a nurse because of Nilima's constant support and encouragement. Even after the death of Nirmal, she could continue to live there because of her strong ties with the place and people.

Piya, the central character of the story is a foreigner, truly speaking, as she is a resident of USA. She is not a citizen of India and she considers her research and profession as her home. Though born in Calcutta, she moved to USA as her parents took her there at an early age. She comes back to India on a mission to study a particular variety of sea animal. Her meeting with Kanai, who is also on a journey to Lusibari, makes things easy for her. Though she made arrangements on her own in the initial stage of her exploration, she later sought the support of Kanai and others. Though highly educated with a PG degree from America, the human in her makes her consider Fokir, her illiterate aid, in her research as her equal. Her ignorance of Bengali is really a matter of concern to her and she feels little disgraced because of this. Though her mother tried to teach her Bengali she couldn't succeed in it. But the bigger issue is her communication with her guide here. Things take a different turn as she develops a peculiar language which includes signs, gestures and words to communicate with Fokir. They feel comfortable with this as necessity is the mother of invention, as the old adage goes. Fokir is reticent and more a man of action than of words. The immigrant sensibility in Piya is somehow eased with the coming of Fokir who could do wonders in the ocean. Fokir is also an internal immigrant as he is fond of moving away whenever he gets a chance. His closeness with his son Tutul is a cause of worry for Moyna as he is least concerned with his schooling. She wants her son to have a better kind of life.

Ghosh's writings assume much significance as he mostly deals with the realities of people who are outside the dominant realm of the society. According to Tumos Huttunen, "Ghosh has found a metaphor that represents an erasure of border between what is familiar and what is uncanny, by setting the book in this strange place" (29). Here, human beings are bonded by a commitment of experiences. The tide country, as it is called is, spread in some parts of India as well as that of Bangladesh. Two thirds lies in Bangladesh, one third in India and the diverse forces of history nurture folklore where this divide is obliterated. As Huttunen says, "Space in Ghosh's narrative is manifested as a many factored problematic that brings together time, place (imaginary and real dimensions), location (whether geographical or discursive) and identity (both personal and national/communal/collective)" (21).

The connection between man and nature as well as man and animals, is further probed in the novel. According to Huttunen, "Nature and animals (notably dolphins and tigers) are presented as the others of human beings, their way of being and communicating is compared to those of humans, who are largely presented as inhibited by linguistic totalities that tie them to the self without 'real' access to other humans or to nature and animals" (84). The rough terrain of the land and its marshy land do have an impact on the people of the area. Their backwardness is further precipitated by the cyclonic attacks they face occasionally. But even in the midst of unhappiness, they do find a kind of solidarity among themselves as well as a kind of conciliatory approach to both the nature and the animals there. While most of them would love animals to the extent of sparing them from big mishaps, they wouldn't tolerate animals when they become a threat to their very existence. But Piya, one of the central characters of the novel who comes from a foreign country, doesn't understand the ground reality of the terrain as she doesn't want any animals to be hurt. Even her constant companion and local guide in her research, Fokir was for killing this terrible beast. She seems to be representing a kind of environmental consciousness which could be doubted that of a fundamentalist. This kind of a dichotomy is symptomatic of the modern society. Ghosh has been able to bring endangered species and the refugees to the fore to make visible that both these animals and human beings are victims of the so-called dominant modes of production as well as its corresponding value systems.

It can be well summed up that it is a novel which treats history as fuel for creativity, as it draws inspiration from several historical sources. What is unfolded is the history of a whole region and its people along with the animals and nature. His innovative nature is proved by the fact that he has attempted to disclose the hitherto unraveled stories of the people and places.

Works Cited

Ghosh, Amitav. *The Hungry Tide*. New Delhi: Harper Collins India, 2007. Print.

Huttunen, Tuomas. *The Ethics of Representation in the Fiction of Amitav Ghosh*. Turku, Finland: Anglicana Turkuenesia, University of Turku, 2011. Web.

3

Impacts of Post-colonialism and Post-modernism in Amitav Ghosh's *The Glass Palace*

S. Malathy

Abstract

The Glass Palace, a poignant novel by Amitav Ghosh opens on the eve of a war in Mandalay, as the British Empire prepares to capture the Burmese throne. The author who is diligent in his dexterity, offers an imaginative reconstruction of the most disturbed, troubled conditions of our recent times in history. Ghosh is a great humanist, who raises his powerful voice for the voiceless and for the people who are oppressed, through this novel. He establishes the impacts of imperialism and the immense destruction it has caused on the conquered nations. Ghosh, who is an ardent and creative genius, writes about families and nations and highlights the sense of dislocation, effectively grasping the rise and fall of empires across the twentieth century and thus raising a poignant reminder of national identity and cultural and political identities as well. *The Glass Palace*, as a masterpiece represents the recurrent themes of post-colonial and post-modernist novels like absurdity of wars, colonization, quest, dislocation, fragmentation or disintegration of identity process of growing, exile, etc. combined with a fascinating story of a family saga.

> ...in the hands of Ghosh, historian by training, an adventurous traveller and a sensitive writer of fiction it becomes a confluence of all three. With remarkable sleight of hand, Ghosh juggles history, fiction and travel writing to produce a story that can be read variously as history of Burma over the last two

> centuries, an enduring romance between two family and a travelogue about a forgotten Buddhist territory. (Ira Pande)

The novel *The Glass Palace* by Amitav Ghosh is a complex story of a family saga, a magnificent work of art that weaves historical facts, spanning three generations. It skillfully examines the political and social issues of Burma, Malaya and India during a tumultuous century. Most of his works have historical settings, especially in the Indian Ocean periphery. His writings deal with epic themes of travel and diaspora, love and loss, political struggle, communal violence, history and memory. Formidably learned and meticulously researched, he is remarkable in his crossing the generic boundaries between anthropology and art work. As a creative genius, there is something equally epic about his scale of scholarship and his holistic approach to life that sits behind each of his books.

The Glass Palace, a poignant novel by Ghosh opens on the eve of the war in Mandalay, as the British Empire prepares to capture the Burmese throne. Ghosh gives an account of the dispute between a British timber company and the Burmese King Thebaw that leads to a battle in the year 1885. He narrates the miserable defeat of the Burmese army which surrendered after fourteen days of war, by a force of ten thousand British and Indian soldiers, even without informing their king, Thebaw.

As M.S. Nagarajan observes, "The nomenclature 'post colonialism', is used to refer to all the culture affected by the imperial process from the moment of colonisation to the present day. Post-colonialism examines and analyses the aftermath of colonisation and the effects of colonial oppression." In other words, "it analyses the literature that was affected by the imperial process, the literature that grew in response to colonial domination, right from the time of contact between the colonizer and the colonized down to the contemporary situation" (Nagarajan, 185).

The Glass Palace begins with the Anglo-Burmese War of 1885. Part-I called Mandalay, reveals the treachery of the two senior ministers of Burma, Kinwun Mingyi and Taingda

Mingyi, who are competing with one another to keep the royal family under guard; expecting rich rewards from the British Government for handing over the King Thebaw and the Queen Supayalat and their royal family. In this part of the story, the narrator assiduously depicts the critical situation under which the British occupied Burma. As the King prepares to surrender, the day is marked black—not only by the Burmese public who used to stand aloof in fear and awe in the past and have quickly changed into scavenge and tried to loot whatever they can find in the royal palace—but also by the British and Indian soldiers who have tried their hands in it. Those soldiers who are deputed to help out in shifting the King's precious stones, jewels and ornaments to the ship that is waiting to take the royal family and its servants into exile from Mandalay to Ratnagiri, have also pilfered the treasury. Through this shameful event, the narrator strips the veils off human nature and reveals the crude and brutal greed of man for wealth that drives him 'inhuman' at various levels.

Man's greed, his desire to grab and possess, is marked equally between the ordinary man and big empire builders like the British, the coloniser, to whom it has become like a 'leitmotif'. This single remarkable scene picturizes the unscrupulous greed that acts as an animating force, that is invariably cutting across individuals, groups, nations, caste, creed, racial differences and financial status. This looting and plunder delineated in the opening scene of *The Glass Palace*, is an exposition, drawn at a larger frame, transcending its literal significance to become a metaphor, and it highlights the raw and naked greed of the colonizer that sets the tone of the novel in resonance.

The creator, who is diligent in his dexterity, offers an imaginative reconstruction of the most disturbed, troubled conditions of our recent times in history. As Chitra Divakaruni says, "The struggles that have made Burma, India and Malaya the places they are today are illuminated in this wonderful novel by a master story teller.... A powerful novel with an epic sweep, filled with tender convincing detail. Ghosh is a master story teller". He attempts strenuously to set down things so accurately, carefully with precision, endorsed by his meticulous research—whether it is the scenic delineation of the Royal Palace in Mandalay, the coolies lives, oil wells, rubber plantation, timber trade, army, technicalities of cameras, skills involved in photography, automobiles, air-crafts, clothing or food—every detail is accurate and faultlessly period specific.

As Ruth Scurr writes in *The Times*, "...Ghosh is a deeply serious writer, sure of his human and historical insights and confident in his ability to communicate them. I cannot think of another contemporary writer with whom it would be this thrilling to go so far, so fast". Indeed it is a prodigious effort of the novelist to alter the received historical opinions without evading notions of historicity or historical determination. Pastiche and parody which highlight the self-reflexes of both modernist and postmodernist works help in reminding the reader that they are not real but fictional, constructed and are consciously ambiguous and give way to multiple interpretations. Historiographic metafiction is a term coined by Canadian literary theorist Linda Hutcheon, that includes those postmodern works, usually popular novels, which are both intensely self-reflexive and paradoxically lay claim to historical events and personages (literariness.org). Most part of this historiographic metafiction adheres to the conventions of both history and fiction and there is an equal subversion of both. As Meenakshi Mukherji aptly points, "No one is directly indicted in this novel, not a single person idealized.... For all its vividness of description and range of human experience, *The Glass Palace* will remain for me memorable mainly as the most scathing critique of British Colonization, I have ever come across in fiction".

To reconstruct the history of the transition of Burma, from a kingdom to a republic (between 1885-1995), the novelist uses materials derived from a variety of sources—diaries, notes, books and official records; recollections and remembered accounts of his father, uncle, friends and several others whom he has met and acquainted with. In this novel, history is so skillfully woven into fiction and thus an epic saga of the colonial regime in Burma and India is created by the novelist. Both the Burmese and Indians, who are bound in the same colonial situations, find it so difficult and suffocating, and this is well-wrought by the narrator. The novelist makes an attempt to seek an understanding of the past to have a bearing upon the present. As Bill Ashcraft says, "The alienating process which initially served to relegate the post-colonial world to the 'margin' turned upon itself and acted to push that world through a kind of mental barrier into a position from which all experience could be viewed as uncentred, pluralistic and multifarious" (Nagarajan, 12). The narrator remembers the past not as a dead, remote period but he peers on into the present and presents post-colonial situations of multi-ethnic, pluralist societies. He denotes the boundaries and mutations of nations imposed by the colonial rulers and their complex cultural diversities and consistent political struggle for democratic system, so powerfully.

Ghosh is a great humanist, who raises his powerful voice for the voiceless, for the people who are oppressed, through this novel. He makes a persistent call against domination of man by man at all levels—economic, political and military. He establishes the impacts of imperialism and the immense destruction it has caused on the conquered nations. Melvin Jules Bukiet who appropriately describes the novel says that it is enriched with "A century of traumatic subcontinental history, provides the architectural background to the intimate details of Ghosh's characters' lives. He conveys all of this with serenity and moral strength in the face of overwhelming turmoil. His book is a singular achievement."

The colonized who suffer a "cultural cringe", "adopt" the phenomenon of imitating the west, called "mimicry", develop a "double consciousness" and perceive the world through the consciousness of the colonizer as well as through their own vision provided by their native culture, is termed "unstable or double identity", and hence their divided self is referred to be "unhomed" or "unhomeliness" (Nagarajan, 187). *The Glass Palace* examines the individual psychological conflicts and dilemmas posed by colonialism. For example, Arjun, an Indian officer in the British army during the Second World War exclaims in pain that, "What are we? We have learned to dance the tango and we know how to eat roast beef with a knife and fork. The truth is that except for the colour of our skin, most people in India wouldn't even recognize us as Indians", shows his plight (*TGP*, 439).

This constant, unsatiated quest for personal identity, longing for recognition, both seem to be lost and found, figures prominently in this novel. The role of Indian soldiers in the British armed forces remains a significant one throughout the novel. One of the most remarkable aspects of the novel arises when Ghosh attempts to mark the 'outsiders' and foreigners'—how the Indians in Burma are also taking advantage of the situation created by the colonisers. Though it is an undeniable fact that the Indians themselves are victims of colonialism, they have also made use of such circumstances in their favour. The rapacity and greed inherent in the colonial process is seen concentrated, demonstrated well in showing what happened in Burma, that is, how the Indians become willing collaborators with the British Empire in their enterprise. Marina Budhos aptly comments in "The Los Angeles" that "Still there is something irresistible about the novels' ambition and how thoroughly it dissects the impact of the 'British colonial enterprise' *The Glass Palace*, like its far ranging subject, is capacious, it reflects the author's own curiosity and hunger for understanding".

The novel exposes barely the process by which Indian agents like Rajkumar, the protagonist, becomes rich by transporting indentured labourers to work in the rubber plantations. Rajkumar and others in the novel never mind compromising as they owe much of their success to the British Empire, while the Burmese who are uncompromised, are presented entirely as victims. But this scenario also changes and a complicity in disguise crops up, with the British Empire specifically regarding Indians serving in the British armed forces.

The writer elaborates the colonial experience and its memories which are heavily loaded with a sense of forlorn pain and suffering of the large numbers of people who have had badly lived through those phases of history. Ghosh in his letter to the Common Wealth Foundation, clearly indicates the directions in which history is to be remembered. When they announced an award for *The Glass Palace*, he registered his refusal politely and wrote, "I would be betraying the spirit of my book if I were to allow it to be incorporated within that particular demoralization of the Empire that poses under the rubric of the Common Wealth." *The Glass Palace* reveals the spirit, the spirit that indicts the colonial rule effectively. The novelist is more concerned with the impact of the colonial encounter on the political, social and cultural and geographical entities—space, distance and time. The narrative in this novel is extended to three generations with many stories which are beautifully woven together.

The novel portrays many characters, sagas of families, their lives and connections with each other. The twists and turns that these characters face in their lives become the main source of interest in the novel. It is addressed evidently to certain specific period, historical circumstances and it seeks the reader to interrogate his role in looking back at his colonial past. The narrator's account of the British invasion starts off well, contrasting the story of a young orphaned Indian boy Rajkumar with that of the imperious but doomed Burmese royal family. Akshay Kumar in the *Sunday Tribune* states: "The novel outdoes theory as well as history in terms of its subtle treatment of colonialism. *The Glass Palace* is an instance of novel overtaking history as an authentic and reliable source of understanding the micro-level subtleties of colonial politics".

The Glass Palace encompasses the colonial rule that had lasted for nearly a whole century, in Burma Malaya and India starting from the Anglo-Burmese War of 1885. It is often during war or in such circumstances as revolution, forced population movements, mass evacuations and so on, that nobody has the choice of stepping away from destiny. Ghosh makes an ardent attempt to chronicle the impact that these events happened to have on families and individuals.

When the British soldiers come to dominate the nation, it is Rajkumar, an eleven-year-old Indian orphan, who informs a crowd at a food stall, that the booming sound they hear is a "British Cannon". "English Cannon", he said in his fluent but heavily accented Burmese. "They're shooting somewhere up the river. Heading in this direction" (*TGP*, 3). As Ghosh is a beguiling and endlessly resourceful story teller, he opens his novel with an arresting account of an Indian boy, Rajkumar whose name means 'Prince', but he was anything but princely in appearance with his oil-splashed vest, his untidily knotted longyi and his bare feet with their thick slippers of callused skin" (*TGP*, 4). This poor boy who is lifted on the tides of political and social chaos creates an empire in the Burma's teak forest.

When the royal family of the Glass palace and its servants are sent on exile, this boy befriends Dolly, Queen Supayalat's youngest maid who looks after the two princess. She is the girl whose love shapes his life later. Unable to give up his love, he goes in search of Dolly from Mandalay to Ratnagiri, as he always remembered his gesture at Dolly, more a sign than a wave "I will see you again" (*TGP*, 36) that he has promised on the day of his first meeting with Dolly. On the day of exile, Rajkumar gives Dolly "handfuls of palm sugar sweets wrapped in a banana leaf" (*TGP*, 45) by working his way slowly into the crowd.

At the time of evacuation, everyone including Rajkumar rush inside to loot whatever they can find in the palace, where he encounters his future wife Dolly, who is also an orphan like Rajkumar. "Rajkumar's eyes fell on a girl...slender and long-limbed.... She was by far the most beautiful creature he had ever beheld, of loveliness beyond imagining" (*TGP*, 34). During the procession, "The king walked out of the pavilion, flanked by the Queen Supayalat and her mother.... The procession passed slowly through the corridors of the palace.... Two carriages were waiting by the east gate.... Just as he was about to step in, the king noticed that his canopy had seven tiers, the number allotted to a noble man not the nine due to a King" (*TGP*, 43).

The King like an errant school child, who is publically demoted, realizes that the English colonels after all have taken their revenge and cries: "of all the affronts Thebaw could have imagined", this becomes "the most hurtful, the most egregious"

(*TGP*, 44). This unceremonious removal of the King and his pregnant queen to the west coast of India, an astute move by the conquering British, is more humiliating to the Royal couple. By this menial way of exile, the British had tried to erase their trace completely from their soil and from public memory at home.

Rajkumar who is transported to Burma, accidentally gets employed as an errand-boy boy in a small food-stall run by a matronly lady Ma-Cho, who is a half-Indian and a mistress to Saya John. On his first meeting with Ma-Cho, he receives a thorough rebuke and scolding from her, as he has approached her for a job, "What do you think—I have jobs under my armpits, to pluck out and hand to you?" (*TGP*, 5). Soon, this boy who is a well-travelled orphan, establishes himself "bold and remarkable". Rajkumar is known for his keen perception and his ability to take calculated risks as he desires "the wealth or the rewards that he knew, with utter certainty, would one day be his" (*TGP*, 14). With an exploring spirit, the spark and the nature to pursue adventure, sets him on the path to achieve his goal. It is strange that he loves to exaggerate his age just to enjoy the feel of it, the feel to be an adult. Despite Ma-cho's warning, he ventures into the fort at Mandalay, as his fancy takes him. He leads a joyful life as he has none to guide or take care of him.

It is Ma-Cho who delineates the Glass Palace to Rajkumar in the opening of the novel. She elaborates on its exquisite structure, "It's very large.... It's a city in itself, with long roads and canals and gardens.... Beyond lie the apartments of the Royal Family and their servants—hundreds and hundreds of rooms, with gilded pillars and polished floors...a vast hall that is like a great shaft of light, with shining crystal walls and mirrored ceilings. People call it the Glass Palace" (*TGP*, 7). This Glass Palace which is the title of the novel can be regarded as an indication to the central theme; the Glass Palace of the Burmese King is standing as a dazzling emblem of the country's elegance and self-sufficiency until devastated by the British. The title might be representing not only the destruction, depredation and exploitation but also the leitmotif of the British that they have practiced in all other British colonies as well.

It is through a young research scholar's writing on *The Glass Palace Chronicles*, one of the few survivors, Dinu, and the vast saga of intertwining families is rediscovered in the final part of the novel called *The Glass Palace*. Dinu, the younger son of Rajkumar who has lost his lady love Alison is seen to be running a modest photo studio named *The Glass Palace*, where the young people gather to discuss pictures, books, ideas, politics, etc. The narrator's diligence and persistence enables him to imbue the title with images of loss as well as hope in retrospect, even without denoting a symbolic point. As Heather Hewett, a Christian Science Monitor aptly marks, "Ghosh spins—his tale with harrowing precision and insight, leaving the reader with a lingering disquiet about how the forces of history can irrevocably alter the lives of ordinary men and women."

Rajkumar's association with Saya John is a significant one. It is Saya John who notices "Something unusual about the boy—a kind of watchful determination...his eyes were filled with worldliness, curiosity, hunger" (*TGP*, 30). He saves Rajkumar from the Burmese, as they have started treating Indians as enemies, supporters of the British. When Rajkumar comes to understand the desire of the British to control Burma's territory for its wood, he quickly senses wealth in teak. This exploring boy, a complete destitute in an alien land, forms friends. Being receptive, he soon learns to see the world from others point of view, and develops a sense of belonging. He has learnt to 'adapt' and 'modify' himself to suit indigenous requirements. His transition is much supported by Saya John, his mentor and teacher. He teaches him the practicalities of life; to deal with people and to understand the other side of every picture. When Rajkumar gets angry with his assistants', behaviour, he advises saying, "You have no business to be angry...." You should learn "to bend the work of nature to your will; to make the trees of earth useful to human beings" (*TGP*, 74-75)

Being a strenuous worker and willing to take up any challenge, he grows up well into a successful and respected businessman in Burma. He traces Dolly who has been living with the deposed king and his Queen. Queen Supalayat, who is feared and admired blindly in Burma, an expert in court intrigues and palace politics, banished the king's mother, her sisters and other wives of the King to a corner of the palace, and has also systematically slaughtered seventy-nine princes of the royal family, is now leading a life of shabbiness and obscurity in an alien, unfamiliar territory while Burma gets depleted of its riches, valuable natural resources like petroleum, ivory, precious stones and its teak wood.

Exile and return are the themes that lie at the core of the novel. The exiled King and the Queen return to Burma like Dolly, who also returns. Dolly, who is more beautiful than the princess she attends, manages the youngest princess who shouts on every trivial reasons, so well. She gets a chance to befriend Uma Dey, wife of the District Collector Beni Prasad Dey who dies at sea. After the sad demise of her husband, Uma Dey moves to Europe and becomes the leader of the movement to free India and later she joins Gandhi's Ashram in India. It is Uma Dey who comes to rescue Rajkumar and the marriage between Dolly and Rajkumar is arranged by her. Rajkumar fathers two sons, Neel and Dinu. When Dinu goes to meet Alison, who has lost her parents in a car accident, he happens to stay there. After Neel's death, his wife Manju, her child Jaya, Rajkumar and Dolly who have joined some thirty thousand refugees have been trying to cross the river in order to escape the impending doom in the form of Japanese attack on Burma. At that time, Manju drowns herself, leaving Rajkumar and Dolly all alone in this exodus. Then Dolly and Rajkumar settle down at Uma's flat.

The Glass Palace also refers to the mutiny of British soldiers, as the Indian army of British Empire revolted against the military. Arjun, Uma Dey's nephew, an Indian officer in British army pours out his emotions, "The old loyalties of India...destroyed long ago; the British had built their Empire by effacing them. But the Empire was dead now—he knew this because he had felt it die within himself" (*TGP*, 441).

"Theories of globalization have moved...the compression of the world and the intensification of the consciousness of the world as a whole". These issues are also focused by Ghosh who portrays a capitalist economy that has mingled with colonial power in Burma and thus he relates the economic and political changes that Burma underwent. *The Glass Palace* deals with the wealth involved in teak trade and rubber plantations and how the conquerors have been trying to steal her riches, her resources. As Mathew, the son of Saya John who fears and foresees, "There is going to be a war", the impending doom in the form of Japanese attack starts in Burma, as an onset of the Second World War. Helen Hayward comments in *Times Literary Supplement*, that "By the careful accumulation of a throng of inter-connected stories, Ghosh succeeds in elaborating a complex canvas which, evocative of the diversity of individual experience, depicts the matrix of political and economic pressures in which it is caught".

Ghosh's *The Glass Palace* is a genuine attempt made on the re-inscription of the past history of the colonial era. Ghosh, who is an ardent, creative genius, writes about families and nations and highlights the sense of dislocation, effectively grasping the rise and fall of empires across the twentieth century and thus raising a poignant reminder of national identity and cultural and political identities as well. While talking about the epic dimensions of the novel, Ghosh tells the reporter of the *Times of India* that, "It is just a story that triggered *The Glass Palace*.... But then, the book...showed me a way of living that really had a transforming impact". *The Glass Palace*, as a masterpiece represents the recurrent themes of post-colonial, post-modernist novels like absurdity of wars, colonization, quest, dislocation, fragmentation or disintegration of identity process of growing, exile, etc. combined with a fascinating story of a family saga.

Works Cited

Ghosh, Amitav. *The Glass Palace*. New Delhi: Harper Collins, 2000. Print.

Ghosh, Amitav. "Ghosh's Letter to Administrators of Common Wealth Writer's Price". 18 March, 2001. www.amitavghosh.com.

Ashcraft, Bill et al. *The Empire Writes Back: Theory and Practice in Post-colonial Literatures*. London: Rutledge, 2002. Print.

Nagarajan, M.S. *English Literary Criticism and Theory*. Orient Blackswan Private Limited, India, 2006. Print.

Munshi, K.M. *The Ruin That British Wrought*. Bombay: Bharatiya Vidyabhavan, 1946. Print.

Mishra, Binod et al. *Indian Writing in English*. New Delhi: Atlantic, 2006. Print.

www.complete-review.com

www.amitavghosh.com

www.booksbrowse.com

4

Culture Speaks: An Ethnographic Study of Amitav Ghosh's *In an Antique Land*

Prasaja VP

Abstract

Ethnography, the branch of anthropology which involves the systematic study of people and culture, has a significant position in the academic discipline since the nineteenth century. It has been discussed widely in the context of arts especially literature, and the academicians are busy in analyzing the relation between ethnography and literature. An understanding of the ethnographic details like places, people and culture is possible through the study of travel narratives as it gives a clear picture of the areas that had been explored and documented by the traveler. A genuine and credible account is attainable when it is given by an anthropologist. Amitav Ghosh, the novelist-cum-anthropologist, cuts a new path in literature with his travel book *In an Antique Land*, which portrays the eclectic notions of fact, fiction, history, autobiography, anthropology, and travel narrative. The work came as a result of the writer's pursuit of the identity of a twelfth-century Jewish merchant who came to India via Egypt around 1130 AD, and his unnamed slave. Ghosh, with his magic marker, beautifully sketches the ethnographic map of Europe and interprets aspects of the culture of its various social groups. The paper entitled "Culture Speaks: An Ethnographic Study of Amitav Ghosh's *In an Antique Land* attempts to analyze the non-fiction from the perspective of ethnography.

Among the leading Indian English writers, Amitav Ghosh has earned a unique position by experimenting varied forms of novels. Ghosh displays a distinctive voice in literature, a voice which is profound and is different from the common run of his contemporaries. He receives myriads of accolades for his novels including *The Shadow Lines*, *Sea of Poppies*, *In an Antique Land*, *The Calcutta Chromosome*, *The Glass Palace*, *The Hungry Tide*, *The Circle of Reason*, etc.

Among his works, *In an Antique Land* (1992) cuts a new path for itself, by portraying the eclectic notions of fact, fiction, history, autobiography, anthropology, and travel narrative. "The book is not recognizable as a novel, nor is it simply an historical investigation: it is a new genre, something that blends an anthropological record with a travelogue, a diary, and perhaps some imagined sections" (Hawley 89). It came as a result of the writer's pursuit of the identity of a twelfth-century Jewish merchant Abraham Ben Yiju who came to India via Egypt around 1130 AD, and his unnamed slave whom Ghosh provisionally calls as 'The Slave of MS H.6'. To trace the story of the slave as a part of his research, he sets off his journey to the antique land of Egypt, mainly the villages of Lataifa and Nashawy.

Ghosh's desire brings him to the land of Egypt, the land where medieval customs and culture juxtaposes with modern desires and discontents. But even as he seeks to revive the history of his Indian predecessor Abraham Ben Yiju, he found himself caught in the life and culture of the Egyptian people. Combined with the observer turned writer's own descriptions of people and places, he also represents the people's own voices. The narrator interweaves the complex history of medieval Egypt during the twelfth century with his own personal experience in Egypt. There is interconnection between the two timelines—the medieval world of Ben Yiju and of the modern world of the narrator himself. This postmodern technique of multi-vocality gave enough scope to reveal the intangible essence of European culture.

Being an anthropologist, Ghosh is interested to study how ethnography can affect the study of human culture and behavior in past and present. Ethnography is a field of anthropology that involves studying people in a particular society by observing them in their natural setting. It includes the scientific study of the culture, region, tradition, history, religion, politics, and behavioural patterns of a distinctive group of people. It primarily aims to describe and interpret aspects of the culture of various social groups. By its nature, ethnographic writing is largely autobiographical and subjective. The observer who is injected into the alien land must have a purpose of his own. Ghosh elaborates an account of his experience as an outsider in the land of Egypt, 'the mother of the world' (80). An anthropology student, he begins his travel as part of his research and places himself in the story as a research scholar.

In the words of E.B. Taylor, the founder of cultural anthropology, "Culture or Civilization, taken in its wide ethnographic sense, is that complex whole which includes knowledge, belief, art, morals, law, custom, and any other capabilities and habits acquired by man as a member of society" (178). It is culture that makes human being different from other species, and gives them a distinct characteristic. In order to get a clearer understanding of the places, people and culture, it is necessary to delve deep into the heart of the land. It is possible through the study of travel narratives as it gives a clear picture of the areas that had been explored and documented by the traveller. *In an Antique Land* thereby presents the world of Egypt through the magnifying lens of a travel writer.

Travel accounts of colonial countries have been done by Eurocentric nations. The Eurocentric traveller is prejudiced towards the culture, tradition, religion and rituals of the country they visited. There emerges the possibility of distortion as the traveller has the tendency to demean the culture of the country they visited. However, Amitav Ghosh succeeds in portraying the real picture of the country he visited. Being a traveler from a colonized country, Ghosh realistically displays the culture of another colonized country.

Ghosh transports his readers to fresh pastures and new locales and gives them a plethora of ideas regarding the new land. He portrays the people and culture of the place in minute details through vivid descriptions. He familiarizes the readers with the new foreign culture. With his narrative, he invites the readers to the land of Sphinx. Thus, the text acts as the carrier of culture.

The narrator acts as a preservative which can preserve the qualities of the society depending on the power of representation. The manner in which the traveler views a particular place will be different from the way in which the people living in that place perceive it. The travel writer usually highlights the quality of the place, its culture, custom, and people that acquires only secondary importance in the accounts of the narrative of an indigenous person of that region.

Ghosh succeeds in outliving the linguistic barrier which could occur during his visit to Europe, the alien land. The issue of language barriers is particularly critical during intercultural encounters. Linguistic constraints make the writer fail in understanding a new culture that he encounters during the course of the travel. As a way to bridge the linguistic barrier, he learns Arabic, the native language of Egypt. The awareness of the language makes him possible to intermingle with the people and understand more about their culture.

Geographical and historical descriptions are an inevitable part of ethnography. In his endeavor to explore the identity of the place, Ghosh ponders over the etymological details of the country. The name Egypt is derived from the ancient 'Masr', which means 'to civilize' or 'to settle'. The word has historical significance in Arabic. It occurs in *Quran* but was in use even before the advent of *Quran*. Towards the south of Egypt is the famous fortress called Babylon. The fort was built by the emperor Trajan in 130 AD. Several changes happened to the fortress as time passes, and its popularity is denoted by the narrator by saying "millions of visitors pour through it every year" (35). For centuries, Alexandria, founded by Alexander the great in 332 BC, served as the capital of Europe. But when the Muslim conqueror Amr ibn al-As invaded Egypt, the capital changed from Alexandria to Masr. Amr laid out a new city around his tent called Fustat, and later Fustat served as the capital. It was the markets of Fustat that first attracted Abraham Ben Yiju to Egypt.

Amitav Ghosh is brilliant in character descriptions. The characters portrayed in the work are ordinary people whom Ghosh encounters during his visit. The daily encounters of these characters are shown with minute details. Their religious rites, social customs along with their eccentricities and whims are effectively portrayed.

The villages of Lataifa and Nashawy constitute of agricultural people. The rich fertile soil, the favorable environment, and the water from the Nile river promoted the development of agriculture. Majority of the people in the village are agricultural men or *fellaheen*. Agriculture is still very traditional and yet to be modernized. Males and very often poor women work in the agricultural fields. Poultry, cattle rearing are some of their common livelihood.

The fading glory of agriculture is shown through the character of Shaikh Musa, Ghosh's friend. Musa took pride in being a *fellah*. He had two sons—Ahmed and Hasan. Ahmed, the elder one worked as a clerk in a factory near Damanhour. He was thus counted as a '*mowazzaf*', an educated salaried man. Ahmed was the most dutiful of the sons and he helped Shaikh Musa on the land as often as he could. Unlike him, Hasan is uneducated. He had been restricted to go to school at an early stage. Shaikh Musa had brought up his son Hasan as a *fellah*, so that at least one of his sons would profit from the land their ancestors had left them. "It was that shared background perhaps that lent Shaikh Musa's voice a special note of affection when he spoke of Hasan" (42).

Egyptians accord high importance to religion in their daily life. Egypt is a Muslim-dominated country. The people whom Ghosh encounters are all religious. The narrator minutely observes the nuances of these religious people. Ustaz Mustafa, one of the informants, had a habit of flicking back the cuff of his *jallabeyya* every few minutes. He seems busy and often does a quick look at his watch. The narrator later discovered that "this gesture was rooted in an anxiety that had long haunted his everyday existence—the fear that he might inadvertently miss one of the day's five required prayers. That was why he looked much busier than anyone else in Lataifa" (46).

Ghosh demonstrates the two indispensable factors of Nashawy society: Politics and Religion. A blending of religion and politics is discernible in their lifestyle. In Nashawy, Ghosh had "soon discovered that salaried people like Mustafa, rural *mowazzafeen*, were almost without exception absorbed in a concern which, despite its plural appearance, was actually single and individual religion and politics—so that the mention of the one always led to the other" (50). Religion is closely associated with politics. The discussion of one leads the way to the other. When Ustad Mustafa, the religious man of Nashawy, confronts the narrator for the second time, he started his conversation by enquiring about Indian politics.

There is also an analysis of how the difference in religious approach creates social difference. During his expedition, Ghosh along with Mustafa, happened to see some of the relatives of Mustafa who were working in a farmland. On meeting the narrator, they unfold their bundle of questions regarding the soil and crops in India. Mustafa apologetically said, "They are fellaheen. They don't have much interest in religion or anything important" (51). Based upon Mustafa's comments, Ghosh recognises that the poor are less interested in blending religion and politics than the rich and educated Muslims.

Social hierarchy is apparent in Egypt since it determines people's access to power and position. Within the community, there is the distinction of upper-class and lower-class. Ghosh uncovers the social stratification. The prominent classes in Egypt are al-Badawy and Abu-Kanaka. al-Badawy is a class of people of the Bedouin origin settled in the Delta. These Bedouin descendents worked on the land as *fellaheen* and they were later called al-Badawy. Gradually, the village of Nashawy was filled with Badawy families that came to be known as the pre-eminent lineage of the village. The other group was from a lineage of barbers and healers, a family called Abu-Kanaka. They were highly religious people. They earned their living by healing and cutting people's hair. Latifs and Jammal were the other social classes.

Superstitions and moral upbringing of a society also have a lot to do with its culture. So many people get caught in the muddle of false beliefs, blind faith and superstitious practices. The traditional Egyptian people firmly believe in the presence of supernatural beings and mysterious occurrences. The story of Sidi Abu-Kanaka and the people's belief of the presence of his ghost and its extended protection over Nashawy are suitable examples that heighten the superstitious beliefs of the people.

An important superstitious character is Amm Taha, the caretaker of the narrator. Amm Taha is a part-time witch who is always ready to cast a spell for a little extra money. Once he happened to visit the room of the narrator. There he saw a hoopoe bird. On seeing it, he becomes happy and he caught it using his jallabeyya and breaks its neck. To the astonished narrator, Taha narrates the use of the particular bird. He says, "I need it for a spell, for women who can't bear children" (129). It may turn funny and ridiculous to the alien narrator, yet he perceives it as the crucial part of their culture.

On another occasion, the narrator visits Amm Taha at his home. There he saw Taha lying on his bed. The narrator enquired the reason. Taha angrily replied: "What do you think has happened? It's the Evil Eye of course—somebody's envied me, what else?" (131). Later in order to ward off the evil eye, he had assigned a woman to break the spell. From time to time Ghosh details the primitive practices of the people and he takes it all with the humility.

Ghosh also compares certain cultural aspects of the country of his visit with that of his own land. He is showing the similarities between two distinct nations, Middle East and South Asia. Though they are separated by different land masses and different cultural patterns, both the nations have a lot in common. The author gets fascinated by identifying something common in both cultures. The mutual support which both these nations exerted upon each other is praiseworthy. Ustaz Sabry narrates the cultural similarities of the two countries with these words:

> Our countries were very similar, for India, like Egypt, was largely an agricultural nation, and majority of its people lived in villages, like the Egyptian fellaheen,

> and ploughed their land with cattle. Our countries were poor, for they had both been ransacked by imperialists.... It was difficult task and our two countries had always supported each other in the past: Mahatma Gandhi had come to Egypt to consult Saad Zaghloul Pasha, the leader of the nationalist movement, and later Nehru and Nasser had forged a close alliance. No Egyptians could ever forget the support that his country had received from India during the Suez canal crisis of 1956, when Egypt had been subjected to an unprovoked attack by the British and the French. (134)

The influence of westernization on the life of Egyptians is unforeseen. Eight years after his initial visit, Ghosh revisits Egypt. His mind is still crammed with stories about the land and its inhabitants. He was shocked by the sudden changes caused by the advancing years. Ghosh, to prove this, gives the story of the Imam, "man of religion" (141), who through traditional teachings of medicine used to cure the people of Nashawy. Later the Imam is convinced that his methods are worthless in comparison to Western knowledge and the intrusion of Western technology in the field of medicine. He bemoans the loss of the old traditional medical practices and decides to switch over to the new practices. Ghosh tells us that the Imam is now learning "the art of mixing and giving injections" (236).

Being a Hindu in a Muslim majority country, Ghosh becomes increasingly aware of the exclusion he feels. During the time of Ramadan, he spent his days amidst a handful of people who were not fasting. He discloses his wish to join in the fast. But everyone insisted: "No, you can't fast, you're not Muslim—only Muslims fast at Ramadan" (75). He realizes that Muslims all over the world are going through the same sacred ritual, and he is bewildered by the attraction of that global community. Ghosh admits, "A phenomenon on that scale was beyond my imagining, but the exercise helped me understand why so many people in the hamlet had told me not to fast; to belong to that immense community was a privilege which they had to re-earn every year, and the effort made them doubly conscious of the value of its boundaries" (76). Though a Hindu, Ghosh could understand the religious bend of his Muslim neighbours. During the Ramadan time, he has gifted Shaik Musa an illuminated copy of the *Quran*, the most aspiring gift one could give to a Muslim. This shows the importance Ghosh assigns to their religion.

A better understanding of the text is possible when studied with the perspective of anthropology and ethnography. Within the limited time, Ghosh could comprehend the wealth of culture and tradition of the Egyptian people. He generates an interest among the readers by perceiving the uniqueness of the culture. In short, *In an Antique Land* enshrines the cultural specificities of Egyptian culture viewed through an Indian eye. Ghosh's attempt is didactic as he instructs the readers the valuable lessons of respect and cultural tolerance.

Works Cited

Burnett, Edward Tylor. *Primitive Culture: Researches into the Development of Mythology, Philosophy, Religion, Art and Culture*. London: John Murray, 1871. Print.

Ghosh, Amitav. *In an Antique Land*. New York: Orient Longman, 1992. Print.

Hawley, C. John. "The Ebb and Flow of peoples Across Continents and Generations". *Contemporary Indian Writers in English: Amitav Ghosh*. New Delhi: Cambridge University Press, 2005. 89. Print.

5

Giving Voice to Subaltern in the Select Novels of Amitav Ghosh

P. Premchandar

Amitav Ghosh is a postmodern Indian English novelist, who has mastered the art of recounting with new styles and modern techniques. He is one of the English writers, who are perceptive to the incidents of history, issues of cultural implication and political significance. Amitav Ghosh is the most modern and persuasive Indian voice in the present world of English literature. Amitav Ghosh is an insightful and thought-provoking writer, who tries to talk about many modern issues and tries to give precious insights to his readers. About the vital insights in the novels of Amitav Ghosh, Tapan Kumar Ghosh observes—"profound historical sense, a strong humanitarian drift, a witty but compassionate insight into man and his society, an attempt at interlacing the time past and the time present in the crucible of memory" (*The Shadow Lines,* 151). Amitav Ghosh has included diverse aspects of human life into his novels, and through his novels, he tries to rise above the limits between a historian, researcher, social anthropologist, journalist and a traveller.

The novels of Amitav Ghosh can be treated as socio-historic documents because in his novels, he reconstructs the private history of the subalterns from the historical past and also voices their plight and sufferings. In this attempt of reconstructing the subaltern history and express the subaltern, he uses history, postcolonial aspects and postmodern traits as significant element of his narration. Amitav Ghosh is one of the selective and thriving writers of the present day in India. His writings comprise both fiction and non-fiction.

His fiction covers chief novels. As a novelist, he has written nine novels, *The Circle of Reason* (1986), *The Shadow Lines* (1988), *In an Antique Land* (1992), *The Calcutta Chromosome* (1995), *The Glass Palace* (2000), *The Hungry Tide* (2004), and the three volumes of the Ibis trilogy—*Sea of Poppies* (2008), *River of Smoke* (2011) and *Flood of Fire* (2015). For this proposed research, the first six novels of Amitav Ghosh, namely *The Circle of Reason, The Shadow Lines, In an Antique Land, The Calcutta Chromosome, The Glass Palace* and *The Hungry Tide* have been selected to study and analyze his ways of expressing the subalterns in his novels by using history, post-colonialism and postmodernism description, and critical tools.

Under subaltern theory, the word 'subaltern' is used in broad viewpoint as synonym for minorities, dalits, and colonial subjects, the illiterate, helpless women and children, whose voices and deeds have been muted. Amitav Ghosh reconstructs the private histories of the sufferers of public history and gives voice to these weak and speechless subalterns.

According to this theory in *The Circle of Reason,* the illegal migrants in al-Ghazira like Alu, Zindi, Karthamma, Kulfi and others are subalterns because they don't have work permits and passports. They felt alienation and insecurity, and they keep on moving secretly from one place to another place. They represent millions of migrants in the Gulf countries struggling for their existence.

In *The Shadow Lines,* the characters like Tha'mma have been treated as subaltern because she is an inhabitant of Bangladesh, who migrated to Calcutta during Indian Partition. Tha'mma as a widow struggled a lot in the alien land to settle and brought up her family. Tridib is a subaltern because he was a sufferer of the communal riots. He was killed in the streets of Dhaka while helping his grandfather.

In his next novel *In an Antique Land,* Bomma, the Indian slave, who worked with the Egyptian merchant, has been treated as subaltern because he has no individual life. He spent his whole life in the service of his master and he has nothing personal. In *The Calcutta Chromosome,* the characters Mangala and Latchman have been treated as subalterns because they were brilliant Indian lab assistants who worked with Ronald Ross. They are the real master minds at the back of Nobel Prize winning invention. They remained at the back of curtains and their talents were unrecognized.

In *The Glass Palace,* Rajkumar, Dolly, Saya John, Dinu, Neel have been treated as subalterns because they were victims of the Second World War. During the war, they lost everything, left Burma and migrated to their native places in helpless condition. In *The Hungry Tide,* Kusum and the other settlers in the Marichjhapi Island have been treated as subalterns because the economic blockade, police attacks made them helpless and voiceless. They didn't get any help from the outside world due to the imposition of Section 144 in that area.

After the study of these novels of Amitav Ghosh in terms of subaltern, it can be felt that Ghosh seriously tries to voice the subalterns and their sufferings. John Thieme in his essay "The Discoverer Discovered" observes:

> Ghosh appears to subscribe to the view that the western discourse silences alterity by denying its very capacity for utterance.... Gayatri Spivak asks the question 'Can the subaltern speak?' All of Ghosh's work to date seems to have been directed towards wanting to answer this question in the affirmative. (Thieme 130)

Amitav Ghosh's voicing the subaltern can be studied in four different parts. First one is reconstructing personal histories which were shadowed by the public ones. The dissimilar tools used by Amitav Ghosh in reconstructing these personal histories constitute the second part. The third part is juxtaposing the public histories and personal histories side by side to study how public histories showed horrific effect on the individuals and made them subalterns. The final part is how Amitav Ghosh voiced these powerless or the speechless subalterns.

In *The Circle of Reason,* Ghosh writes about the effect of the Indo-Pak war of 1971 on the people of Lalpukur, a village on the Indo-Bangladesh border. In the post-war developments,

Alu from Lalpukur escapes to al-Ghazira. In this novel, Ghosh reconstructs the private history of Alu and other migrants living in the Middle East to bring out the emigrational problems they faced.

In *The Shadow Lines,* Ghosh writes about the effect of Indian partition of 1947 on the ordinary people like Tha'mma and the effect of communal riots of 1964 on the lives of helpless people like Tridib. In this novel, he reconstructs the private histories of Tha'mma, to show how the Indian separation affected the ordinary people and also he reconstructs the private history of Tridib to show the dilemma of the victims in the communal riots.

In *In an Antique Land,* Ghosh writes about the result of the historical Indo-Egyptian trade of twelfth century on the life of ordinary people like Bomma, Ashu, etc. In this novel, he reconstructs the private history of Bomma, an Indian slave worked with an Egyptian merchant, Abu Ben Yiju during the Indo-Egyptian trade of twelfth century.

In *The Calcutta Chromosome,* Ghosh writes the historiography of Ronald Ross's discovery of Malaria broadcast through mosquitoes. In this novel, he reconstructs the private history of two Indian lab assistants Mangala and Latchman, who helped Ronald Ross in this discovery. This private history brings the shadowed lives of brilliant Indian lab assistants worked with their English masters.

In *The Glass Palace,* Ghosh writes about the result of the Second World War on the millions of Indians lived in Burma then. In this novel, he reconstructs the private history of Rajkumar and other victims of the Second World War to show how the Second World War made millions of Indians as helpless and voiceless.

In *The Hungry Tide,* Ghosh writes about the effect of the Marichjhapi incident on the lives of thousands of migrants like Kusum. In this novel, he reconstructs the private history of Kusum and other migrants suffered in the Marichjhapi incident of 1979. Thus, Ghosh reconstructs the private histories of the individuals, who became helpless or voiceless subalterns due to the horrifying effect of the historical incidents.

In the art of fictionalising the history, Ghosh uses history against imagination or actuality against fiction. He employs his imagination and creativity; his research abilities and questioning mind in historicising the fiction. This fictionalised fact is a reality which brings the private histories of subalterns into limelight, which was shadowed by the public histories. It can be analyzed that the novels of Amitav Ghosh help the readers in better considerate the history.

In reconstructing the private histories of the subalterns, Amitav Ghosh typically uses postcolonial aspects and postmodern techniques as tools. He has also used postcolonial aspects like the uncanny, demanding stereotypes, valorisation of cultural individuality, counter discourses, metanarratives, hybridization and imitation. They are helpful in bringing out the psychology and thinking of the subalterns.

In the process of reconstructing the private histories of subalterns and voicing them, Ghosh uses postmodern techniques like magical realism, travel motif, maximalism. They help in preparing the ground for the rebuilding and voicing. The postmodern qualities like non-linear narration, satires, metaphors, pastiche and multiple narratives are helpful in reflecting the estrangement, anxiety, helplessness and voicelessness of their lives. Intertextuality in the form of documents, diaries, memoirs; letters, notebook, etc. play a key role in reconstructing the private histories and voicing the subalterns.

Amitav Ghosh places public history and private history side by side and discusses the effect of the public history on private history. He portrays individuals as victims of the historical events and brings out the horrific effect and unhealed wounds they caused on the minds of the common people.

In his novels, Ghosh discusses riots, violence, colonialism and partition but his main focus is on the helpless individuals or the subalterns who were crushed under the wheels of these historical incidents. Protagonists of his novels are not historical figures but ordinary people, who are the exemplifying figures for thousands of victims at that time of history.

Amitav Ghosh does not question the public history but through his writings, he questions its biased nature and its lack of comprehensiveness. He questions the way it has neglected the private history of voiceless subalterns. He looks at the history not from the centre but from the periphery.

Historical facts in the form of public history and imaginary facts in the form of private history go hand in hand in parallel lines. The parallel narratives of public and private histories bring out certain new things into limelight, which were not documented by the historians. Thus, this juxtaposition of public and private histories brings the shadowed parts of the history into limelight and adds new facts to the existing historical facts.

Amitav Ghosh voiced the helpless and voiceless subalterns by using history, postcolonialism and postmodernism. In *The Circle of Reason,* he voiced the illegal migrants in al-Ghazira. The readers could listen to their plight and sufferings in the words of Zindi. At the end of the novel, the voice of the subalterns is heard through the words of Zindi as, "I wondered what would happen to me if I died in a desert in a foreign land, without a house or friends to help me....I'm too old and Boss is too young....Boss and I are going back home, Alu. Boss is going to build me a house someday." (*The Circle of Reason,* 454)

In *The Shadow Lines,* Ghosh voiced the plight of the refugee migrants during the Indian separation of 1947. He also voiced the plight of the victims of communal riots. Ghosh gave voice to the anguish of the migrants over partitions and communal riots through the words of the old man, who was killed in the communal riots:

> I know everything. Once you start moving, you never stop. That's what I told my sons when they took trains. I said I don't believe in India-Shindia. It's all very well, you're going now, but suppose when you get there they decide to draw another line somewhere? What will you do then? Where will you move to? No one will have you anywhere. (*The Shadow Lines,* 237)

In *In an Antique Land,* Ghosh voiced the silence of Bomma who remained in the darkness of history. We could listen to his silenced voice in the Geniza documents. In *The Calcutta Chromosome,* Ghosh voiced the unrecognized talents of Mangala and Latchman through the research of Murugan. We could listen to Mangala and Latchman seriously discussing about transmission of Calcutta chromosome, in the research article of Murugan.

In *The Glass Palace,* Ghosh voiced the plight and anguish of the Indians in Burma during Second World War. We could listen to their voices in the words of Rajkumar. During the Second World War, Rajkumar lost everything in Burma, and he was forced to leave Burma and went to India. The readers could listen to the subaltern voices of the victims of the Second World War in the words of Rajkumar, when he said: "My father was from Chittagong and he ended up in Arakan; I ended up in Rangoon; you went from Mandalay to Ratnagiri and now you're here too. There are people who have the luck to end their lives where they began them. But this is not something that is owed to us" (*The Glass Palace,* 310).

In *The Hungry Tide,* Ghosh voiced the plight and sufferings of the settlers in Marichjhapi. The readers could listen to the plight of the migrants through the words of Kusum, when she said, "the worst part is not the hunger and the thirst. It was to sit here, helpless, and listen to the Police making announcements, hearing them say that our lives, our existence was worthless than the dirt or dust" (*The Hungry Tide,* 261). The subaltern voices of the migrants can be heard in their cries wafting across the water, "Amra kara? Bastuhara. Who are we? We are dispossessed" (*The Hungry Tide,* 255).

About voicing the subaltern by Amitav Ghosh, Santwana Haldar observes, "With a piercing insight, he explores historical events that were sidelined in government records and upholds the issue related to imperialism and multiculturalism. An active member of the Subaltern Studies Project, Ghosh likes to present those events from the perspectives of the subalterns" (Haldar, 308). In this study of voicing the subaltern, four interesting observations can be made. The first one, in every novel wherever the story happens or whatever the theme may be, it is more about Indians and Indian sub-continent. The second observation is all the protagonists of his novels are the victims of the history. This shows Amitav Ghosh's revisionist approach towards history. The third observation is most of the characters were on migration for different reasons and he writes about their problems as migrants. The fourth interesting observation is that all the protagonists are subalterns and the novelist tries to voice them. This shows the humanistic vision of the novelist.

The interesting themes, innovative narrative techniques, richness of language, portrayal of history, reconstruction of subaltern histories, discussion of contemporary social issues, and subaltern voices of Ghosh's novels promote his position from an Indian English writer to the status of a World Writer. About the writings of Amitav Ghosh, G.J.V. Prasad, in his article, "Rewriting the World: *The Circle of Reason* as the Beginning of Quest" rightly observes:

> With an anthropologist's sense of detail and a historian's grasp of facts and chronology and with a creative writer's curiosity about causation and effects and great narrative skill and imagination, Ghosh weaves together a pluralistic and self-reflective view of the world – one that challenges the smugness of accepted narratives and point of view and certainties of post colonial borders as well as generic boundaries. (Prasad, 56)

It can be summed up that a close study of the novels of Amitav Ghosh is a rewarding experience because it provides a lot of knowledge and presents various new ideas and discusses many contemporary issues. It provides a lot of information and knowledge about different places, its people, and their culture. They are brilliant narratives of complexities of postmodern life. In this regard, it seems that he is responding to Edward Said's call in *Culture and Imperialism*:

> The major task is to match the new economic and socio-political dislocations and configurations of our time with the startling realities of human interdependence on a world scale. We need to go and to situate these in a geography of other identities, people, cultures, and then to study how, despite their differences, they have always overlapped one another, through non-hierarchical influence crossing, incorporation, recollection, deliberate forgetfulness, and of course, conflict. (Said, 402-03)

It can be inferred that a close survey of the novels of Amitav Ghosh is an exciting experience, because it takes the readers into the depths of the historical past to show the shadowed parts of the history. It portrays the history from below. It shows the horrifying effect of history on the individuals and discusses how the historical incidents pushed the common people to the margins of the society and turned them into subalterns. It gives voice to the plight and sufferings of the subalterns.

It can be concluded that a close analysis of the novels of Amitav Ghosh is an intellectual experience because they discuss social, cultural and subaltern issues and try to voice the subalterns. They provide the readers with many ideas and valuable inputs. They help the readers in understanding the history in right way.

Voicing the subaltern by Amitav Ghosh gives confidence to the subalterns of the contemporary society and boosts up their morale. It shall be apt to say that Ghosh successfully tries to bring the subalterns from the margins of the society to the centre. In this regard, Ghosh justifies the comments made by John Thieme in his "Foreword" to *Amitav Ghosh's The Shadow Lines: A Critical Companion*: "Like Edward Said, Ghosh draws attention to the artificiality of the East-West binaries of Orientalism. Like Homi Bhabha, he demonstrates the hybrid, interstitial nature of cultures, as articulated through language. Like Ranajit Guha and the Subaltern Studies scholars, he endeavours to recuperate the silenced voices of those occluded from the historical record" (Guha, 251).

Works Cited

Ghosh, Amitav (2009). *The Circle of Reason*. New Delhi: Ravi Dayal Publisher and Penguin Books.

——— (2009). *The Shadow Lines*. New Delhi: Ravi Dayal Publisher and Penguin Books.

——— (2009). *In an Antique Land*. New Delhi: Ravi Dayal Publisher and Penguin Books.

——— (2006). *The Calcutta Chromosome*. New Delhi: Ravi Dayal Publisher and Penguin Books.

——— (2010). *The Glass Palace*. Noida: Harper Collins Publishers India.

——— (2011). *The Hungry Tide*. Noida: Harper Collins Publishers India.

——— (2009, Oct. 12). Interview by Michelle Caswell. "An Interview with Amitav Ghosh." Asia Source. Web. 18 May 2013.

Ghosh, Tapan K. (2010). "Beyond 'The Shadow Lines': Amitav Ghosh's Quest for the Remains of an Antique Civilization". Dhawan, R.K. (Ed.), *The Novels of Amitav Ghosh*. New Delhi: Prestige Books. Print.

Haldar, Santwana (2010). "Amitav Ghosh's *The Hungry Tide*: Analyzing Its Complex Range of Concerns". R.K. Dhawan (Ed.), *The Novels of Amitav Ghosh*. New Delhi: Prestige Books. Print.

Prasad, G.J.V. (2005). Rewriting the World: *The Circle of Reason* as the Beginning of Quest. Brinda Bose (Ed.), Amitav Ghosh—Critical Perspectives. Delhi: Pencraft International. Print.

Said, Edward. W. (1994). *Culture and Imperialism*. London: Vintage.

Thieme, John (2003). "The Discoverer Discovered". Tabish Khair (Ed.), *Amitav Ghosh: A Critical Companion*. New Delhi: Permanent Black, 2003. Print.

——— (2008). Foreword. Murari Prasad (Ed.), *Amitav Ghosh's The Shadow Lines: A Critical Companion*. New Delhi: Pencraft International. Print.

6

The Art of Characterization in the Select Novels of Amitav Ghosh

S. Mohan Raj

Introduction

Amitav Ghosh, in his works, presented the quality and soul of the working class individuals and groups. He also presented the arrangement of practising political order and shared forces. The post-frontier and contemporary authors of our time have presented numerous average Indian characters. However, Ghosh's characters are extraordinary. Mostly, they are all working class individuals, who have incalculable dreams for the better prospect of life. They uncover their issues of migration, displacement and alienation. Ghosh connects his characters with the crisis of alienation and the similar sort of issues found in the real life. People migrate in search of livelihood. They even cross national borders for good placement and a better life. For example, Nabeel, *In an Antique Land*, leaves his home and country in order to raise his home in a better position. Ila, in *The Shadow Lines*, wants to migrate in order to free herself from the working class choking influences. Eakambaram unmistakably remarks, "Ghosh's characters go as far as Delhi or London on work or travel and come home to Calcutta or Dhaka only to learn that peace is as elusive as ever (Eakambaram, 236). The two novels *The Shadow Lines*, *The Circle of Reason* and the non-fiction *In an Antique Land* is under study. The characters in these works struggle to establish their identity and existence in the unrestrained social and political disarray. They have different facets of entities such as professionals, friends, family members, spouses and lovers.

The characters in Ghosh's novels authenticate their identity in the backdrop of sturdy challenges and existential crisis. The personas of the works under study share a certain likeness in their construction. They are all middle-class family members and are victims of troubles such as rootlessness in addition to the existential challenges. It was as an outlet of the political and communal frenzy. Ghosh's cleverness is that he chose the life, its meaning and experiences as a focus of his writings. He has drawn it from his actual experiences of human beings, over and above from his detail study of sociology, history and anthropology. He projects such life experiences lively in his creation and characterisation. The characters are wholesome and are presented at the suitable stages of life. Ghosh exhibits better art of characterisation as Brinda Veerappa rightly comments:

> Through the characterisation...Amitav Ghosh makes a touching comments on the lives of many people of old generation of the subcontinent...who have lost their spaces—literal, emotional and spiritual—because of partition.

The diagnostic string of the study discloses that the characters are drawn in an artful way to fit the subject and theme of freedom and its ideas. It explores the meaning of freedom. For a common man, who faces hazards to outwit their individual freedom for enhanced prospect and improved way for earning and upright living to exist. The portrayal of characters in *The Shadow Lines* is a fine example of Ghosh's art of characterisation.

Ghosh's ideas are ingenious, through his analysis of characters. Ghosh discloses that the men and women were of a regular cautious nature. The cautiousness was drawn from the society. The society was dishevelled by political and religion blows arising from the blind beliefs, prejudices and far-reaching domination of violence. Ghosh projects some characters several talent and calibre. For example, in *The Glass Palace*, the character Rajkumar narrated these, "It was Rajkumar's practice never to collect more than a part of his salary, banking the rest with John." Rajkumar wants to run his own business in a headed manner by the acquirer of timber yard and flourish. The character of Jyoti Das, a police officer in *The Circle of Reason* jotted down in a deceitful way. It was drawn by Ghosh through his imaginative and creative skills. Ghosh describes Jyoti Das as "He is clean shaven and pride himself on it for it distinguishes him from his colleagues.... He is pleasant if not good looking...looks younger than his twenty years he is often mistaken for college students" (Ghosh, 123). The character of the police officer is moving.

The portrayal of Uma Verma in *The Circle of Reason* is quite interesting; she acknowledges science over the conventional ideas. She is a microbiologist. She confesses to being a human rather than to be buried in science forlorn. The characters created by Ghosh suit with the thematic consideration. They enable the readers to feel the real-life character touch. For example, the character of Tha'mma in *The Shadow Lines* lively presents the wounds of segregation of nation. Tha'mma was prepared to run an errand for freedom of her country. She ultimately learns from her occurrence and questions the competence of borders between nations by political erroneous believes. Ghosh gives the poignant, touchy portrayal of feelings and sentiments of expatriate and debarred people of natural discreet in the event of bifurcation of the nation. Insights of the affected people are characterised effectively in the novel. Shubha Tiwari rightly comments it as, "*The Shadow Lines* does not have matured characters. Nor...Saints...but their flaws are human; explicable...it is a master stroke of Ghosh at the art of characterisation (Tiwari, 5).

The Circle of Reason is sensibly a distinguished novel from an ordinary form. The characters and their lives are individual; they do not fall into the conventional category. They are all common human beings. The livelihood of those characters in *The Circle of Reason* shows man's hassles of alienation and existential confront. It is obvious in the point of Alu (*Nachiketa*), who moves from Calcutta to Al-Ghazira in search of better living.

Alu's description is tough to describe. He is neither tall or short, nor dark or fair, his uncle Balaram wants to replace Alu from schooling. Balaram wants to inculcate the art of weaving in him. Balaram's character in the novel is projected as a practical thinker and the survivor of beliefs. Balaram's character connotes the title of the novel. He is a rationalist; the art of characterisation is exposed through Balaram. Ghosh describes Balaram as:

> He had a thin, ascetic face, with clean lines, a sharp ridge of a nose and wide, dreamy eyes. His high broad forehead rose to a majestic dome crowned with a thick, unruly pile of silver hair. It was an astonishing forehead: it shown, it glowed, it was like a lamp shade for his bulging Higher Faculties—language, form, Number, the lot, it was striking face even in repose. (Ghosh, 55)

Balaram's character can be typified as a man of reason. Balaram's idea to run a 'School of Reason' is a greenhorn. Ghosh here persuades that the education can bestow qualities in a man, but skilled education may facilitate him to earn his living. Weaving, a skilled art is one of the significant aspects of the novel. Alu wants to be a weaver. Balaram's learning of Phrenology induces him that it is the apt livelihood for Alu. Ghosh mildly relates the loom (weaving) with the man and national boundaries. He writes:

> Man at the loom is the finest example of mechanical man, a creature who makes his own world as no other can, with his mind. The machine is man's curse and his salvation, and no machine has created man as much as loom. It has created not separate words but one, for it has never permitted the division of the world. (Ghosh, 55)

Alu starts to learn weaving from Shombhu Debnath, a depraved man in Lalpukar. Ghosh utilised the space to give a historical perspective to the weaving. He indicates that the human wove, buy and sold clothes since long past. For example, Indian clothes were found in Egyptian rulers' graves and tombs. The silk route can be spotted, it starts from China through Central Asia and Persia until it reaches the ports of the Mediterranean. Then the clothes reached the markets of Africa and Europe. Ghosh indirectly emphasises that the trade connected continents together for centuries, but the narrow rationalistic ideas conceived the borders within. Ghosh intellectually made his character designs to bring out this truth. Alu becomes a trained weaver under the supervision of Shombha Devnath. Maya Shombha's daughter is Alu's first sexual encounter. Alu is construed of his scam activities and he drives away from Calcutta to Kerala and Al-Ghazira. As in other novels of Amitav Ghosh, the character of Alu also faced the problems of migration and alienation.

The characterisation of Jyoti Das is remarkable; he is an Assistant Superintendent of Police. Ghosh described him as an impressive man. He was different from his colleagues. Jyoti Das suspects Alu of anti-social activities and he follows him. The peculiar thing about Jyoti Das is his personality. Ghosh's art of characterisation is publicized through Jyoti Das. Ghosh describes him as, "He is pleasant if not good looking and he looks younger than his twenty-five years; he is often mistaken for a college student" (Ghosh, 123). The character of Jyoti Das deceives critical acclaim. "One of the characters who reappear from time to time is Jyoti Das, a Police Officer by profession, whose real vocation is bird watching. His pursuit of Alu provides a loose connecting thread to the later portion of the novel" (Kaul, 247). Ghosh through the characterisation of Alu and Jyoti Das constructs the picaresque effect in the novel.

The characterisation of Rakesh is notable. Rakesh is a migrant who migrates with Alu from India to Al-Ghazira. He is unable to find a job, though he is a graduate. People used to migrate to find better earning. It was projected through the character of Jeevanbhai Patel. He is a businessman from Gujarat. He is a highly practical man who always wants to rear the money. He moves from place to place, faced the skirmishes in life. He continuously fails and wins but at last commits suicide out of loneliness. His death affects Zindi, a woman who wants to purchase the tailoring house from him. Another character—Nury, an egg-seller's character depiction attracts attention. Ghosh describes Nury as, "In his own small way Nury was a great man. He had the wisdom to see the world cleverly. And like a logician, he drew clear conclusions from what he saw" (Ghosh, 246). Nury's characterisation is much philosophic; he is top in circles of other characters. Ulka Joshi comments, "The characters are trapped in such a non-productive circle that their struggles lead them to nothingness" (Ulka, 32).

One can find the 'reason' for success or failure. This is the circle of life. Middle-class people strive to attain success in this life circle. For an instance, Balaram lives with the reason of self-reliance and work with machines. The characterisation of Balaram personifies reason. The reason put beside things in this novel. Balaram is fascinated by *Life of Pasteur*. He follows Pasteur as his model. However, his scientific temper indicates factual situations. Balaram's characterisation sticks with logic, he cannot look beyond reason. Ghosh characterisation is balanced which throws lights on contradictory elements in the depiction of the character.

The novel is highly unconventional, not strictly organized and episodic. It resembles the picaresque type. The novel is just like a journey, but it is asymmetrical. The characters in the novel are in the state of frenzy. They look forward to the fortune. The protagonist Alu has gone from darkness to purity. Ghosh generously moves from the past, present and future. The novel's episodes are loosely connected and crowded with characters. The novel is illustrative, open-ended with a soothing effect. Ghosh never attempts to preach.

The novel has both historical and mythological elements. Like Girish Karnad, Ghosh moulded the myth and history. In this novel, Ghosh presented his ideas, characters and images with irony and fictional ornamentations. The characters are flung with metaphors and stand for rootlessness. The conception of 'home' is altered. It made thrift in the characterisation. The novel's base moves to and fro from Bangladesh and Calcutta, it reaches the Middle East and Kerala. The story shifts in an indecisive atmosphere, the locations are not stable, but shaky. Alu's character is the only stable element. The characterisation of Alu is hectic. Bhudeb Roy made Alu as a scapegoat and declares him a terrorist. Alu sprints to Calcutta. Alu's characterisation turns like the vagabond and adventurous. Alu's actual name is Nachiketa. It is a mythological name. Nachiketa is a mythical boy son of sage Uddalaka who waits at Yama's doors (door of death) in quest of celestial knowledge. Alu stands in the death door in Al-Ghazira. He is trapped alive in a building collapse. The 'fire' runs in the myth—a cleansing agent; carbolic acid runs in the novel—a cleansing agent. He identifies the truth in scientific reasoning. He wants to be scientific in removing the ills of society. Thus, Ghosh made a medley of characterisation. It gives the impression that everything is in reality is a matter of how we look at it. 'Attitudes matter'. Time in this novel is characterized by remarkable fluidity. The lives that this novel depicts are all lived on the threshold of abnormality. It obeys the saying that 'attitude is altitude'.

The construction of the characters in the novel *The Shadow Lines* (1988) is different. The novel was published in the backdrop of frenzy. It was a period of heavy civil disorder, uproar and rampant in the nation. The assassination of Prime Minister of India evokes great violence and chaos in that time. By then, Ghosh was teaching in Delhi University. He evidenced the violence and riot. The characters of *The Shadow Lines* are created from Ghosh's imprints of communal violence and of national boundaries. The riots and pile slay enriched the creation of characters in *The Shadow Lines*. Ghosh through his skilful characterisation projects the demarcation of lines (national boundaries) divide people but not their memories. For example, the character Tha'mma and her old uncle survive with their memory of their past.

The novel's background is set in Bangladesh, Calcutta and London. The novel deliberates story of three generations. Ghosh's characterisation and projection of individual character are unique. The chief character of the novel includes Tridib, Tha'mma, Ila, May Price, Robi, unnamed narrator and Nick Price are interesting and distinctive. Neelam Srivastava comments about those characters as: "In the text, we get to know various characters, who let themselves be trapped in stories which are not of their own fashioning, as well the narrator, who is simultaneously the most 'gullible' and the most 'doubtful' listener of all" (Srivastava, 60).

The characters in *The Shadow Lines* reflect the ethos of the people who are trapped in rootlessness and existential challenges. Through all the focal characters, Ghosh has marked the life of people who were affected by the violence, riots and re-demarcation of national boundaries. The characters encounter an identity crisis. They belong to middle-class society. The character of unnamed narrator plays a vital role in the novel. The character Tha'mma was born in Dhaka; she is a teacher. She dislikes Ila, granddaughter of her sister Mayadevi. Ila's brought up was different. She was vivacious by living in various places, as her father faced occasional transfers. Through the characterisation of Tha'mma, Ghosh underlines the fate of people who evidenced the partition of India, Pakistan and Bangladesh. The protagonist Tha'mma projected as a specimen of nationalism. Ghosh projects that the demarcating lines drawn by the political machinery cannot divide the memory and experiences of the people. Here, Ghosh depicts that such lines of division are elusive and they are the real lines of shadows.

Tha'mma was born in a joint family at Dhaka. She was strong-willed and stubborn. She lost her husband. She joined a school to face her family needs. She is a proud middle-class woman and a devoted teacher. She rejects the favour, sympathy and help from others and even from her own sister, Mayadevi. She is determined and proud to face life and its toils. Shubha Tiwari comments, "Tha'mma's character is a tribute to so many unrecognized women in this country, who are holding the world of their children and near and dear ones together by their toils and labour" (Tiwari, 34). Ghosh shows that Tha'mma's motivation is to be free with self-respect and national power. The pathos of the middle-class families is very well revealed through Tha'mma. Ghosh writes, "All she wanted was a middle-class life in which the middle classes the world over, she would thrive believing in the unity of nationhood and territory, of self-respect and national power: that was all she wanted..." (Ghosh, 78). Through Tha'mma, Ghosh has extensively evoked the feeling and the meaning of nationalism.

Another important character of *The Shadow Lines* is Tridib, son of Sahib, a high rank diplomat. Tridib stands as an attractive personality and has many admirers. The narrator considers Tridib as his hero. He was pursuing his research in Ancient Indian History of Bengal. People stick to him as he has charming personality, wide knowledge and reading. Tridib's existence hastens impetus to the story and the impulsion to the narrator in the novel. Tridib loves May Price and sends her chatty letters. This love affair causes Tridib's death in the riots. He tries to save May Price and is slayed by the rioters. Tridib's death is most dramatic and penetrating stage in the novel. It reminds Ghosh's experience of the widespread riots and slaughters in 1984. Gita Chaudhari noted the death of Tridib as, "With his death he brings home to the narrator the meaninglessness of artificial boundaries, the falsehood of forcing one individual's idea over another and the disaster of misplaced ideals" (Chaudhari, 97). Living without memory is not possible. Few live with the past memory and the other lives with other's memory. The characterisation of Tha'mma and May Price nailed this point. Living without the touch of historical events is impossible. Ghosh, in his art of characterisation, reveals the historical events as, "...those events of 1964 is the product of a struggle with silence. It is a struggle I am destined to lose—have already lost—for even after all these years.... It is not, for example, the silence of imperfect memory" (Ghosh, 218).

Characterisation of May is indeed different. May has an extra edge and sense of justice. It is clear while she gave a simple explanation on Tridib's death. She had an influence on Tridib. She forces him to stop the car to save a street dog in Calcutta. Tridib obeys her. In another incident at Dhaka, Tridib stops to save her from the rioters. His characterisation is much genuine and epitomic as his name 'Tridib' means 'trinity'. Ghosh presents this character with the touch of Christ. May's character is parallel with that of Tridib. She lives like a penance ever since Tridib's death. She sleeps on floor, fasts; she works for the earthquake relief and other social services. She raises fund for poor people. Only at the end of the novel, she realizes the meaning of sacrifice.

Characterisation of Ila is notable. She is one of the major women characters in the novel. She wants to be free in her ways of living. She also wants to get rid of cultural clutches and family laws. Ila is a representative of a modern woman. She loves to be in London. She finds it as a proper city for her cosmopolitan way of life. The narrator is in love with Ila. The narrator was attracted by her Western cloths. But Ila marries Nick, an Englishman. Eventually, she finds her marriage is not up to her expectations. Ghosh projects her as a representative of a postcolonial female perspective. Anu Chopra comments on Ila's character as, "Even when she starts working for a child organization, she is emotionally so dishonest because she hates children. It is difficult to understand why Amitav Ghosh has portrayed Ila as such a superficial person" (Chopra, 64). Characterisation of May is different from Ila. May is portrayed as a humane and sensible woman. Tridib's love with May and her relationship with Tridib comes to an end at his death. She felt guilty of his death. She felt sad for his sacrifice but she was arrogant enough with him while he was alive. Ghosh brings out the effects of Western culture on the Indians by way of surplus culture. He compares Western free will to India's cultural effects.

Through his characterisation, Ghosh interprets the issues like up-rootedness, national boundaries and riots on political, communal and social differences. He brings out that the lives of all the three generations of characters are deeply affected by the said issues. The novel is drafted in an emotional plane which highlights the universal truths of life. Enchantingly, the novelist has portrayed the psychological condition of children. The narrator remains as an adult rooted in his childhood experiences. His reactions, descriptions and impressions of things and people are from his childhood perception. With this point, it is apt to acclaim childhood as the major theme of the novel.

Characterisation of the narrator is modestly overwhelming. Ghosh throws light on the Child Psychology. Tridib is narrator's cousin. Tridib's charming character had an influence on the narrator's life. They have a special attachment. The narrator tries to imagine Tridib as a child and tries to envision his stories about London from Tridib's child-like perspective. The narrator travels with Tridib with his stories of London, Cairo and other places. The narrator travels, identifying himself with the child's eyes with the impact of his character role model Tridib. The narrator is swathe with the protective presence of Tridib. Ghosh may characterise the narrator and Tridib from his personal experience. The narrator has an uncontaminated child-like love for his uncle Tridib. He spurts with pride at Tridib's intellect and superior knowledge. His delight enlarges when Tridib treats him as an equal and discloses secrets with him. The child in the narrator loves Tridib and the adult in the narrator firmly stands for him. Ghosh beautifully presents the Child Psychology. One odder glance into child psychology happens when the child-narrator comes to know about the death of Tridib. Tridib was close to him and more than a friend, philosopher and guide. His influence on the narrator was extreme.

Love is one of the bases in this novel; love is a very intangible subject. It is an emotion that centres the universe. It cannot be restrained or restricted; it is very wide in its scope. Thiruvalluvar, in his 71st *Kural*, indicates that there is no bar to restrain love. Love and logic are natural enemies. Throughout the novel, love and logic play hide and seek.

The characterisation in *The Shadow Lines* is unique, imagination is the keynote for any literary products, but the imagination never works with the real emotions. The real emotions are found in the darkness and solitude of human mind. The real emotions cannot be penned and can be registered with innate touch. The concept of alienation and displacement is not only for the national boundaries but also for the human boundaries, who clasp their minds with many locks. No one opens the real thoughts, perhaps the real love of May with Tridib is profound in his absence. The boundary of fascination abides her to excel her love, but on later days she suffers and mourns for her sluggishness. The darker part of the human mind is a real shadow thing. The characterisation affixed with the title exactly because the line between the human minds and the real boundaries between the human beings are darker yet unexplainable things. However, Ghosh to a level succeeds in his attempt of characterisation, his choice of title fits like a glove.

Ghosh amalgamates two sets of characters in the novel *In an Antique Land*. The characters can be identified into two, the historical and the present time characters. The amalgamation of characters is in three periods: pre-colonial, colonial and post-colonial periods. It is skilfully drafted in a form of a story. The main characters in the pre-colonial time are Abraham Ben Yiju and Bomma. Ben Yiju is a Tunisian Jew merchant. He came to India via Egypt in 1130 AD. He carries his business in India, Egypt and Aden. Bomma is his slave from India. Through these characters, Ghosh portrays that the life in those days of pre-colonial time was happy. People lived in harmony with fellow men in spite of culture and race. Ben Yiju was born in Tunisia, settled in India and married an Indian girl.

The character of Ben Yiju is historical and discovered by Ghosh. He has retold the life of Ben Yiju and three others. They were Madmun Ibnal Hassen Ibn Badar, Yusuf Ibn Abraham and Khalaf Ibn Ishak. Ben Yiju came to Mangalore in 1132 AD and married a slave girl, Ashu. Ashu belongs to a south Indian Nair family. Ghosh's research work on slave, MSH-6 demonstrates numerous surprising features of human relationship. Though Bomma was a slave, he was trusted with goods. He was sent as a representative of Ben, to the places like Egypt and Adan. Bomma is developed as a business agent of Yiju. Ghosh describes him as, "Bomma probably had to undergo while in Ben Yiju's service, that eventually became a small patch of level ground between them: the matrilineal descended Tulu and the patriarchal Jew who would otherwise seem to stand on different sides of an unbridgeable chasm" (Ghosh, 263).

Ghosh unearths the relationship between India and Egypt in ancient time. Through Ben Yiju's character, Ghosh inscribes history. He also writes his discovery of tradition, culture and harmonious association of men. The multi-cultural and multi-religious believes at Ben Yiju's time were detailed. Ghosh underlines that the foray of Portuguese and Dutch on the overseas business in the Indian Ocean and the Arabian Sea has ended the development of a harmonious association between different culture and religion. Ghosh criticizes colonisation here, as it spoils the existing harmony and accord.

Other sets of the characters that appear in the novel, *In an Antique Land* are fictional. It is based on Ghosh's visit as a research student of Oxford to Egypt, Lataifa and Nashawy. *In an Antique Land* consists of three visits of Ghosh to Egypt. He collects information and according to that, he develops the character of Nabeel. Through the characterisation of Nabeel, Ghosh stirs up the feelings of those people who are away from their homes. Nabeel goes to Iraq to bring in more and to earn for his family. But he himself is thrown out of the family. He becomes an 'outsider'. Though he got better development and position in abroad, he lacks happiness. Nutan Damodar comments, "Nabeel loses his standing within the family as a living emotional being and becomes a money producing machine" (Damodar, 130). Ghosh highlights that Nabeel's position in Iraq is not better than that of a slave in ancient times. Ghosh affirms that Nabeel's stance is that of a bonded labourer. Nabeel is hushed by his boss. Nabeel has added burden by family needs and a sense of alienation. He felt like trapped in a foreign land. Ghosh appears to draw to an extent some similarities between Ben Yiju and Nabeel. Both are forced to leave their homeland for one or another reason. They move to foreign lands with a hope to get a better economic possibility. Ghosh's art of characterisation of Ben Yiju and Nabeel is such that history is repeated after many centuries.

This book underscores the natural history of Indian trade business and commerce before the arrival of Vasco da Gama to India. Ghosh wants to limelight the forgotten period of history. He demonstrates that India's alliance with the Arab and the Chinese was liberal. Through the characterisation of Bomma, he registers the above flow and rapport between nations and peoples. The book is in fact a testimony of Ghosh's deep urge as a tireless, genuine researcher. It covers his research as a social anthropologist over decades. His writing captures the daily encounters of his characters. They are shown with their religious rites, social customs along with their eccentricities and whims. A tale breeds into a story, ordinary thing becomes history, and the anthropology mixes with fiction. It brings a change in the ecology of learning. Ghosh's *In an Antique Land* nurtures in the environment of magical realism. The sense of time is not strict in this novel. Time mixes with blending of fact and fiction. It binds together the different branches of knowledge, sociology, anthropology, history, philosophy and religion. Ghosh's interface is with four languages and cultures. It stretches across continents and centuries. The novel has segmented into six parts as, the Prologue, Lataifa, Nashawy, Mangalore, Going Back and Epilogue. It began in 1942 when Ghosh read an article by E. Strauss. The slave of MSH-6 was denoted here by a merchant named Khalaf Ibn Ishaq in Aden. Ghosh admires that the history of a slave has survived all centuries. History is all about kings and queens, their richness, magnanimity, magnitude, and so on. To find a slave in history is indeed a wonder for Ghosh. So, he begins the novel with that the slave of MSH-6.

Yiju and his acquaintances exercise a language of Northern derivation. Ghosh contemplates that Yiju and other traders used code words in their business communication. Ghosh indicates that that the wholesale trade spot of Varanasi is highly specialized. He admires about the significant and profitable trade and cordial relationships between people of diverse backgrounds, which is indeed astounding. They earn and share their cultures and religions, which is a utopia even today. Indian trade changed forever on 17 May 1498 when Vasco da Gama landed in India. "Within a few years of that day the knell had been struck for the world that had brought Bomma, Ben Yiju, and Ashu together and another age had begun in which the crossing of their paths would seem so unlikely that its very possibility would all but disappear from human memory" (Ghosh, 286). Ghosh seems to be captivated by Egypt and its history. He sees people and their characters live in his mind exactly. However, he does not find the same humbleness from foreigners. Their treatment towards Ghosh is based on their view of India, but very few foreigners like

Nabeel understand Ghosh's agitation and fondly reprimand him. The impact of such incidents over Ghosh is catastrophic. He drew them in mind while he made the characters.

One thing is exacting about Amitav Ghosh is that he is not a conventional writer and he is unpredictable. He is not regular in the production of novels one after another with the basic patterns and the never changing themes. The characters in his novels cannot be described with any such traditional references. His art of characterisation, description and narration is unique and attractive. It's a strange sort of a work, characterisation within the parameters of history and in the mode of searching for something innately.

Works Cited

Primary Sources

Ghosh, Amitav. *In an Antique Land*. New Delhi: Ravi Dayal Publishers, 2001. Print.

———. *The Circle of Reason*. New Delhi: Ravi Dayal Publishers, 2001. Print.

———. *The Shadow Lines*. New Delhi: Ravi Dayal Publishers, 2001. Print.

Secondary Sources

Chaudhari, Gita. "The Narrator in *The Shadow Lines* coming to term will reality", *The Fiction of Amitav Ghosh*. Ed. Indira Bhatt and Indira Nityanandam. New Delhi: Creative Books, 2001. Print.

Chopra, Anu. "May and Ola—The Two Faces of Woman", *Interpretation—Amitav Ghosh's The Shadow Lines*. Ed. Indira Bhatt and Indira Nityanandam. New Delhi: Creative Books, 2001. Print.

Damodar, Nutan. "Roots of Alienation", *The Fiction of Amitav Ghosh*, New Delhi: Creative Books, 2001. Print.

Eakambaram, N. "The Theme of Violence in *The Shadow Lines*", *Amitav Ghosh's The Shadow Lines*. Ed., by Novy Kapadia. New Delhi: Asia Book Club, 2001. Print.

Joshi, Ulka. "*The Circle of Reason*: Caught up in Circles", *The Fiction of Amitav Ghosh*. Ed. Indira Bhatt and Indira Nityanandam. New Delhi: Creative Books, 2001. 32. Print.

Kaul, R.K. "Another Triumphant Entry—Amitav Ghosh: *The Circle of Reason*". *Indian Book Chronicle*, Vol. II, Nos. 11 and 12, Nov.-Dec. 1986, 247. Print.

Pope, G.U. *The 'Sacred' Kurral of Tiruvalluva Nayanar*. New Delhi: Asian Educational Services. xxxi. 1886. Print.

Srivastava, Neelam. "Fictions of Nationhood in Amitav Ghosh's *The Shadow Lines*". *Journal of Contemporary Thought Summer*, 1999, 60. Print.

Tiwari, Shobha. *Amitav Ghosh—A Critical Study*. New Delhi: Atlantic Publishers & Distributors, 27th Edition, 2003. 34. Print.

Veerappa, Brinta K. "*The Shadow Lines*: A Critical Appraisal", *Amitav Ghosh's The Shadow Lines*. Ed., by Novy Kapadia. New Delhi: Asia Book Club, 2001, 166. Print.

7

The Colonial Impact on the Individual and the Social Lives: A Postcolonial Reading of Amitav Ghosh's *Sea of Poppies*

R. Karthika Devi

Every age in the history of the world encounters a transformation due to a new event. And the last quarter of the last millennium witnessed a drastic transition with the advent of European expedition and exploration of the east and the south of the world for various reasons such as adventure, trade, etc. Wherever the westerners established their trade centres and settled themselves, they began to exploit the natural resource, occupy the lands where the natives had lived since time immemorial, subjugate them to serve them as slaves, eradicate their culture and traditional ways of life, make them economically poor by plundering their wealth, introduce English language in order to erase their identity, establish various schemes and missionaries to convert them to Christianity.

When the sons of the soil obeyed them submissively, the whites who established their colonies considered them noble savages. When they protested, the colonizers called them barbarous and considered it the burden the white to civilize them. They brought out negative portrayal of the natives and the Orientals as lazy, barbarous, good for nothing, foolish and superstitious in their history books and literature. In order to fulfil their material ends, the white went to any extreme of butchering the natives wretchedly. The natives were not only physically tortured and socially made subaltern but also internally oppressed. Both the royal people and the ordinary people became victims of the evil effects of colonialism. While history books chronologically recorded the major events influencing the course of human life in general way, most of them have become human construct reflecting the maker's ideology rather than presenting the truth as it is. Hence, many a time, there arise gaps in the history books. Some events fall in shadows being untold. A sensitive sympathizer who gets the opportunity of knowing such unmentioned sorrows and suffering bring out them into light with their historical perspective, literary imagination and knowledge. In fact, by adding their knowledge of the other side of reality, they reconstruct history in a novel way. Amitav Ghosh is such a writer, who being the student of history and having the chance of hearing what actually happened in various parts of India and the world from those who had witnessed the happenings directly, having been brought up as the son of a lieutenant in the British Indian Army, in different parts of India and the world. Ghosh's *Sea of Poppies* is one of the novels which focuses on the negative influence of the colonial rule.

Sea of Poppies, in the manner of an epic narrative, revolves around the lives of the people coming from various social backgrounds and from different parts of the world but assemble in the vessel, the *Ibis*.

The ship, the *Ibis* itself is a symbol of colonial authority, arrogance and colonial inhuman act and attitude to fellow human beings. The ship was originally constructed in order to transport the black people of Africa or Negroes as slaves to work in the plantations and industries owned by the whites in their colonies such as America, the Caribbean and Mauritius. Actually, the black people taken as slaves were not treated as human beings by the ship owners but as "Cargo" (https://en.wikipedia.org/wiki/Atlantic_slave_trade) i.e., because they even did not have the heart and mind of giving these people the status of being living beings with emotions, feelings, thoughts, pains and sufferings. By the middle of the 17th century, slavery had hardened as a racial caste, with the slaves and their offspring being legally the property of their owners, and children born to slave mothers were also slaves. As property, the people were considered merchandise or units of labour, and were sold at markets with other goods and services. The transatlantic slave trade, which is one of the consequences of colonialism which made one man a slave to another man, paradoxically preaching the principles of democracy, resulted in a vast and as yet still unknown loss of life for African captives, both in and outside America. "Approximately 1.2-1.4 million Africans died during their transport to the new world. More died soon upon their arrival. The number of lives lost in the procurement of slaves remains a mystery but may equal or exceed the number who survived to be enslaved. The savage nature of the trade led to the destruction of individuals and culture" (https://en.wikipedia.org/wiki/Atlantic_slave_trade). However, at present organizations such as PETA, which are western-based, talk of compassion towards living beings. At this juncture, works like *Sea of Poppies* remind people of the inhuman treatment of the blacks by the whites. Ghosh describes the dabusa, inside the *Ibis,* where the slaves were kept as animals being hands and legs tied with iron chains. It has been recorded through the observation of Jodu who was rescued during the wreck of his board and kept in the same hold:

> ...Jodu became aware of sickly fetid odour, welling upwards from the darkness below: ...the dabusa had a close, cramped feel-partly because its ceiling was not much taller than a man, but also because it was divided, by timber ribs, into open compartments, like Cattle-pens...he discovered that there were several such chains in the pen, nailed into the far beam; they ended in bracelet like clasps, each fitted with eyeholes, for locks. The weight and heft of the chains made Jodu wonder what sort of argo they were intended to restrain: it occurred to him that they might be meant for livestock and yet the stench that permeated the hold was not that of cows, horses or goats; it was more a human odour, compounded of sweat, urine, excrement and vomit; the smell had leached so deep into the timbers as to have become ineradicable. He picked up one of the chains, and on looking more closely at the bracelet-like clasps, he became convinced that it

> was indeed meant for a human wrist or ankle, he saw that there were smooth depressions in the wood, of a shape and size that could only have been made by human beings, over prolonged periods of time. The depressions were so close to each other as to suggest a great press of people, packed close together, like merchandise on a vendor's counter. (Ghosh, 139-40)

The description of the dabusa where the Negro slaves were imprisoned like lifeless commodities in order to be transported to toil for the prosperity of the whites represents the white man's cruelty and hard-heartedness. Such inhuman ill treatment of the blacks later led to a number of bloody protests and assassination of great leaders like Abraham Lincoln. The sufferings and the migration of the blacks is one of the consequences of the colonial expansion and it has been touched by Amitav Ghosh while he has actually dealt with the migration of the South-East Asians as indentured labourers in his *Sea of Poppies*. The racist arrogance of the colonizers towards the others has been recorded by Ghosh.

The formation of new diaspora community of indentured labourers comprising not a single racial group but a mingling of a variety of people belonging to different communities, races and nations speaking different languages, is one of the results of the colonial spirit of the imperial powers. The only common characteristic existing among the members of this new, diaspora is poverty which was cunningly exploited by the colonizers for their own benefits.

Deeti from upper caste but economically poor family; Kalua from socially oppressed class but a physically strong being; Neel Ratan Haldar from a royal family; Poulette, a French girl disguised as a Bengali lady, were the different persons sailing in the ship. However, their identities had to be erased and their individuality was eradicated except as the labourers of the whites. For example, Kalua and Deeti joined as indentured labourers in order to escape not only from poverty but also from social injustice. Hence, they had to hide their identity and Kalua gave his father his name and his father's name to himself. But, these two names were altered by the English man, and it has become another name "Maddow Colver" which gave him an entirely a foreign identity. This loss of identity was very common during the colonial rule. Ghosh comments on this:

> Later, within the dynasty that claimed its descent from him, many stories would be invented about the surname of the founding ancestor and the reason why "Maddow" occurred so frequently among his descendants. While many would choose to recast their origins, inventing grand and fanciful lineage for themselves, there would always remain a few who clung steadfastly to the truth; which was that those hallowed names were the result of the stumbling tongue of a harried gomusta, and the faculty hearing of an English pilot who was little more than half-seas over. (Ghosh, 278)

Names are not merely a facility to call somebody but they fix a certain identity to people or a particular group. However, the colonizers were not ready to consider these people as belonging to other races, but only entities without any identity. Hence, they did not give much importance to their names except for recording them in their registers as safety measure. Actually, these people became victims of the white man's racist prejudice. Deeti and Kalua also suffered from the racist discrimination.

Deeti was actually wife of Hukam Singh and mother of Kabutri living in a small village some fifty miles east of Benares. Her husband was not only crippled but also an opium addict. He used to be taken to the opium factory everyday in the ox-cart run by the low caste Kalua, a strong gigantic man. One day Hukam Singh died and there was no other option for Deeti other than to be the victim of *sati*, a practice of entering the funeral pyre of husband to go to the other world along with him, as she did not want to be sexually exploited by her brother-in-law.

Being the victim of gender violence at her husband's house, Deeti belonged to the oppressed community. In the same way, Kalua too is portrayed as a member of the subaltern society, as he belonged to the low caste which is actually a human construct. When the novel opens, Kalua comes as the ox-cart driver to pick up Hukam Singh, Deeti's husband to go to work in the opium factory run by the Britishers. At that time, he used to cover his face not to be seen by the upper caste people, as the high caste happening to see the face of the low caste was considered an ill omen. In spite of their oppressed condition, both of them are shown as strong people who endure their sufferings stoically. When the sufferings exceed the limit, the white's decision of taking the local people as indentured people to far away new lands was favorable for them to escape from the critical situation. However, it was only a temporary relief. Both of them knew this fact. Yet, they had decided to begin a new life in the foreign land.

When for the first time, Deeti happened to hear the rumour of the whites taking the people to work in places like Mauritius in exchange of money, she wondered how it was possible to leave one's own land without enjoying the warmth of kith and kin:

> ...What it would be like to be in their place, to know that you were forever an outcaste; that you would never throw your arms around your mother; never eat a meal with your sisters and brothers; never feel the cleansing touch of the Ganga. And to know also that for the rest of your days you would eke out a living on some wild, demon—plagued island? (Ghosh, 71)

Even before taking a decision to leave the native land, her heart was filled with the terrific fear of encountering an utter loneliness in the alien land. Yet, they had to endure the alienation in order to escape from the wrath of the upper-caste people, who could not tolerate the union of a low-caste man and an upper-caste widow.

However, their escape turned to be a story of falling into fire being afraid of mosquitoes. When their identity was revealed in the ship by the Subedhar, the captain of the ship Chillingworth gave orders to give sixty whippings. Zachary, the American carpenter of ship wondered at the punishment and asked him whether he was sure to award Kalua sixty floggings. Zachary told the captain that Kalua would bleed to death, if sixty strokes were given. Further, the captain revealed his racist prejudice and arrogance when Zachary expressed his displeasure saying that a coolie's choice of his wife did not matter to them because the punishment was ordered to Kalua because of his marriage with Deeti. When Zachary Reid questions the Captain "...we can't let him be flogged for it while he is in our custody" (468), the latter speaks:

> I am amazed, Reid, that you of all people – an American! Should pose these questions. Why, what do you think would happen in Maryland if a white Woman were to be violated by a Negro? What would you, or I, or any of us, do with a darkie who'd had his way with our wives or sisters? Why should we expect the subedar and his women to feel any less strongly than we would ourselves? And what right do we have to deny them the vengeance that we should certainly claim as our due? No Sir.... (468)

The argument of the captain proved the fact that with all their intellectual pursuits and scientific enquiry of life and truth, they were fundamentally barbarous ones, who cannot consider their fellow beings equally. The whites used to point out the caste system as one of the evils of Indian society but they themselves equated it on par with the natural distinction between the whites and the blacks. The talk with reference to the difference between the upper caste and the lower caste in association with the anomaly between the whites and the blacks and the Captain's readiness to kill the low caste, proves the cruelty, narrow mindedness, and selfishness, racist and parochial temperament of the whites. Further, the Captain's reference to the American of what he would do if a white woman would be violated by a Negro, raises several critical questions. America is a multicultural country where people are naturally able to appreciate each other's ways of life. That is why, perhaps, Ghosh might have portrayed Zachary, an American to be a sympathetic person. However, it should be recognized here that the United States of America itself was a colony of England. Also, Zachary Reid is a mulatto, an offspring of a white father and a black mother like Abraham

Lincoln, who too had fought against the typical white man's aversion towards the Negro. He worked and struggled a lot for the abolition of slavery.

Zachary Reid, being a mixed breed, did not consider the division of human beings on the basis of race, creed, language, nationality, religion, etc., as the whites did. The new races of mixed bread and the formation of their own culture and ideologies towards life is another effect of colonialism and this impact can be observed throughout the world. In addition to the creation of character of Zachary, Ghosh has presented another picture of the cross breed resulting from the union of a Parsi of Indian origin and a Chinese woman. The spread of mixed breed culture is found in a number of countries. For example, in Canada, half breeds or the Metis, who are originally the offsprings of the French male and the Aboriginal female, constitute a district group which has undergone innumerable sufferings at the hands of the mainstream white society.

Writers like Maria Campbell and Beatrice Culleton in an autobiography and semi-autobiographical manner have discussed the sufferings of the mixed race people in their *Halfbreed* and *In Search of April Rain Tree* respectively. These mixed race people have to either assimilate into mainstream culture or to suffer from identity crisis. They cannot establish their own identity. Further, it brings them inexpressible psychological suffering. They undergo the burden of the feeling of aloofness. In their isolation, some will be open and broad minded and some would become opportunists. Both the characters have been delineated by Ghosh. While Zachary was able to question the English man who gave orders to flog Kalua with whip sixty times, Ah Fatt urinated on his friend at the command of the first mate of the ship, Mr. Crowle, due to the fear of being punished. Yet, the intermingling of different races had became so common only after colonialism, though history says that even two thousand years back, the southern part of India had mercantile ties with the Greeks and the Romans. It is also true that the ancient trade culture was limited with the exchange of goods but the colonial trade interest resulted in a master-slave relationship, leading to the exploitation of one man by another man or one country by another country, to an irretrievable condition. Not only people such as Deeti, Kalua and Ah Fatt, who belong to the subaltern community but also persons belonging to the royal families were victims of the white man's policies based on racist prejudices and economic exploitation. Ghosh has seriously and severely portrayed how the British were indiscriminate towards the upper and the lower class people in their inhuman treatment of them in a cruel and arrogant manner, through the life of Neel Rattan Halder.

Neel Rattan Halder is the Raja of Raskhali. He possessed all the noble qualities of an aristocrat such as compassion, benevolence and generosity and a sense of responsibility towards his dependants as well as the loose morals of the high born community, such as a wayward, luxurious life, not bothering about the expenses and lack of knack of money management. He was betrayed by his own people and cheated by Benjamin Burnham, the owner of the ship, *Ibis*. He had been initially prosperous in his opium business which was actually initiated in India by the British merchants, who later became rulers. Actually, a Raja should not be involved in such a drug business which would lead people to a dangerous path of life. A Raja must involve himself in only those concerns which would bring good to people, according to *Kshatriya dharma*, but Neel Rattan Halder, due to the colonizer's influence, did opium business but in a careless manner. Opium trade earned him a lot of money. He spent all the money lavishly for those who were around him. He had even given a luxurious dinner to Zachary Reid, Doughty and Benjamin Burnham, the owner of the *Ibis,* who later became responsible for his arrest after being charged with forgery. Though he involved in opium trade for making money, he was not money-minded. What he had earned, he used to spend it for his dependants without calculating lose or gain. At last he became bankrupt. His bankruptcy was cunningly exploited by the money-minded English merchant, who is the product of Colonialism. During the nineteenth century, various schemes were planned and executed in order to annex the states of Hindustan. Subsidiary Alliance was introduced and implemented by Lord Wellesley to expand the British Empire. Lord Dalhousie proposed of Doctrine of Lapse, according to which if the native king did not have his own legal heir, his state would be taken by the British. Even in the judicial courts, only the English judges tried the cases for English people. Ilbert Bill, introduced during the viceroyship of Lord Rippon, was vehemently opposed as it recommended that the Indian judges and advocates could deal with cases involving the English people. In such a situation, for his debts, Neel Rattan had to lose his estates to the English man Burnham, to whom he had given a luxurious feast. Because of the influence of Burnham, the Raja was convicted as a forger and given the sentence of seven years of imprisonment and transportation to Mauritius as an indentured laborer. He was put in Alipore jail. There he was tortured in a humiliating manner. His attire was torn and he was made naked in order to check his physical health and body and to find identification marks. He endured everything stoically. When he happened to sail in the *Ibis*, it was tattooed on his forehead, "forgerer, Alipore 1838" (286). Amitav Ghosh in a masterly way describes how violently and inhuman way, the physical body of the Raja was examined by the servants of the English.

> ...they quickly tore off the remnants of his clothing; then they held him upright, pinioning his limbs so as to fully expose his naked body to his jailor's scrutiny...the touch of the orderly's fingers had a feel that Neel could never have imagined between two human beings.... It was as if his body had passed into the possession of a new owner, who was taking stock of it as a man might inspect a house he had recently acquired, searching for signs of disrepair or neglect.... (282-83)

Neel, in spite of being examined roughly, got the gesture from the orderly for forgiveness. And the person who tattooed on the forehead of Neel too gave him a ball of opium to reduce the pain of tattooing and after the work, he told Neel that he had used only diluted ink for tattooing, which will disappear in a very few months. He further said that his family had been given shelter and other privileges and survival by his ancestors in his estates. Throughout the description of the painful experience of Neel at Alipore jail, Ghosh has never portrayed Neel suffering psychologically. But, he always tried to talk in English with the English people in vain and was humiliated by them.

While Neel spoke in refined English, other simple characters such as Serang Ali, the head of the group called laskars, also used English as lingua franca in a rough way. The spread of English language was one of the chief effects of British colonialism. However, when the language was used by different people, it underwent different changes, new words were formed and various accents were produced. Ghosh records this fact in an interesting way through the tongues of the various nations and natives. As far as the upper-class people are concerned, speaking in English language means a standard of stylish life. When Neel tried to make friendship with Zachary speaking in English, the carpenter turned to the second mate of the ship in futile. Though he had given grand feast to the foreigners, including Zachary, who was willing to have friendly relationship with him, could not continue it because of the pressure given by the whites. Yet, Neel maintained his balance as a royal man even during the most adverse moments. For the sake of fun, Neel and Ah Fatt, the mixed breed was ordered to entertain the first mate of the ship Crowle. Neel was compelled to urinate on Ah Fatt, but he refused and so was severely attacked. But he never budged while Ah Fatt readily urinated on Neel when he was tempted with a ball of opium. However, after urination, instead of being awarded with opium, his mouth was filled with goat dung. This incident was narrated to show the cruelty of the white men and also to bring into light the various ways in which the colonized were tortured as subalterns.

In addition to portraying the representatives of the existing groups of Indian society, Ghosh has also given the picture of a peculiar group consisting of poor people belonging to different parts of the world and hence different races. This group is entirely new to Indian English fiction. Ghosh's historical knowledge has given the opportunity to the readers to have a glimpse of this group of people who work together with a leader. They would work for cheap remuneration but, they should be either taken together for a task or not at all.

As a postcolonial writer, Amitav Ghosh has presented the impact of colonial rule on Indian life with the backdrop of the opium war between the British and the Chinese during the nineteenth century. The major events that took place on the ship, Ibis, originally built for transporting the black slaves, were currently used for trading opium in 1838. While dealing with the life and delineating the characters of different personages, Ghosh reveals his true nationalistic sentiments. Almost all Indian characters except a few like Subedar Bhyro Singh, are endowed with noble qualities. Raja Neel Rattan Halder was a man of integrity throughout his life. While the whites considered themselves superior in general, he proved himself to be superior among the foreigners practically. When he was prosperous, he used to give feast to them. On such occasions, when the guests feasted, he would fast as he was not willing to eat with unclean beef eaters. For example at one dinner, when Zachary Raid tried to give his hand to Neel for shaking, Neel was not willing to do that because of his sense of cleanliness. Even the English man Mr. Doughty knew that. The situation is described in a humorous way.

> The two Englishmen merely bowed
> Their heads in response, but
> Zachary startled Neel by moving
> forward as if to shake hands
> He was rescued by Mr. Doughty,
> who managed to intercept the
> American. 'keep your hands to
> yourself, you gudda of a griffin,'
> whispered the pilot. 'Touch him
> And he'll be off to bathe, and we
> won't be fed till midnight'. (105)

In the same way, Deeti is endowed with occult powers. She was a pious lady keeping a shrine like set up at her home for everyday *pooja*. She had the pictures drawn by her own hand. She drew the picture of the ship which she had mystically visualized but only after drawing she saw it the *Ibis* in which she had many thrilling experiences later. This mystical power of Deeti has once again been mentioned by Ghosh in his *River of Smoke* also in a higher level:

> ...she had shown the storm to be wrapped around an eye. This bespoke an understanding of the nature of storms that was, for its time, not just unusual but revolutionary: because 1838, the year of that storm, was when a scientist first suggested that hurricanes might be composed of winds rotating around a still centre—an eye, in other words.... How was it possible then that Deeti, an illiterate, frightened young woman, had been granted this insight? And that too at a time when only a handful of the world's most advanced scientist knew of it? (Ghosh, *River of Smoke,* 20-21)

Thus, Indians have been portrayed in positive terms while the American, Zachary struggles to maintain his balance; the half-Chinese Ah Fatt utterly fails in the strength of his character while urinating on Neel Rattan Singh.

The whole novel moves fast with the movement of the characters from one country to another above the sea waves on the ship, Ibis. This transfer from place to place or migration causes not only agony, sense of alienation and identity crisis, but also leads to the emergence of a multicultural society. In this, new diaspora blooms in a new world in the multicultural society, not only the natives adopted and assimilated the Western culture or became uncultured, but the westerners also accepted the Indian way of living and learnt the Indian language. Poulette, a girl of French origin, brought up in Bengal, sailed in the Ibis as a Bengali lady like other Indians, who travelled without knowing their fate. They suffered, struggled and survived, and whether they gain or lose would be discussed in *River of Smoke* and *Flood of Fire*. However, the only man of confidence was the British merchant, the seed of colonialism, who sailed with a single motive of gaining profit by his trade at the cost of the life of anybody/the colonized.

Works Cited

Ghosh, Amitav. *Sea of Poppies*. New York: Picador, 2008. Print.

———. *River of Smoke*. New Delhi: Penguin Books, 2011. Print.

8

Food as a Metaphor in Amitav Ghosh's *In an Antique Land*

S. Barathi

Introduction

Food represents a country's culture and thus, it could possibly be studied to identify post-colonial ideologies present in a text. India and other Asian countries are globally acclaimed for their food culture. This food does not just stop with preparation and tasting, it has been carried beyond its scope to the field of literature. In this context, it is worthwhile to quote the words of Jennifer that, "Food connects humans, and perhaps all living things, by a common need for it that all share. It is in many ways an ordinary thing, but it is essential to all. Through globalization, food now connects people in very literal, physical ways" (3). Thus, the role of food in every culture portrays some values. These aspects are found in Ghosh's *In an Antique Land*, a travelogue based on his experiences in Egypt. In this work, Amitav has blended the cultures of both India and Egypt, which is an excellent epitome of the role of food in Eastern culture. The paper deals with the writer's artistic portrayal of his experiences in an alien land as well as the depiction of the Egyptian culture with specific reference to food.

The New York Times has praised the book as a "hybrid of history, cultural investigation and travelogue". All works of Ghosh carry a unique and distinct character left by him. His earlier works display his quest for identity, immigrant sensibility and other diaspora elements. Besides, one could locate a great thirst for identity in the alien land by identifying his native culture with that of the alien culture. All his works cleverly blend the native culture with the alien land. The present study has been made in *In an Antique Land* that describes the experiences of the writer in Egypt as a social anthropologist, trying to trace the life of a slave MS4 brought to India by a Jewish Trader named Ben Yiju.

The narrative is neatly packed with his quest to trace the past life of the slave, Bomma and his adventures in Egypt where the people had some wrong notion about the Hindus. Instead of justifying the practices of his religion, Amitav just remains silent but at the same time, he never tries to emancipate the other religion. His only fault is, he was unable to justify certain practices in his religion to the non-natives who had no knowledge about his religion. They had certain false ideas about Indian culture. Rather than breaking such notions, Amitav tries to move on by remaining silent.

In any culture, food plays a crucial role; especially in a country like India, food is a part of its culture. Similarly, even in the Egyptian land, food is intertwined with the culture of its people. Egyptians share similar culture to that of Indians. The hospitality they provide to the author, an Indian, is an evidence of their friendly attitude. Amitav as a diaspora writer, tries to connect to his roots in India through his country's culture. In one of the reviews, the work has been appreciated as "...a leisurely blend of travelogue, history and cross-cultural analysis" ("*In an Antique Land* Book Review") by Ghosh that has reconstructed or recreated a 12th-century master-slave relationship in the modern concept of slavery.

Background of the Study

Clifford in his review notes that, "The Third World anthropologist now conceives his research as extending a long history of intercultural relations, contacts not defined by European expansion or the dichotomy of East and West" (*London Review*). Beneath this cross-cultural and cross-questioning, there is an undercurrent of sorrow which is evident when Ghosh narrates his past to his new friends, explaining the religious practices of people in India like burning their dead. He is reminded that in India, how the Hindus were routinely slaughtered by the Muslims, and the Muslims in turn by the Hindus for not doing so.

The story of Ghosh himself, known in the village as "...the Indian doctor, the uncircumcised, cow-worshiping kaffir who would not convert to Islam" demonstrates how the veritable culture of his native land affects him on an alien land. The story combines a variety of every day conversation and research scholarship intertwined with the history and relationship between the two nations, Egypt and India, for more than ten centuries. A reviewer of *In an Antique Land* remarks that it is not an anthropologist trying to reap on the years of tedious study because Ghosh writes with a great care and tenderness and is honest, funny and wry—all the great qualities of a travel writer. The only shame is that he overstretched himself with the dual narrative theme, a challenge that few ever manage to pass off successfully and even more unlikely a stunt when dealing with ancient anthropology. Commenting on the narration, he further remarks that Ghosh reveals himself to have an accomplished turn of phrase and a humble voice that lends itself to evoking the values and beliefs of a poor, peasant society. It makes the reader wonder why he attempted the dual narrative approach at all (*In an Antique Land*).

A reviewer in *Publishers Weekly* has remarked about how Ghosh has pointed out in his work about servitude as:

> a career opportunity, the principal means of recruitment into privileged strata of the army and bureaucracy. Researching in letters and documents in Egypt.... He also writes vividly of southern India, a tapestry of castes, cults and worship of spirit-deities. (*Publishers Weekly*)

Not only this, many other critics also have pointed out how people across the globe in the past had commercial contacts, especially trading the spices with other parts of the world. Cliford rightly points out that *In an Antique Land* has reached back to a 12th-century cosmopolitan world that links Arabs, Jews and South Asians, a world not yet structured by five hundred years of Western economic and cultural expansion.

However, Ghosh has presented a submerged tradition of contacts between South Asia and the Middle East in his work. This past situates, in a sense authorizes, his own late 20th-century ethnography—a series of disturbing encounters with worldly peasants in the Nile Delta (*London Review*). Throughout the work, one could feel the aroma of Egyptian soil through Ghosh's description of the Egyptian business men and their lifestyle.

Egyptian Culture

In the opening of the story, the prologue mentions the purpose of the writer on finding a particular slave who has come along with a Jewish trader originally from Tunisia travelled through Egypt and came to India as a trader. He had amassed great wealth as his trade flourished and references related to this were discovered in Genzia. The author begins his narration by sharing his experiences during his stay in the two villages Lataifa and Nashawy. He stayed in the house of Abu Ali, a prominent person in the village. The writer describes how women often force-feed geese to make them fat. Abu Ali has prospered through his shop which sells things like "sugar, tea, oil and the likes, at government subsidized prices" (13) as his shop was one of a kind, he fixed a high price for the goods based on their demand. If the customers refused, they would find is no other shop nearby and had to walk some pretty distance to another village. Thus, Abu Ali ruled the rooster.

Another interesting thing which the author notices is that the women force-feed their geese by pushing the corns down the throats of the birds with their forefingers. Shaik Musa's son Ahmed gives a description of the corn grown by them which is "harvested before winter, towards the start of the Coptic year which begins with the month of Tut..." (13). Throughout the story, Ghosh uses several things associated with food that reflects Egyptian culture.

Abu Ali always relishes food that comprises of mostly thick meat. Later, while describing an incident where Abu Ali drives his moped, the writer comments that in his jallabeyya, he looks like a "gargantuan lollipop" (15). Thus, even for describing a person Ghosh has casually made use of the reference of food.

Then, the writer moves on to depict the character of Abu Ali, who has a materialistic outlook. His eating habit could be evident from these words "he was normally to be found lying inert upon his divan, resting after his midday meal". This shows the culture of the people. During the meet he expresses displeasure with the rent paid for his stay, however, on the other hand he says that he treats the author as their own family stating, "You are lucky to be staying here with us. We will cook for you, wash your clothes for you, and provide you with anything you need" (17). Though his words are customary, it reflects the Egyptian hospitality towards the guests.

The author moves on to compare Cairo and Egypt. He finds that the word Egypt itself a metaphor. The country's civilization is found on the banks of river Nile and its delta with thick growth. In the prologue, Ghosh briefs on the connection between the two countries—Egypt and India, which is principally on Trade. India is a major exporter of spices like cardamom, pepper and metals like Iron and Brass to the Middle East countries. This is evident from the details about Ben Yiju's Business, where his partner overseas "...acknowledges certain goods received from Ben Yiju—a shipment of areca nuts, two locks manufactured in India and two bowls from a brass factory" (5-6). Readers also come to know that apart from the goods imported by the trader in India, he receives some food materials as gift from his friend, which the writer has noticed as "things which have no price and no value. The list seems to hint at a sweet tooth of Ben Yiju: 'two jars of sugar, a jar of almonds and two jars of raisins'" (6) all of which demonstrate the Jewish Trade's taste for the manufactured sugar for in India, only palm candy sugar was available and the Jewish trader did not like its taste. He rather prefers the sugar manufactured from sugarcane juice.

The book is an exemplar of cultural adaptation and it abounds with comparison of native and alien culture through the view of the natives. The story moves around the two villages Lataifa and Nashawy and then moves back to Mangalore and again returns to the two Egyptian village. Tracing the life of Ben Yiju, Amitav Ghosh conveys to the readers that when he came to Masr, it was the markets that attracted him first and later he refers to Babylon as his spiritual home.

Friendly Attitude of the Natives with the Writer

During his stay at Lataifa, the author visited some of the families that are friendly to him and one among them is Sheik Musa. He lived with his son and two grandsons. He has often invited the author to his house and during the authors visit to his house, his friendly attitude and hospitality made Ghosh feel at home. This is evident from the lines: "Sheik Musa, his son Ahmed, his two grandsons and I were eating out of one tray, while the women of the household were sharing another.... It was something of a special occasion for I had just crossed the invisible barrier" (25). Usually, he was served tea and snacks at 'mandara', the guest room where usually the male guests are received, but this time he was invited to dine with them inside the house. He gives a detailed description of the trays filled with food, "each tray was as big as a cartwheel" (24) and hence, every one could have their share of food. An interesting aspect noticed by Ghosh is the freedom the women enjoyed in that village. Though the women of the village never wore veils, the writer who had limited knowledge about Arab custom and culture never looked at them for the sake of modesty. However, now he feels strange shaking hands with them and sitting together for dinner. All these demonstrate that the Egyptians are cordial to their guests.

Cultural Conflicts

The story also represents the contrasting cultural aspects of both countries (i.e.) India and Egypt. The story of Khamees the Rat, the notorious impotent (already twice married); of Zaghloul, the weaver determined to travel to India on a donkey; of one-eyed Mohammad, so obsessed with a girl that he spent nights kneeling outside her window to listen to the sound of her breathing; of Amm 'Taha, part-time witch, always ready to cast a spell for a little extra money; and, of course, the story of Amitav Ghosh himself, known in the village as the Indian doctor, the uncircumcised, cow-worshiping kaffir, who would not convert to Islam ("www.amitavghosh.com"). When he lands at the village of Nashawy, the million dollar question of the young boys was whether he was circumcised. Even the educated villagers try to convert Amitav to their religion thinking that his religion does not teach him the right way. Further, there are instances where the teenagers misunderstand the attitude of the author and thinks of him as an immature man. Though India and Egypt share some common tradition and habits, yet Egypt has its own culture which leads to the misrepresentation of all Indians as Hindus. Ustaz Mustafa, though educated, had some misconception about Indian culture and tradition. Based on his readings, he tells Ghosh about the use of plenty of chilli in Indian cuisine and about Sati. But Ghosh defends his country's culture trying to explain to him that not everything he has heard is true. Another vital factor about India is that it is a multicultural land which is not much understood by the Egyptians who follow monoculture.

Role of Food

Indian vs Egyptian Culture (Cultural shock of the natives)—Egypt is rich in its culture which is evident from the various names given to the same place. The author is astonished by the variety of names people used to refer to the same place. He calls Cairo "an archipelago of townships" (20). The author notices the fortress and twin towers separated by the steel gate that serves as a gateway to Babylon.

Food as a Cultural and Personal Identity

Food imagery helps readers to understand their characters' true identities, because in many ways, food defines people and cultures. The article "Food in Literature—Introduction" from Thomas J. Schoenberg and Lawrence J. Trudeau's *Twentieth-Century Literary Criticism* elaborates on the relation of psyche and eating practices which essentially identity the self and are instrumental in defining family, class, and even ethnic identity.

Food could possibly signify the belief systems, religious rules and complex ideologies of a particular person or character, or even that of an entire community or culture, that may not be possibly explained explicitly in a text. In the chapter titled Lataifa, he describes the food culture of Egyptians:

> A large pile of rice were dishes of fried potatoes, cheese preserved in brine, salads of chopped tomatoes and fresh dill, plates of cooked vegetables, large discs of corn meal bread, and bowls of young Nile perch, baked tomatoes and garlic. Everything was fresh and full of flavor, touched with the unnameable quality which makes anything grown in the soil of Egypt taste richer, more distinctively of itself, than it does anywhere else. (28)

This richness of food is specific for South Asian countries. Another aspect revealed by the writer here is that food products are much cheaper and fresh in the countryside than in the cities. Moreover, the unique dish made from Nile perch is unavailable to the rest of the world. The writer also gives a detailed description of the process of cooking with the ingredients used, all of which certainly evokes interest in the readers to visit the place and relish those dishes at least once in their lifetime.

Food: The Universal Metaphor

Food represents universal cultural truths—aspects of the Indian cultures represented that seem to permeate all nations and cultures. Kunow describes the semiotic quality of representation as "a stand-in, a sign of something that is (or was made to be) absent" (151). He further states, "Food has, of course, always functioned as representation: ethnographers and cultural studies specialists have long been demonstrating how food not only feeds but also organizes us, how the making, taking, and disposing of aliments are socially and culturally inflected" (151). Although food imagery had been used in literature from the past, psychological theories had examined the role of food and eating as a universal experience.

Conclusion

Throughout the book, Amitav discusses the cultural issues and food, right from the beginning. Like our Indians, he mentions, Egyptians too offer tea and biscuits to their guests. Though there are differences in the method of cooking and spices used, the writer has relished all the dishes which is reflected in this work. Further, food shows the acceptance of one's culture, where the writer gets adapted to the Egyptian foods while in Egypt. Though Indian Foods were available, he did not choose it due to the high cost. Thus, Egyptian food becomes his nourishment throughout his stay there.

Works Cited

Burcham Whitt, Jennifer. *An Appetite for Metaphor: Food Imagery and Cultural Identity in Indian Fiction.* East Carolina University. Masters Thesis, May 2011. pdf.

Clifford, James. "Looking for Bomma: *In an Antique Land* by Amitav Ghosh." *London Review of Books.* Vol. 16.6 (March 1994): 26-27. Print.

<https://www.lrb.co.uk/v16/n06/james-clifford/looking-for-bomma>.

Ghosh, Amitav. *In an Antique Land.* New Delhi, Penguin Publishers Ltd., 2008. Print.

Iyer, Pico. "The Nile of Time: *In an Antique Land* by Amitav Ghosh." *Los Angeles Times.*

<http://articles.latimes.com/1993-04-11/books/bk-21703_1_amitav-ghosh>.

"In an Antique Land." 2011.

<https://www.amitavghosh.com/antique.html>.

"Review of *In an Antique Land* by Amitav Ghosh." *Publishers Weekly.* Jan. 1993.

<https://www.publishersweekly.com/978-0-394-58368-6>.

9

Inclusion and Exclusion: A Postcolonial Reading of *The Shadow Lines*

Charles Joseph

Post-colonialism is an academic discipline that analyzes, explains, and responds to the cultural legacy of colonialism and imperialism. Post-colonialism speaks about the human consequences of external control and economic exploitation of the native people and its lands. Drawing from postmodern schools of thought, postcolonial studies analyse the politics of knowledge (creation, control, and distribution) by examining the functional relations of social and political power that sustain colonialism and neo-colonialism. The depiction of imperial regime demarks the social, political and cultural ambit of the colonizer with reference to the colonized. As a genre of contemporary history, post-colonialism questions and reinvents the manner in which a culture is being viewed and challenges the narratives expounded during the colonial era.

Anthropologically, it records human nations between the colonists and the peoples under colonial rule, seeking to build an understanding of the nature and practice of colonial rule. As a critical theory, it presents, explains, and illustrates the ideology and practice of neo-colonialism with examples drawn from history, political science, philosophy, sociology, anthropology, and human geography. It also examines the effects of colonial rule on the cultural aspects of the colony and its treatment of women, language, literature, and humanity. A major aspect of post-colonialism is the rather violent-like, unbuffered contact or clash of cultures as an inevitable result of former colonial times; the relationship of the colonial power to the (formerly) colonized country, its population and culture and vice versa seems extremely ambiguous and contradictory. This contradiction of two clashing cultures and the wide scale of problems resulting from it must be regarded as a major theme in post-colonialism. For centuries, the colonial 5 suppressor often had been forcing his civilized values on the natives. However, when the native population finally gained independence, the colonial relicts were still omnipresent, deeply integrated in the native's minds and were supposed to be removed. Hence, decolonization is a process of change, destruction and, in the first place, an attempt to regain and lose power. While natives had to learn how to put independence into practice, colonial powers had to accept the loss of power over foreign countries. Both sides have to deal with their past as suppressor and suppressed.

This complicated relationship mainly developed from the Eurocentric perspective from which the former colonial powers saw themselves. Their colonial policy was often criticized as arrogant, ignorant, brutal and simply naïve. Their final colonial failure and the total independence of the once suppressed, made the process of decolonization rather tense and emotional. Post-colonialism also deals with conflicts of identity and cultural belonging. Colonial powers came to foreign states and destroyed main parts of native tradition and culture; furthermore, they continuously replaced them with their own ones. This often led to conflicts when countries became independent and suddenly faced the challenge of developing a new nationwide identity and self-confidence. It is an academic discipline featuring methods of intellectual discourse that analyze, explain and respond to the cultural legacies of colonialism and Imperialism.

Post-colonialism responds towards the human consequences of controlling a country and establishing settler for the economic exploitation of the native people and their land drawing from post-modern schools of thought, post-colonial studies, the politics of knowledge by analyzing the functional relations of social and political power that sustain colonialism.

Ghosh's, second novel is more sombre, less fanciful in its politics, and quite stunning in the power with which its formal experiments in sequence and location resonate thematically. *The Shadow Lines* traces nearly a half-century of interlocking relations among three generations of two families, one Indian and one British, giving perhaps the definitive fictional demonstration of Benedict Anderson's dictum—those nations are "imagined communities." When the same Hindu-Muslim conflict can take place simultaneously in Dhaka and Calcutta, the unnamed narrator must abandon his common-sense assumption "that distance separates, that it is a corporeal substance," and his belief "in the reality of nations and borders." The self, like the cosmopolitan cities it lives in, becomes a palimpsest, sedimented with history, memory, and others that the self has absorbed. The narrative mode echoes this intricate layering with its looping, Russian-doll-like nestling of story within story, place within place, and memory within actuality. The unnamed narrator, with his internationalized consciousness, wallows in an empowering sense of simultaneity and correspondence. Growing up with Tridib in Calcutta, he can "know" war-time London neighbourhoods and see the English boy Nick Price as a spectral mirror image. His grandmother's confusion between her childhood Dhaka and the present-day foreign city becomes symptomatic of the violence done to people by artificial borders and partitions (poignantly allegorized in her family's divided house). If the novel valorises the search for unbounded space and co-existing time, however, it refuses to endorse self-serving appropriations of "other" realities. When Ila compares her pleasure at bohemian 9 living with that of war-time radicals, the narrator criticizes the "easy arrogance" by which she assumes "that times and places are the same because they happen to look alike, like airport lounges." However, after a futile argument about whether her London or his Calcutta is the site of real history and important politics, he realizes the shaky ground on which he too claims possession of people and places he has largely invented.

Ghosh, thus recognizes the political stakes involved in drawing connecting lines, thus airline routes, across the shadow lines "of national boundaries and historical periods". His globe-shrinking project enables not only integration, but also juxtaposition. The controlling metaphor of the airport lounge makes this point brilliantly. It is full of complex cross-cultural encounters, the shadow lines makes a unique contribution to the debates over 'difference' and 'otherness' that galvanized the contemporary post-colonial world. The discovery process shared by Murugan, the reader and author follow a narrative roller coaster that at times resemblances a fun-house, a laugh of dark 'ride' with a carefully timed sequence surprises popping out at every turn. In stylized prose, emphasizing dialogue and description, Ghosh employs conventional devices of the mystery. The high-tech thriller, the hard-boiled detective novel, the science-fiction adventure and the Victorian ghost story, all with such boldness and panache that it can be hard to tell if he is parodying the genres or doing them in earnest. However, after the novel's controlling plot lays down the last bit of secret knowledge, it turns out to be very much about control and knowledge and although Ghosh typically does not wear his politics on his sleeve, the implication of this novel's secret history is that control of medical knowledge is wrenched away from European in the past and bestowed on Indians in the past, present and future. Understanding of the disease is reclaimed and redefined on distinctly Indian terms; in Ghosh's version it has significance not just for science and bodily health but also for spiritual health and worship, fate and predestination, reincarnation, time cycles and other notions more dear (by and large) to Indians than Westerners.

"At the origin of India and Pakistan lies the national trauma of Partition, a trauma that freezes fear into silence, and for which *The Shadow Lines* seeks to find a language, a process of mourning, and perhaps even a memorial." The year 1947 spelt for India a heightened consciousness of the very idea of a nation. Not only was freedom from the colonial rule ushered in and a long cherished desire of a free country made available to the Indians, it also meant that the arrival of freedom signalled a virtual dislocation for a big fraction of the population; the birth of the free nation was accompanied by excruciating labour pains of the event of Partition. Histories of both sides portray this event in passing as a misfortune that arose out of the power interests of the 'other' side. In the history textbooks, the struggle for Independence is seen to have concluded successfully; it was hailed as a model of the practice of the new philosophy of ahimsa. It can however, legitimately be called non-violent only if we chose to gloss over the very existence of the event of Partition that accompanied the midnight decree of freedom—the biggest migration of human population that the subcontinent or perhaps the world has ever witnessed.

It entailed loss of human life on both sides. In its magnitude, it was one of the most important events in the Indian history and it affected the life patterns of thousands of families who travelled in caravans, horses, carts and cattle from West Punjab and in homemade boats from East Bengal. How does history talk of these migrants? How does history justify this act of the state at that time? Urvashi Butalia, in her book *The Other Side of Silence* says that the state has strangely made no memorials to mark this momentous event. However, the memory of Partition has very well been preserved by the communities in the confines of their homes through stories and anecdotes told by the way of mouth and passed through one generation to the other. Of late, this interest in the documentation of the private experience of Partition has been performed by our Literature. Indian Writing in English has seen a spurt in the publication of Partition related Literature.

The Shadow Lines is, among other issues, a book about the Bengal Partition. The experiences of Tha'mma through the trope of the divided house (as discussed earlier), clearly brings out her side of the story about the event. The story of the old uncle, Jethamoshai, captures the poignant side of the human experience of Partition and of course, the depiction of the penury and destitution of Tha'mma's poor relatives capture the economic effects of Partition. Community and Communal Strife: *The Shadow Lines* takes up the issue of Partition (1947) and the author presents through it an elaborate critique of the whole idea of a nation as it emerged in the circumstances. Community, as a condition prior to Partition, is seen as an ideal state and the narratives that the community produces, are seen as being more representative of their experience than history. The natural community in the Indian subcontinent across Punjab and Bengal got split into two nations following the call for Partition. What followed was the physical dislocation of 15 million people from the places that their communities had traditionally called home. Those who crossed over to the Indian side arrived landless, clueless and resource less to be a part of the rejoicing in Delhi on the eve of country's Independence.

The Partition had thus disrupted the existence of natural communities. A classification about natural and interest oriented communities is used by Sudipta Kaviraj to draw up an elaborate case about the difference between nation and community. He draws heavily on the work of the sociologist Toennies to discuss two kinds of communities Gemeinschaft which is the primary, traditional group, and which according to Kaviraj one does not make an interest actuated decision to belong. On the other hand is Gesellschaft, similar to modern nations, which are based on the convergence of political and economic interests. The Partition necessitates the disruption of Gemeinschaft embodied by the old communities in Bengal and Punjab in order to create Gesellschaft India and Pakistan. Further, these imagined communities can place their boundaries in time and space anywhere they like, 'unlike the former which have naturally limited contours.' So, whereas the former state reflects a cultural bonding, the latter is based on political interest. These groups are also then linked with their own forms of narration. Narratives, according to Kaviraj, are always told from someone's point of view '...they try to paint a picture of some kind of an ordered, intelligible, humane and habitable world...literally produce a world in which the self finds home.'

The Gemeinschaft, therefore has its own community specific narratives and Gesellschaft acquires it in due course. Whereas the former lives in age old stories, shared in various forms by the community, the latter finds a home in histories. Community also comes to us as a concept through the reading of the experience of Partition. Community, as it appears through the government documents, gets reduced to numbers that bear the brunt of state policy. These communities are visualised by the state as characterised by one single characteristic-language or religion. These are the communities on paper and convenient as subjects for policy formulation. But real communities lie outside the ambit of these documents and as Melville talks of places such as kokovoko, an island far away to the West and South, which is not down in any map because true places never are, these communities too are only lived, seldom represented. The Partition of India was based on the justification of communal tension between Hindus and Muslims but our literatures have presented to us far more complex designs of communities with composite structures, that have for considerable time, shared a common culture in spite of religious differences. In this regard, Bhalla argues that there are hardly any chronicles, songs, *kissas* and *tamashas* in Punjab, which record a long history of irreconcilable hatred between Hindus and Muslims. What the governments never addressed was that culture, instead of religion, could be an equally valid characteristic defining communities, that culture far predated religion as a constituent of a community, that it was absurd to lump together culturally alien Muslims of Bangladesh and Pakistan as one nation and force the East and West sides of Punjab and Bengal respectively to be declared a part of India. Subsequently, the Nationalists construct the other side as a country politically, ethically and inherently opposed to itself. The Partition of India, in this sense, was an important event because it cartographically relocated what were once closely existing natural communities and instead formulated an imagined community of the nation. The history of India being the narrative of the modern nation rather than the primordial (and now secondary) community told the tale of the nation and obliterated that of the society. Riots between communities, as a characteristic 20th century phenomenon, figure in the book prominently. The author also focuses on how they are portrayed variedly by the newspapers and the author's imagination. Whereas in the author's imagination, they have stood out as a single most important event of his childhood, in the newspapers and other sources, they do not even merit a mention. The author looks for reasons that lead to this silence in portrayal of riots by the state. The reason, of course is not far to find—the difficulty in representing an enemy that arises from within rather than without. The new age stories (literature) therefore, become the narrative of the communities and make up for the silence in history when it comes to the portrayal of events like partition and riots. It records what happened to the partition victims and subsequently, victims of the numerous civil strife, whose point of view always remains under-represented because these incidents undermine the very notion of a nation that history purports to create. It is also ironic that post partition, people across the border share all their old stories but from a point, completely separate histories. As Ghosh points out the nature of this relationship is governed by...that indivisible sanity that binds people to each other independently of their governments. And that prior, independent relationship is the natural enemy of government, for it is in the logic of the states that to exist at all they must claim the monopoly of all relationships between people. It is shown how when the communities give way to nation their narration is taken over by a totalizing history. In *The Shadow Lines*, Tha'mma receives her ideas about the new nation that she comes to inhabit after Bangladesh becomes another country. Some voices in the contemporary Indian Writing in English have studied the writing and historical justification of partition in this light.

Historians have tried to read a communal angle into the event and tried to trace a genealogy of such events with a retrospective intelligibility that leads to a known and expected end. It is interesting to note, therefore, in this light that while they highlighted stray incidents of communal violence in the pre-partition time to give a historical justification to the inevitable phenomenon of Partition, in *The Shadow Lines*, on the 33 other hand riots, civil strife and communal riots do not find expression in the official records. This happens because the same incidents, which at one time supported the political decisions, will at the present only go on to hamper its legitimacy. In both cases, the community experience and its depiction suffers. The accounts of partition completely ignore the fact of the composite quality of relationships that existed between people of different religions and that there were other potent factors of their cohesion like a shared cultural ethos. *Train to Pakistan* by Khushwant Singh talks of such a definition of community in the village of Mano Majra.

Some of these books show the existence of an alternate religion, with people of different faiths looking upon a common shrine (in this case a sandstone slab) as religious. Interestingly, this feature about close-knit cohesive communities, later gets transported to the imagined community of the state of otherwise riot-ravaged India. Home/Homelessness: In the novel *The Shadow Lines,* home is in an allegorical relationship with nation. Tha'mma talks of her upside-down house in Dhaka and the story of that house is indeed the story of partitioned India. As children living in a joint family in Dhaka, Tha'mma and her sister Mayadebi are witness to the feud between their father and his brother. Things come to such a pass that they think of dividing their house. This division is so tangible that an actual line is drawn in the middle of the house dividing everything including the commode. In this ludicrous detail, the partition comes out for the reader as an event that was both irrational and avoidable. Another aspect of Partition of the house that is later applied to the nation is about the ideological division that follows this material division. Once the Partition has taken place, the other side of the house becomes inaccessible to everybody including the two girls, Tha'mma and Mayadebi.

Since Tha'mma is the elder one, she talks of the house as the upside-down house, in which everything is the opposite of how things naturally are. The two nations, just like the two parts of a household, were united at one time but the course of history (or failure of vision) divides them, and for sustaining their separation, the difference has to be created. These stories that Tha'mma creates to bring alive to her younger sister the situation of the other part of the house, are in spirit comparable to the modern version of fake national pride that is also likewise based on false stories of difference. Her decision to go to Dhaka, which is her erstwhile home, in order to bring back her old sick uncle, is a very unsettling time for her. Routine activity of furnishing her personal details while finishing the documentation for her visa forms, raise fundamental doubts about her identity. For the first time, the sure-shot and composed Tha'mma, goes through pangs of some fundamentally disturbing interrogation. She wonders as to how the place of her birth had come to be messily at odds with her nationality. She cannot resolve the chaos that surfaces in the patterns that are so essential to her identity. The book has two sub-sections: Going Away and Coming Home. Both phrases indicate the queer sense of home and homelessness that the Partition victims have experienced, that allows them to dispense with a fixed point that signifies a point of departure.

Major characters in *The Shadow Lines*: *The Shadow Lines* is one of Amitav Ghosh's most outstanding novels and may be regarded as one of the masterpieces in the field of Indo-Anglian fiction. The novel focuses on the meaning of political freedom and the force of nationalism, as well as the personal experiences of the narrator of the novel. Told in first person, the story of *The Shadow Lines* is of a growing boy, who lives in the shadow of the man he idealizes and of an individual drawn into history as well as social and political turbulences. Tridib gives the boy, who is the narrator of the novel—worlds to travel in mind...eyes to see with them with. The narrator's grandmothers, Tha'mma is the third central character to the structure in the novel. As an eight-year old child, the narrator (35) sees England through the eyes of Ila and Tridib as a 26 years old, he realizes the truth when merges from the shadows of Ila. Tridib and Tha'mma. Tha'mma is an important character, as she plays a foil to the younger generation and also a critic of those who she thinks have deviated from Indian mores. She is the grandmother of a narrator, a retired headmistress, a disciplinarian head of the family. Like old persons, she has faith in old accepted values of life and looks down upon those who do not fall in line with her. She was born and brought up in a joint family in Dhaka. Tha'mma was married to an engineer with railways in Burma, therefore she passed the first twelve years of her married life in railway colonies. The protagonist of the character belongs to a boy, who grows up in a middle-class family; he is the narrator's uncle. He is in love with May and occupies the central place in several incidents of the novel.

He is the son of Mayadebi and Data Chaudhary, who is in diplomatic services in India. Therefore, his parents always live abroad and come to Calcutta only when his father is on leave. Ila is the daughter of Jitin, who is an economist in the U.N.

She travelled widely with her father, who is transferred from one country to another. She comes to Calcutta during holidays, but is not moored with any culture. Naturally, she is a character that stands exposed, unprotected in the armour of convictions, though nature has given her features which are similar to those of her kith and kin. She is the narrator's cousin, who lives in Stock Well, London. The narrator is in love with her, but she marries Nick. May Price is the grand-daughter of Lionel Treawsen, who was discovered by his death, had been a prolific inventor, and had taken no less than twenty-five parents for different mechanical gadgets. However, Treawsen was a man of varied interests. He got interested in setting homeopathic hospital in a village near Calcutta and also in the theosophical society of India and séances by a lady in Chowrin ghee. She is the Price family's daughter. She is in love with Tridib and blames herself for his death. Robi has a unique place among the character of the shadow lines since he is not designed either to be a contrast or to coalesce with any character of the novel. He is a shade different from others, a class in himself. There is nothing in him for whom he can be censured, but he is the only character for whom Tha'mma puts in a good word. He is the son of Sahib and Mayadebi and the younger brother of the Tridib. He is a favourite of Tha'mma because she believes that he resembles her and he has a strongly built body.

Racism is a product of the complex interaction in a given society of a race-based worldview with prejudice, stereotyping, and discrimination. Racism can be present in social actions, practices, or political systems (e.g., apartheid) that support the expression of prejudice or aversion in discriminatory practices. The ideology underlying racist practices often includes the idea that humans can be subdivided into distinct groups that are different in their social behavior and innate capacities and that can be ranked as inferior or superior. Racist ideology can become manifest in many aspects of social life. Associated social actions may include xenophobia, otherness, segregation, hierarchical ranking, supremacies, and related social phenomena. While race and ethnicity are considered to be separate in contemporary social science, the two terms have a long history of equivalence in popular usage and older social science literature. "Ethnicity" is often used in a sense close to one traditionally attributed to "race": the division of human groups based on qualities assumed to be essential or innate to the group (e.g. shared ancestry or shared behavior).

Racism and racial discrimination are often used to describe discrimination on an ethnic or cultural basis, independent of whether these differences are described as racial. According to a United Nations convention, there is no distinction between the terms "racial" and "ethnic" discrimination. The UN convention further concludes that superiority based on racial differentiation is scientifically false, morally condemnable, socially unjust and dangerous, and there is no justification for racial discrimination, anywhere, in theory or in practice. Today, the use of the term "racism" does not easily fall under a single definition. It is usually found in, but usage is not limited to law, the social and behavioral sciences, humanities, and popular culture. Leela Gandhi's concept of Indian imperialism: It is lunch time late in the century before last and the young Indian man, whom we must imagine standing hungrily on Farringdon Street, is not charmed by London.

In time, true to that psychic distortion, which makes us homesick for those places in which we were foreign, he will come to Miss London bitterly. For the moment, however, his homesickness is rather more conventional; an acute state of corporeal disaggregation, a maladjustment of the body, ill at ease among sofas, carpets, cornices, porticoes, vestibules, flower-beds, pavements, morning suits, bread, porridge and potatoes. Mostly, bread, porridge and potatoes. For, to put it plainly, he is distraught about food, its lack and it's unrecognizable. No stranger to meet eating and its guilty pleasures, his sojourn has only been authorized by the elders of his community under condition of vow to abjure the triple temptations of liquor, meat and sex, and so to suffer a staple diet of oatmeal porridge... bread, butter...meat and potatoes ad libitum.

In his compelling and histrionic autobiography, *My Experiments with the Truth*. M.K. Gandhi rates his encounter with salts over as a life-changing experience and in deeded over the remaining three odd years of his legal studies in London. Gandhi's involvement with his legal studies in London. It is with early phase of Gandhi's formation that this chapter concerns itself; seeking in his enmeshment with late—Victorian radicalism raw materials for the transnational or non-indigenous of his anti-imperial polemic. For, I will argue, the culture of *Fin de siècle* animal welfare (of which vegetarianism was but one subsidiary) exerted profound influence on Gandhi's politics and ethico-ideological lexicon, giving substance to his critic or imperialism, shaping the complex of etymology of Gandhian *Ahimsa*.

From his earliest writings on the subject, Gandhi is quick to recognize the zoophilia of his English companions as a variety of xenophilia, that openness to outsiders, aliens, strangers, foreigners, ratified in the enduring Epicurean challenge to the Aristotelian circumscription of community, consolidated in its transmission as a flight from self-identical, self-confirming sociality.

Contrary to popular perception, there is no generalized or undifferentiated response to the partition among those who have chronicled it. Reactions vary from nostalgic lament for a lost age to attaching blame and apportioning responsibility for the terrible misfortunes that befell those who had been affected, in some way or the other, by the events of 1947. While there is a general agreement that the murder and mayhem that accompanied the partition was a human tragedy of epic proportions, there is far more ambivalence in the ways of dealing or accepting the consequences of partition. While the majority of writers made a conscious effort to hold up the tattered fabric of secularism in the face of communalism, bitter and painful memories also find expression, especially in a range of first-person accounts, diaries, etc. It seems difficult to discern a commonality of concerns, or any coherence and unity of thought, save the obvious assertion that countless innocent lives were lost due to the political decisions of a mere handful. In the wake of continuing interest in the partition, both among the students of history and literary historians, not to mention the average reader, a spate of anthologies on the partition have appeared. Anthologies, as a necessity, must have a peg, ideological or otherwise. Their editors have tried, in different ways and through different voices, to highlight different aspects of a single, traumatic, shared experience. In a sense, therefore, each anthology and its editor invariably have an 'agenda'. Often, these 'agendas' appear to be at cross-purposes with each other.

Alok Bhalla, one of the ablest and most diligent chroniclers of the many partition narratives, points out the 'real sorrow' of the partition, namely that it 'brought to an abrupt end a long and communally shared history.' In his deeply insightful introduction to the four volumes of stories, he shows a clear-eyed understanding of the tensions within the communities, which occasionally burst into spurts of outrage, yet did not, he believes, impair 'the rich heterogeneity of the life of the two communities.' That is, till the partition, at the 'ordinary and local levels, even as late as 1946,' Bhalla notes, the daily life of Hindus and Muslims remained 'so richly interwoven as to have formed a rich archive of customs and practices, that explains why there is a single, common note which informs nearly all the stories written about the partition and the horror it unleashed—a note of utter bewilderment.' It is this bewilderment that is common across barriers of ethnic, linguistic and cultural identities, not to say religious ones, that come out in this selection of stories translated from Urdu, Hindi, Punjabi, Sindhi, and Bangla.

A diaspora is a scattered population, whose origin lies within a smaller geographic locale. Diaspora can also refer to the movement of the population from its original homeland. Diaspora has come to refer particularly to historical mass dispersions of an involuntary nature, such as the expulsion of Jews from Judea, the fleeing of Greeks after the fall of Constantinople, the African Transatlantic slave trade, the southern Chinese or Hindus of South Asia during the coolie trade, the Irish during and after the Irish Famine, the displacement of Palestinians in the 20th century and the exile and deportation of Circassia's. Recently, scholars have distinguished between different kinds of Diaspora, based on its causes such as imperialism, trade or labour migrations, or by the kind of social coherence within the Diaspora community and its ties to the ancestral lands.

Some Diaspora communities maintain strong political ties with their homeland. Other qualities that may be typical of many Diasporas are thoughts of return, relationships with other communities in the Diaspora, and lack of full integration into the host country.

The term 'hybridity' has become one of the most recurrent concepts in postcolonial cultural criticism. It is meant to foreclose the diverse forms of purity encompassed within essentialist theories. Bhabha is the leading contemporary critic who has tried to disclose the contradictions inherent in colonial discourse in order to highlight the colonizer's ambivalence in respect to his position toward the colonized other. The simple presence of the colonized order within the textual structure is enough evidence of the ambivalence of the colonial text, an ambivalence that destabilizes its claim for absolute authority or unquestionable authenticity.

Works Cited

Ahmad, Aijaz. Canonical Criticism of Cosmopolitan Post-Colonials Appears. *In Theory: Classes, Nations, Literatures*. Verso. 1992. Print.

Alam, Mohit. The Question about the Location of Culture: A Study of Amitav Ghosh's Novels: *The Shadow Lines* & *The Glass Palace*. Bangla Journal. Ontario: Canada: 2008: Vol. VI. Issue 14. Print.

Bhaduri, Seema. *Of Shadows, Lines and Freedom: A Historical Reading of The Shadow Lines. The Novels of Amitav Ghosh*. Delhi: 1999. Print.

Dixon, Robert. *Traveling in the West: The Writing of Amitav Ghosh* in Tabish Khair, ed. Spivak, Gayatri: The Post-Colonial critic; Interviews Strategies, Dialogues, Sarah Harasym: Routledge. 1990. Print.

Ghosh, Amitav. *The Shadow Lines*. UP: Penguin, 2002. Print.

Memmi, Albert. *The Colonizer and the Colonized Boston*. Beacon, 1965. Print.

Moore, R.J., *Escape from Empire: The Attlee Government and the Indian Problem*. Oxford: Clarendon Press. 1992. Print.

Mukharjee, Meenakshi. *Realism and Reality: The Novel and Society in India*. New Delhi: Oxford Press. 1985. Print.

———. *The Perishable Empire: Essays on Indian Writing in English*. New Delhi: Oxford Press. 2000. Print.

10

Significance of History and Human Influence in the Select Novels of Amitav Ghosh: A Critical Overview

N. Asharudeen

Abstract

Amitav Ghosh is a recognized Bengali writer. He is also deeply inspired by historical matters of the eastern and the western countries. Ghosh's attention of America is deeply committed to the search of philosophical truth, observing the grandeur and wealth of America. He believes that America is the only country where he can be free to expose his ideas. The study attempts to give a critical overview that deals with some of the Ghosh's novels as the sign of history and human influence. History, no longer remains an unchangeable, but is reconstructed with his style of narration about the hidden past that he has represented in the novels. This critical overview approaches the discussion of present and past of human society which Amitav Ghosh has clearly narrated in *The Circle of Reason* (1986), *The Shadow Lines* (1988) and *The Glass Palace* (2000). Ghosh's representation of different characters in his novels deal with the experience of displacement, trauma and nostalgia, that plays a vital role in determining and shaping the characters to different intolerable situations. Amitav Ghosh's fictional world is restless and his central characters are travelers. Ghosh's conflation of time and space of distinct places is even more powerful in the plot of roaming imagination. Diaspora becomes a main issue in humanities today which instigates Amitav Ghosh to deal with reminiscences of his life in his writings. It is definitely the root cause of the Ghosh's lying around the dealing of past events in socio-political issues.

Amitav Ghosh is a recognized Bengali writer and he is one of the celebrated writers in India. He spent his childhood and adulthood days in different places of Asia, Bangladesh, Sri Lanka and Iran, however, he was born in Calcutta, India in 1956. Ghosh is known for the excellent candor and clarity of his prose and brilliant perception of the understanding of human relations in different societies. He is a resourceful craftsman in fiction and has exhibited his ideas and earned substantial critical compliments. The study is based on the overview that some of the Ghosh's novels are the sign of history and human influence. History no longer remains unchanged because it can be reconstructed with its style of narration about the hidden past as Ghosh has represented in his novels.

Amitav Ghosh has had plenty of experience in studying the history of socio-political and cultural events of India. He often interprets the relationship among the societies and individuals in the nation. His style of narrating history, politics, culture and humanities is distinctive.

Ghosh's attention of America is deeply committed to the search of philosophical truth, observing the grandeur and wealth of America. Ghosh seems influenced from the country as the land of a new world. America has developed a good civilization, which symbolizes the significance and nobility of humans and is based on morality. He believes that America is the only country where he can be free to exhibit his ideas. This perception has made him to settle in America for attaining a prosperous life as a Professor at New York University. Amitav Ghosh has manipulated the style of American life in the cultural conflicts, linguistic boundaries, partition of nations, riots and everything which also influenced him greatly.

Indian writing in English is the uphill to bring the glorious impact of Indian society to the universe, and Amitav Ghosh's part is vital in the circle of Diaspora. His novels have earned many literary awards. *The Circle of Reason* (1986) is his first novel which won the Prix Médicis Estranger. His second novel, *The Shadow Lines* (1988) received India's most prestigious literary award, Sahitya Akademi Award of 1990 and earned

Ananda Puraskar for the same book. Ghosh's *The Calcutta Chromosome* (1995) received Arthur C Clarke Award in 1997. *The Glass Palace* (2000) became an international bestseller and sold more than a half-million copies in Britain, which earned the grand prize for fiction at the Frankfurt International e-book award in 2001. The Government of India honoured Amitav Ghosh by conferring the Padma Bhushan award.

Ghosh is well versed in many languages such as English, Bengali, Hindi, French, Arabic and Italian. The language skills have helped him to realize the reality of every individual society what he has experienced with. Amitav Ghosh has been greatly influenced by the cultural, social and political stance of present and past of different countries.

Ghosh's dear friends, Gautam Mukopadhya, Ranajit Guha, Dipesh Chakraborthy, and Parth Chatterjee have got influenced in the thinking of present and past of human society which Amitav Ghosh has admitted in an interview given to Biswarup Sen in Charlottesville. Amitav Ghosh is much grateful and thoughtful towards his friends.

Salman Rushdie might have got influenced by Ghosh's dealing of the relationship between national issues and the individual ones, that can be observed in Rushdie's *The Midnight's Children*. It seems Amitav Ghosh focuses on individual quest for his personal meaning and existential problems from the past. He is also deeply inspired by historical matters of the eastern and the western countries. In Introduction, Michael Holquist explains about the differences in novel and history:

> Histories are like novels in that they insist on homology between the sequence of their telling, the form they impose to create a coherent explanation in the form of narrative on the one hand and the sequence of what they tell on the other.... The novel differs from history in that it dramatizes the gaps that always exist between what is told and the telling of it, constantly experimenting with social discursive and narrative asymmetries. (28)

Amitav Ghosh's novels encompass with both historical and political assessment of the past. His novels, *The Circle of Reason* and *The Shadow Lines* deal with the historical events though they are not exactly historical novels. *The Circle of Reason* deals with the theme of Diaspora, this is the appropriate illustrative from the prolific writings of Amitav Ghosh. The protagonist of *The Circle of Reason* Alu, who is a novelist, his life starts in Lalkpur, and then he migrates to Bengal, Bombay and finally ends his odyssey in Algeria. The novel unfurls the risks of migration and adaptation and reminiscence are the most significant themes of the novel. The novel sharply talks about the problems of migrant labourers in the Gulf countries. The author discusses the dreams of the Diasporas through the different characters, the reason and consequence of displacement on the migrated people. The novel clearly exhibits the sufferings of the migrated people which happens due to their displacement and also reveals how their dreams are shattered to the healing in their land, the exploitation of the small matters in the migrated land and the various causes of displacement are argued by the author through his characters. Amitav Ghosh narrates the migration of people from their hometown to different places within the country and outside the country. He portrays the characters are helpless, where they don't have any choice but to escape from the place. Zindi is also an important character of the novel and she is abandoned by her husband, finding her a barren. She adopts the profession of prostitution to support her brothers. She sends them money to build houses for them but she is not allowed to enter the house when she is badly in need of them.

In *The Shadow Lines,* Ghosh narrates the historical events skillfully as war devastation in England, civil conflict in post-partition of Bengal and riots of Calcutta are entrenched in the novel. The novel seems to show ridicule even at the idea of exclusive national identity and pride because riots break out in Dhaka and Calcutta. As a result of the incident, cultural bonds are broken in Bangladesh, England and the Middle East and they become a recurring image in the novel. In *The Shadow Lines*, Ghosh makes matters worse by the conventional mapping of the world into East and West with two parts, "Going Away" and "Coming Home". Ghosh has tried to fill his sense of belonging, national identity, cultural, rituals and tradition which create the basis of postcolonial fiction in the consistency of *The Shadow Lines*. The novel draws a few historical events like the freedom struggle in Bengal, the Second World War, and the partition of India in 1947, the continuous communal agitation in the form of riots in Bangladesh and India. There is a collective expression of pains in Indian History, a revelation of all religions in which Muslims, Sikhs and Hindus alike included. The narrator concludes that the lines which divide the two nations are only shadow lines. Amitav Ghosh, a postcolonial writer, has conferred the story of post colonialism by his own style, without the account of British canon. He attempts to reconstruct the effect of the events what happened in the past. The events of four decades are clearly narrated in the novel, even though it depicts the events of past but it also comes across the recent style of living.

Amitav Ghosh is also involved in non-fiction writings such as *Countdown* (1998), a book on India's Nuclear policy, *The Imam and the Indian* (2002), a collection of essays on different subjects of historical incidents, Egyptian culture and literature, and *Dancing in Cambodia, At Large in Burma* (1998) and some more writings published in the same distinct way. As his writings revolve around the past events, it is understood that how strongly he has given more importance to the historical events.

Ghosh's works lie in his skill to weave Indo-nostalgic elements which become more serious and heavier themes. Amitav Ghosh's fictional world is restless and his central characters are travelers and diaspora. Ghosh's conflation of time and space of distinct places is even more powerful in the plot of roaming imagination. Diaspora becomes a main issue in humanities today which instigates Amitav Ghosh to deal with reminiscences of his life in his writings. It is definitely the root cause of past events in socio-political issues.

More number of Indians have moved out of the other countries and subsequently they have set up small communities all over the world. The displacement forms people to flow towards social networks and their fictional world. The issues like identity crisis, homesickness, displacement, trauma and nostalgia are aroused by migration which makes the person think of past events in his life.

The Glass Palace takes in its epic sweep, the stormy social disorders that impact the lives of three generations in three nations. The narrative spans nearly a hundred years of pre and post colonial period in Burma, India and Malaya, brilliantly fusing the historical with the fictional. Ghosh draws complex socio-political effects through the experience of loss, exile and search for identity by the central character Rajkumar's family, which is scattered through the post-imperialist dislocation in various parts of the South Asian countries. The novel depicts the entangled histories of Burma, Malaysia and India under the British dominion and provokes the question about the nature of deployment of its historical sources to attain the desirable aesthetic response. Historical incidents and creative fiction are subtly interconnected into the narrative structure of this novel. The British invasion of Burma in 1885 made a disruption in the history of Burma. The war continued only for fourteen days, but it had strong and deep reaching consequences. The satisfaction of the Burmese King and his bombastic queen got disturbed all of a sudden. They were not given time to protest. The King of Burma was deposed from the throne and the royal family was banished to the remote regions of Ratnagiri in India, which is between Goa and Bombay. The Indian soldiers in the British Indian army devotedly served the Empire to depose King Thebaw and Queen Supayalat. This great historical event was carried out forcefully but quietly in the novel by Ghosh. Ghosh is very much influenced by his father and uncle, the narration of the forgotten history of Burma through *The Glass Palace* is a typical attempt of reconstruction by Amitav Ghosh. Amitav Ghosh states in *The Glass Palace*, "The seed of the book was brought to India long before my own life time by my father and uncle. In attempting to write about places and times that I know only at second and third hand I was forced to create a parallel, wholly fictional world"

(*TGP*, 549). Ghosh's representation of British colonization and its outcome is in the three countries which interplays the fact in a deceptive place of imagination to create an awareness of the reality of postcolonial worlds.

Amitav Ghosh's novels *The Circle of Reason*, *The Shadow Lines* and *The Glass Palace* deal with the experience of displacement, trauma and nostalgia, play a vital role in determining and shaping the characters to different intolerable situations.

Works Cited

Bakhtin, Mikhail Mikhailovich. *The Dialogic Imagination*. ed. Michael Holquist, trans. Caryl Emerson and Michael Holquist. Austin: University of Texas Press, 1981.

Ghosh, Amitav. *The Circle of Reason*. Delhi: Ravi Dayal, 1986. Print.

———. *The Shadow Lines*. Delhi: Ravi Dayal, 1988. Print.

———. *The Glass Palace*. Delhi: Ravi Dayal, 2000. Print.

11

Marginalisation and Uncertainty in Amitav Ghosh's *Sea of Poppies*

X. Anita Arul

Abstract

Life is full of uncertainties. Nothing can be of sure unless it is God's own plan. Life has all its perplexities and it is intertwined with problems, unanswered questions related to fate. God's thinking and his judgement is completely different from that of human beings thoughts and attitudes. We are all living a life of confliction. Life doesn't spare even persons who live a life with a wealthy background too. Sometimes indecisiveness leads to all our living. Life is a package of unpredictability that keeps life quite interesting. Amitav Ghosh in *Sea of Poppies* has chiselled his characters to show that life is a challenge and we have to live a life as it goes and no one can change it according to their own plan. Uncertainty is an emotional element as well as a process. It defines life as a wretched one and it helps to get transformed into a well-being in all forms.

> "For my thoughts are not your thoughts, neither are your ways my ways," declares the Lord. Isaiah 55:8

As per the Biblical verse, God's plan alone can be declared to be in existence. Human beings live on this earth without any kind of determinacy. This principle of uncertainty can be applied to the novel *Sea of Poppies*. A kind of ambiguity prevails in the characters of this novel. *Sea of Poppies* is a package of characters that are ready to take risk in life. Indefiniteness is a feature associated with people who leads a life without any kind of determination. During the first opium war, countries engage themselves in coolie trade. People are used as materials and traded between countries to work on the farm. In "Sea of

Poppies" the lascars, thugs, and other indentured labours are traded to Mauritius. Some people make others their slaves and make them work for their selfishness. On the basis of bonded labour, people are sent to other countries to work no matter to what caste they belong to instead "they be young and able-bodied and willing to work" (205). So many of them are carried by the triple-mast schooner named the 'Ibis'. "Lascar on the Ibis knew themselves to be from one part or another of the subcontinent" (188). The Indian prisoners are shipped to the British Empire's network of Island prisoners.

When the people's inefficiency, uncontrollability and their poor situation does not sync with the society, they start to seek a deviant way for their survival. Such is the situation that prevails during the first half of 18th century. Social disorder is the accelerator that takes people to choose a deviant life when they face so many uncertainties.

The novel begins with the vision of uncertainty seen by one of the major characters in the novel, Deeti.

> The vision of a tall-masted ship, at sail on the ocean, came to Deeti on an otherwise ordinary day, but she knew instantly that the apparition was a sign of destiny for she had never seen such a vessel before, not even in a dream: how could she have, living as she did in northern Bihar, four hundred miles from the coast? (1)

Sea of Poppies sails around the 'Ibis', "a schooner of old-fashioned appearance" (11) and it is built to transport slaves from one country to another. The ship sets sail with opium factory workers, lascars, coolies, convicts and so many other passengers. When there is uncertainty in life, risk plays a vital role in each and every circumstances. Instability in life automatically paves way for others to interfere in our life. Where our native grip faces a kind of shiver, there a path has been created for the aliens to get into and disturbs our conviction and leads to rule us by all means. Slavery is not like any other relationships. It is hard to manage people who have been under slavery. They may have so many psychological issues. People are exploited by the one who enjoys money power in society during colonial period. Enslavement is a severe unacceptable cruelty that is formed to feed some layers of society. The authoritative layers keep the labourers under their control and spoil them to the core, making them come out of their originality to work for them.

Deeti is an intelligent character who knows how to handle persons and overcome problems in conflicted situations. She is from a village "so far inland that the sea seemed as distant as the netherworld" (1). She is given in marriage to a crippled impotent man Hukam Singh, a sepoy who completely spends his life with opium without having any consideration towards the people who lives around even his wife. Deeti's hopelessness after marriage leaves her within a focus of uncertainty towards life. She is forced to be a subordinate to her husband, mother-in-law and brother-in-law. She managed to live this life with a great acceptance of transition. Eventually, she being offered a well-rewarded option of her uncertainty situation she starts her life with Kalua, a low caste ox-cart man after her husband's demise.

Deeti has undergone an emotional life. She is a woman with all natural feelings. She undergoes silent emotional domestic torture by her in-laws. She experiences many unpleasant events. She is being tortured by her brother-in-law to be his mistress. There, she has been so skilful enough to solve the issues. She has been threatened making use of her misfortune by that time. She is forced to accept her husband's brother as though she is a property. It is a kind of crime against womanhood. Her helplessness is being used by them and this is the situation of the women in the society. As Martin Seligman observes it as a "learned helplessness", is a kind of condition where the mind accepts the situation, though it is worse. The mind is set for this inescapable situation.

> It was useless, she knew, to be seized by regret now, on the very night was her fate had been wedded to his: it was as if the shade of Saturn had passed over her face, to remind her of her destiny. (34)

Being a woman, she is forced to control her emotions without being tempted. The feel of loneliness makes her get emotionally attracted towards Kalua, who is an ox-cart man. Fate plays a significant part in uniting Kalua and Deeti, though it sounds so strange. Since ancient days, women and not men have been given the label to protect the chastity of the whole society. It is difficult to manage things in an uncertain place. In this novel, Deeti's concealed emotions are enticed by Chandan Singh in various situations as,

> Your Husband and I are brothers after all, of the same flesh and blood. Where is the shame? Why should you waste your looks and your youth on a man who cannot enjoy then? Besides, the time is short while your husband is still alive—if you conceive a son while he is still living, he will be his father's rightful heir. Hukam Singh's land will pass to him and no one will have the right to dispute it. (157)

Deeti has to patiently bear all the mocking comments that are thrown at her by her mother-in-law. Deeti's mother-in-law remarks her as Draupadi, a female character in Hindu epic, *The Mahabharata*. She is considered to be the very beautiful woman of that time who has five husbands. Being a daughter-in-law, she cannot overcome the bad situation in which she has been tied up. Deeti has to go in search of peaceful existence. Especially towards women, there is much violence that takes shapes at home.

Deeti, who lives a life of subjugation, at one point gathered her courage and she decides to be with Kalua. Deeti has gained positive strength and energy. She can take decision so boldly out of uncertainty. The stressful life that she leads makes her so stubborn in her decision that she escaped from *sati* pyre. She acquires immunity and strength to overcome the obstacle set down by her brother-in-law, Chandan Singh. It takes Deeti through a tremendous breakthrough as:

> She had shed the body of the old Deeti, with the burden of its karma; she had paid the price her stars had demanded of her, and was now free now to create

> a new destiny as she willed, with whom she chose and she knew that it was with Kalua that would be lived, until another death claimed the body that he had torn from the flames. (178)

Deeti has transformed herself into a mighty woman empowering herself to an extent that she fights for a woman, Munniah in 'Ibis' for her freedom.

Zachary Reid, whose legitimate rights has been denied because he is caught by the very cruel label racism. This made him represent himself as he does not belong to the 'black' and he presents himself as a gentleman. He is often blackmailed by Mr. Crowle in 'Ibis' as he has known to him with his masked identity. His unemployment forces him to sail in 'Ibis' as a carpenter. The struggle he encounters each day is so well delineated in this novel *Sea of Poppies*. He has been selected to refit the 'Ibis' that "Swims like a Swan and steers like a shark" (77). The role this kind of people play in the world of stage is very important. This vital preference is best understand by the one who is denied of all this importance. There is a clash between an identity and the self. They experience the differences in power. Living this inevitable life itself is an unpredictable threat for slaves. Anything may happen in their life. No one can question their masters. So many of them may lose their life even before they reach their destination of work. They are shifted from their own native land to Mauritius to work in the plantain farm. The plantation workers are treated so badly that they will not be provided enough food, not paid well, harshly punished and no shelter will be provided.

Racism causes many problems to individuals and the society. Racism is an evil system in society that blocks the people of the lower strata society to such a great extent that they cannot survive. They are isolated from all the good things in the society. The discrimination brings all the advancement in society to a halt. These stages of ill-treatment keep some particular sect of people in a very low position. A particular vast community are denied of educational and employment opportunities that make the society an imbalanced one. They start developing a feeling of low self-esteem among themselves. They face harassment often or regularly. Young people are compelled by the pathetic situation to move away from their native land.

In *Sea of Poppies*, Zachary represents himself as a person who is the son of a white father and a quadroon. Zachary's uncertainty of life gives him an inert ability to sail on 'Ibis' apart from the fact that this is for slaves. He wishes to learn the sailor's trade. His eagerness that lies within him is the outcome of his pure understanding of life that is with hopelessness. His life is filled with darkness due to the label that he bears, the 'Black'. He is ready to take risks that are one of the features of people who live a life of uncertainty. He misses the feel of connection between him and his own people, as he is the son of a freed woman. The determination and courage mould him to learn so many ways of construction successfully. Zachary has transformed himself from being a 'black' to a gentleman as addressed in Calcutta once. He becomes a second mate in 'Ibis'.

Raja Neel Rattan Halder, Zamindar of Raskhali, is picturised as a very great man, rich with wealth and human power. During the course, he is being humiliated and exiled from his place for imprisonment. Though he is surrounded by a vast crowd of his own people, his uncertainty still persists. His endless fear may be because of his inefficiency towards keeping up his morality. Taking decisions in uncertainty must be done carefully. Neel is in a position that most of his property has been given to the people around by his father and he is in financial crisis. Now he is struggling to manage things. He thinks Burnham will help him to come out of his crisis, but it results in vain. Raja is accused of forgery and sentenced to death for seven years. His uncertainty in life regarding his property and settlement gives him an encounter with a negative and unsuccessful life. He is being imprisoned and at last shipped in 'Ibis' to Mauritius. His wife Malathi is the sole sufferer, who lives in a small home because of his immorality.

Paulette, a French orphan who was brought up by Jodu's mother, Tantima, as her mother died during childbirth. Jodu's mother helps her father who is a Botanist, in bringing up Paulette. Her first language is Bengali, and the food she has for the first time is rice-and-dal *Khichri*, which is cooked by Jodu's mother. Her life is also unpredictable, as she is oscillating between her own nativity and her adopted environment. She is too submissive in nature. After her father's death, she is in the hands of Mr. Benjamin Burnham. Benjamin Burnham is the son of a Liverpool timber merchant whose "intention in moving to Calcutta was to position himself to bid in the opium auctions of the East India Company" (76). Jodu is not so certain about finding Paulette. However, his mother, before she passes away from this world insisted him to go in search of her. In dilemma, Jodu starts his journey and fortunately finds Paulette. His uncertainty results in success and his mother's wishes have been fulfilled.

Benjamin Burnham compels Paulette to marry Kendalbushe. Meanwhile, she falls in love with Zachary. Burnham is the one who can be associated with masculinity, superiority and the dominance of trading slaves from one place to another. An unhealthy situation pressurises her to travel to Mauritius. As some imbalanced situation occurs in a place she lives in, there comes a chance of going for an option in search of her own identity. She has decided to go to the next level of taking risks. So, she makes her mind to go to Mauritius, trusting that her future will be better, once she reaches there. She is such an obedient sort of girl who does this due to an uncertain life and she is worried about her existence under Burnham's control.

Whenever there is a tumult in society, the people of marginalised sect try to establish their identity in the society by any means. By all means, they prove themselves to the society that they are fit to live a life which is useful to others and they can live without being a burden on the earth. Uncertainty brings mental agony, distress, frustration, loneliness, fear, anxiety to individuals. Because of emotional distress, they may be pushed to a period of time that they can't imagine continuing their life except taking the option for suicide. Individualism is questioned by the society and at the same time it leads to many adventurous journeys too.

An uncomfortable feeling exists in everyone's mind in this novel that arises out of the problems they face in their daily walk of life, challenging their livelihood. Humanity has met with an end as slavery was predominant everywhere. Their ordinary lives are in agitation. Taramony, *guru ma* of Baboo Nobo Krishna Panda, *gomusta* of Burnham, lives a kind of spiritual life after Baboo's uncle's death. His uncle wants Baboo to accompany his wife to Brindavan to build a temple. There was a ray of temptation which runs between Baboo and Taramony, a kind of uncertainty. As a woman of power, she controls her feelings and they both live in a small house in Ahiritola. "Never once did Taramony permit him to touch her in an unchaste way" (161).

Finally, there is a transformation in all the major characters and it is only because of the feeling of uncertainty that sticks to everyone's life. All the major characters like Deeti, Zachary Reid, Paulette, Malathi, Taramony took a positive spin in their life to get transformed after a heavy painful process of uncertainty. It brings a lot of difference in their lifestyle. It gives a feel that so many changes are easy to make in our own life. It empowers each character and helps them to come out of their frustration, melancholy, anguish and desperateness to become independent of themselves.

Marginalisation and uncertainty are quite unavoidable in a place of colonial set up. Those marginalised people are in unimportant positions. Their identity is crushed to the core. They are pushed to the least floor. They are away from the benefits provided to the other groups. They cannot easily climb up the socially upward ladder. All these deprived sects joined hands together to create a feel of oneness under the sky in 'Ibis' and they come out with their multiple aspects including intolerance and acceptance.

> On a boat of pilgrims, no one can lose caste and everyone is the same: it's like taking a boat to the temple of Jagannatha, in Puri. From now on, and forever afterwards, we will be ship-siblings—*jahaz-bhais* and *jahaz-bahens*—to each other. There will be no differences between us.

This answer was so daring, so ingenuous, as fairly to rob the women of their breath. Not in a lifetime of thinking, Deeti knew, would she have stumbled upon an answer so complete, so satisfactory and so thrilling in its possibilities. In the glow of the moment, she did something she would never have done otherwise; she reached out to take the stranger's hand in her own. Instantly, in emulation of her gesture, every other woman reached out too, to share in this communion of touch. Yes, said Deeti, from now on, there are no differences between us; we are *jahaz-bhai* and *jahaz-bahen* to each other; all of us children of the ship" (356). Uncertainty results in changing reality, a mass transformation.

Works Cited

Ghosh, Amitav. *Sea of Poppies*. New Delhi: Penguin. 2008. Print.

Seligman, E.P. Martin, Steven and Christopher. *Learned Helplessness: A Theory for the Age of Personal Control*. Oxford University Press, 1993. Print.

<https://www.thoughtco.com/anomie-definition-3026052>

<https://judithcurry.com/2012/06/10/psychology-of-uncertainty/>

12

Postmodern Historiography: A Study on Amitav Ghosh's *The Glass Palace*

Prasaja VP

The popular genre of historical novel changes its course of flow during the postmodern scenario. Historical fiction made a sudden leap from the traditional sort of historical narrative to the much more experimental form executed by the postmodern writers. It deviates from the actual representation of historical events to the rather more fictionalization of the facts. The influence of postmodernism flouted the monolithic approach to history and reality and demands a pluralistic approach to them. It blurs the boundary between history and fiction by "making the transition from one realm to the other as jarring as possible" (McHale, 90).

Postmodernism pushed the boundaries of cultural convention and effected a shift in perception and representation. Postmodern writers adopted a novel way of questioning the entire paradigm of the representation of the real. They are of the view that there is no ultimate reality and the 'real' is just a representation or construction. They resist to mirror these constructed reality, and instead they reshape the reality on their accounts. They challenged the objective rendition of old historiography, making the process of documenting reality increasingly fluid by a subjective version of reality. These transformations lead to the distortion of meta-narrative or grand narratives which marks affinity to the dominant hegemony. The postmodern strategy of mini-narratives which rejects the portrayal of elaborate formal aesthetics gradually takes the stance.

Postmodern historical novels constantly battle against logocentrism, phallocentrism, ethnocentrism and imperialism of Western history. They question the truth-value of history as dominant Western discourse and challenge its monology by commingling the fact and the fiction. The traditional canonical texts were blind to questions of race, class, and gender. Within the institutionalization of postmodern literature, a progressive step was taken by the writers to dethrone these canonical texts by deconstructing the Western binary. This drastic change in the attitude of the academicians is largely due to the result of an emphasis on the philosophy of subjectivity, relativity and equality. Thus, feminist, postcolonial, and ethnic texts were incorporated into the accepted canon.

History is a record of the dominant ideology. It is a human construct, as is literature. It is the prejudiced representation of the people on the periphery by the dominant class, who are in the centre. By extolling the feats and glory of the dominant historical figures, it often submerges the simple annals of the socially deprived class. Often the voice of the marginalized groups is unheard or is silenced by the hegemonic ideologies. To subvert this reality propounded by the dominant class, the postmodern novelists insert history into fiction and rewrite them from a perspective different from the accepted interpretation.

History and marginality are of utmost importance as themes in postmodern and postcolonial writing; there is the general tendency to insert historical events into the literary text to undermine dominant ideology. Postcolonial writers, in this context, point out the fact that colonized are excluded from history, which comes to represent the hegemony of the colonizers. Thus, postcolonial historiography serves as a liberating genre for colonized writers that enable other histories to be verbalized.

Contemporary writers hailing from the colonized country of India, explore varied forms of life that existed during the British rule. Among the leading postcolonial writers in English, Amitav Ghosh displays a distinctive voice in literature, a voice which is profound and is different from the common run of his contemporaries. The particular themes and techniques that Ghosh employs in his novels allow him to be labeled both as a postmodern and a postcolonial writer. Ghosh has a particular interest in the Indian colonial history and the contribution of the English language in the postcolonial world.

In most of the novels of Amitav Ghosh, history forms a major element. Amitav Ghosh is among those handful of writers in the world who have the capacity to interweave history with fiction to make a gracious and elaborate story. His debut novel *The Circle of Reason* (1986) takes a peep at the various angles of the Nationalist movement. His second novel *The Shadow Lines* (1988) is largely set against the backdrop of major historical events such as the Second World War, the partition of India, the communal riots of 1963-64 in Dhaka and Calcutta, the Maoist Movement, the Indo-China War, and the Indo-Pak War. Ghosh's non-fiction *In an Antique Land* (1992) is a historical investigation of an ancient merchant who came to India via Egypt around 1130 AD. Even though a sci-fi *The Calcutta Chromosome* (1995) has no exception, as it portrays the life of Sir Ronald Ross, the Nobel Prize-winning scientist who achieved a breakthrough in Malaria research in 1898.

Among his works, *The Glass Palace* (2000) cuts a new path for itself, by challenging the institutionalized perspectives of the colonial history. The novel is shaped by a historical moment that is integral to the plot. It is set against the backdrop of three countries—Burma, India, and Malaya, which were once under the colonial power. It provides a detailed account of the royals in the Konbaung Dynasty of Burma, their uprooted life due to the complex socio-political factors and the resultant loss of identity. It also focuses on the plight of Indians in their own land and in the neighbouring land of Burma and Malaya. As Pico Iyer remarks, "The Glass Palace performs an invaluable service in showing us how the events of the last century, and especially the war, looked to many people in Burma and India, whose voices have seldom been heard before in the West" (28).

Ghosh is of the opinion that the conventional historical record is faulty and incomplete because the contributions of the colonised have been left out. So, in *The Glass Palace* he departed from the version of factual narration and thereby destabilizes the hegemonic historiography. Ghosh challenges the truthfulness of the narrative and revolutionized the conventional narration by the act of fabrication.

Ghosh offers alternative versions of history in the novel by foregrounding the silenced lives, and desires of the colonized people. The novel is tied around the characters who are helpless victims of the forces of history. It encompasses the colonial rule of a whole century right from Anglo-Burmese War of 1885 to the chaos of the two World Wars. It spans a period from pre-independence era and ends in post-independence era. It attempts to narrate the history of the colonization of Burma from the viewpoint of Rajkumar, a migrant Bengali, who right from his childhood adopts Burma as his homeland.

The postmodern version of History is always subject to *subversion.* In the novel, the dominant voice of history is refracted through subversion and gives way to other voices that have been suppressed. As the critic Jayita Sengupta says:

> The postmodernistic version of history is always subject to subversion, reformulation, and interrogation. However natural the presentation of fact are, the element of personalization cannot be ruled out in the process of selection of material and in drawing forth different subjective response through constant interrogation. So history is never objective and historiography metafiction always goes through a process of ontological re-formulation where history and fiction collide to make a sense of the world of representation. Ghosh's rendering of British colonialism and its aftermath in the three countries is interplay of the fact and fiction in an illusory place of imagination top create an awareness of the experiential reality of the post-colonial world. (4)

Through the subjective lens of a subaltern, Ghosh details the story of the colonial past. As a mouthpiece of the ordinary people, Ghosh exposes the angst and aspiration, the pain and pleasure that they have confronted by giving voice to fictional characters and thus tries to depict the impact of great historical events upon their lives. He manages to convey the representation of the colonial past on metaphorical levels by means of his pivotal character, being a half-breed. Through this revisionist history, he attempts to make us rethink the subaltern's alternative history through the portrayal of the central fictive protagonist, Rajkumar.

The subaltern experiences are often veiled by the colonialist historiography. However, Amitav Ghosh daringly reconstructed the history by inventing a fictional character who is a subaltern, and narrates the major historical events from his point of view. Ghosh describes Rajkumar as an Indian, a 'kalaa', who migrated from his native land to the alien country of Burma. The name Rajkumar reminds one of a royal persona but Ghosh's Rajkumar is a poor orphan. As Ghosh says, "His name meant Prince, but he was anything but princely in appearance, with his oil-splashed vest; his untidily knotted loungyi and his bare feet with their thick slippers of callused skin" (1).

Ghosh's inclination towards the marginalised people will be read through a juxtaposition of historical and ahistorical characters. In the novel, Ghosh gives a perfect amalgamation of the two worlds of history and imagination. The novel deploys an array of fictional characters like Rajkumar, Dolly, Saya John, Uma Dey who reflect their lives in the historical events and impact of colonial rule of British. Ghosh has also presented the royal family of King Thebaw, the last king of the Konbaung Dynasty of Burma and his queen consort Supayalat and their subsequent exilement due to British colonization, to render the historic atmosphere. He brilliantly interweaves these fictitious characters into the plot of the historical story.

For this act of historicizing, Ghosh became the butt of criticism. In a letter written to reject the nomination of his book *The Glass Palace* for the Commonwealth Writer's Prize, Ghosh reveals his opinion regarding the writers' freedom in reframing history. He acclaims: "That the past engenders the present is of course undeniable, it is equally undeniable that the reasons why I write in English are ultimately rooted in my country's history. Yet the ways in which we remember the past are not determined solely by the brute feel of time: they are also open to choice, reflection and judgement" (*Journal of Commonwealth Literature*, 21).

Amitav Ghosh's remarkable effort in this novel has been to offer an imaginative reconstruction of the most troubled times of our recent history. He paints the insecurities in the human existence, which is one of the postmodern traits. *The Glass Palace* starts with the tumultuous condition of war. The impending arrival of the war was anticipated by the central character. The author begins, "There was only one person in the food-stall who knew exactly what that sound was that was rolling in across the plain, along the silver curve of the Irrawaddy, to the western wall of Mandalay's fort. His name was Rajkumar and he was an Indian, a boy of eleven—not an authority to be relied upon" (3).

Rajkumar is a man of determination who creates an empire in the Burmese teak forest. His life becomes inextricably interlinked with the political, national, and religious events of his time. He becomes a part of the history when he visits the royal palace of King Thebaw during the time of colonial loot, and meets Dolly, the queen's maid who is most beautiful. His love to Dolly culminates in their marriage and the novelist details the life span of their three generations. Apart from this main plot, there are subplots that details the critical life of Indian soldiers, which the authorized history failed to etch. Ghosh is frustrated by the silenced voices of the colonized lots in the recorded history. He narrates:

> It's not been written about at all.... It's strange—there were over half a million people on the Long March, over 400,000 of them Indian, and there is such a silence about it.... There was no need for the Indians in Burma to flee when the Japanese approached—many Indians did stay back. It makes you realise the degree to which Indians felt themselves to be the sheep of the British; the delusions that governed their lives. (68)

The novelist adopts the postmodern technique of pastiche to create a new narrative voice. He frames the body of the novel by mixing the elements of a romance, narrative fiction, adventure fiction, and historical fiction. He incorporates all the elements of a novel to create fragmentation. Ghosh uses the romantic genre to chart the characters who reflect on the history of colonialism in Burma. It is also a narrative fiction that employs a complex narrative structure. It is adventurous as it displays the escapades of the hero. It can be read as a historical novel for it portrays the history of a nation. There was so much detail, it felt like an autobiography—which it probably was—in part. The diasporic identity of Rajkumar, a confused Indian refugee in Burma, is similar to that of the novelist who straddles both the Eastern and Western worlds regularly.

The Glass Palace can be analysed as a text which is primarily parodic in its relation to the traditions and conventions of the genre involved. Even though a historic novel, it constantly distorts the traditional historical narrative. Here, Ghosh also employed the element of irony, which is key to postmodern narratives. The novelist approaches the subjects like Second World War and communal riot from a distant position and choose to depict their histories ironically and humorously. In the novel, the characters of Queen Supayalat and Arjun were displayed with a tinge of irony. Queen Supayalat, even after being captured by the British, does not lose her pomp throughout the novel. The portraiture of the Queen is too ironic. Arjun, basically an Indian, is completely affected and influenced by the Western ideology. He imitates the West in his dressing sense and food habit. He is not aware of the fact that he is being used as instrumental to inflict pain on his own people.

The title of the novel itself connotes postmodern element. The title itself is ironic. *The Glass Palace* is the vast central hall of the Burmese king, which is covered entirely with transparent glass. It is mentioned only twice in the novel after its appearance in the opening section. Ghosh uses the 'glass' as a metaphor. The royal couple, on the one hand was able to study what was happening around the country through the glass, and at the same time they made themselves dissociated from the city by remaining inside the glass palace. The palace is an emblem of British colonisation. The destruction of the glass palace connotes the destruction of the colonized people.

The common features of a non-linear narrative mode as well as chronological shifts are discernible in the novel. The novelist uses third person narration. He also uses the flashback technique to show forth the inner recesses of the personality of the characters. There is a perpetual presence of past in the characters' lives and focus on the ways the past re-emerges and shapes the present. He also uses the technique of shift, the technique in which the author from one story switches on to another story. Jayita Sengupta in her review article "Ghosh's *The Glass Palace* through Post Colonial Lens" shares her view regarding the narrative technique:

> The writer's device which is central to the artistic deployment of his material in the novel is the metaphor of the camera. Leitmotifs of mirrors, lenses, and binoculars are scattered throughout the text. The artist's eye reflects, bears, witness to the historical events as a kind of photomontage, a series of snapshots over time whose details are filled in. (26)

Ghosh writes his novel with historical background against which he weaves the stories of the subalterns. *The Glass Palace* is indeed a masqueraded history. Ghosh made a fine work of art by carving the fiction with the tool of past. As the American historian Dominick LaCapra rightly says, "texts are both historical events in their own right and a crucial basis for our inferential reconstruction of other events; the problem of how to read and interpret them should be considered vital for the historian" (431). Thus, Ghosh proves his mettle as a postmodern historian by rereading and reinterpreting history and give subalterns a prime place in the pages of his books and thereby in the annals of history.

Works Cited

Ghosh, Amitav. *The Glass Palace*. New Delhi: Harper Collins, 2000. Print.

Iyer, Pico. "The Road from Mandalay: Review of The Glass Palace." *New York Review of Books*. 48.4 (2001): 28-31. Print.

LaCapra, Dominick. "Intellectual History and Its Ways." *The American Historical Review,* 97, No. 2 (April 1992): 425-39.

McHale, Brian. *Postmodernist Fiction*. UK: Routledge, 2003. Print.

Sengupta, Jayita. "Ghosh's *The Glass Palace* through Post Colonial Lens." *The Quest*, Vol. 16, No. 1, June 2002, 26-32. Print.

13

The Shadow Lines: A Futuristic Post-colonial Voyage

Gobinda Sahoo

> Nationalism is not the awakening of nations to self-consciousness: it invents nations where they do not exist. (Ernest Gellner in his book *Thought and Change,* 169)

Amitav Ghosh's *The Shadow Lines* is a postcolonial artifact of Indian writing in English with a different approach to nationalism. Published in 1988, this novel work of art has been widely acclaimed as one of the most significant postcolonial fictional products during the contemporary period. If we peep into the pages of the novel with a critic's vision, we find almost all the postcolonial features in it. *The Shadow Lines* is a series of uninterrupted record of the effects of colonization. The whole plot is but a memoir of the past experiences by an anonymous narrator and conception of nationalism in the voice of the grandmother, one influential matriarchal character of the novel.

The Shadow Lines puts a very big question mark on the national boundaries which are but mere imaginary lines to separate the nations. The novel may be called a mouthpiece of the emergence of multiculturalism, an offshoot of postcolonial literature, dealing with the borderlines as mere blurred lines between nations and finally between families and even within one's own self-identity. The storyline is a dramatization of the inner conflicts of the union of dissimilar but interrelated cultures and the superficial conflicts between families and friends, that have been imposed by geographical discord. Generally, the Indian English novels are based upon the curiosity of the westerners to travel in India. However, things are opposite here. In this respect, the novel seems unconventional in terms of postcolonial literature, as it shows the colonized people moving to the land of colonizers. The very first line of the novel gives us the reference:

> In 1939, thirteen years before I was born, my father's aunt, Mayadebi went to England with her husband and son Tridib. (*TSL*, 3)

The plan of attempting a novel with a dream of a world sans boundaries, comes through a personal experience of the writer. In a seminal essay entitled "The Ghosts of Mrs. Gandhi", published in 1995, Amitav Ghosh shares his experience of anti-Sikh riot of 1984 in Delhi and acknowledges how his experiences of the riot has influenced him in shaping *The Shadow Lines*:

> Within a few months I started my novel, which I eventually called *The Shadow Lines*, a book that led me backwards in time, to earlier memories of riots, ones witnessed in childhood. It became a book about the meaning of such events and their effects on the individuals who live through them.
>
> When I went back to my desk in November 1984, I found myself confronting decisions about writing that I had never faced before. How was I to write about what I had seen without reducing it to a mere spectacle? My next novel was bound to be influenced by my experiences....

Ghosh's approach has been very novel in *The Shadow Lines*. The narrative does not catalog any of the socio-political harrowing turmoil occurring in the subcontinent. Rather, the bildungsroman indexes each of his character living through emotional trauma, a consequence of either freedom movement in Bengal, the Second World War, the partition of India or the communal riots that broke out in East Pakistan (now Bangladesh) following the Hazratbal Shrine incident in Srinagar in 1964.

The whole story of *The Shadow Lines* moves back and forth between the two families, one is Indian, that of the narrator and the other English, the Prices, and tries to emphasize on the hybrid identity of the narrator. The characters in the novel are caught between two worlds. The narrator is Indian in origin but educated in England and it is through a hybrid use of English language, a heterogeneous version of India is portrayed. The narrator renders a contrast of opinion between Tha'mma and Ila. While Ila prefers to live in London, the grandmother does not accept her decision. In her view, she does not belong there as "she has no right to live there" (*TSL*, 76). Each country, she affirms, exclusively belongs to the people who fought long wars for its independence at the cost of the lives of their ancestors. She claims that the borders have been drawn with the blood of the ancestors.

The novelist makes the characters travel to the West, as a result of which, they gather first-hand information of the life of the colonizers. The story shifts from London to Calcutta to Dhaka as told by the anonymous young narrator. The stories interweave life in Dhaka before partition, life in London during the war and the narrator's life in Calcutta during 1960s and in London during 1970s. The narrator gives an account of the people and places Tridib has described to him twenty years back in flashback along with an exhilarating life of modern London. To the narrator, his imaginary renovation of the past is more real than that of the present. Ila considers present rather past as real. She does not fake refuge in the past.

The Shadow Lines covers three generations of the narrator's family spread over Calcutta, Dhaka and London and his English family friends, the Prices. The novel has been written at the backdrop of the civil strife in the post-partition East Pakistan and the riot-hit Calcutta. The period covered in the narrative is from 1939, the year of outbreak of World War II to 1964, the year of eruption of a cycle of violence in India and Pakistan. In 1939, the narrator's ideal Tridib, aged 8, is taken to England, and in 1964, he is killed in a riot near his mother's ancestral home in Dhaka. Tridib's murder irks everyone. His younger brother is much moved by the incident. He questions on the meaning of freedom by drawing lines on a map. Amitav Ghosh questions on the geographical boundaries that divide and separate the people of one land from their own people on the pretext of religion and community.

> Why don't they draw thousands of little lines through the whole subcontinent and give every little place a new name? What would it change? It's a mirage; the whole thing is a mirage. How can anyone divide a memory? If freedom were possible, surely Tridib's death would have set me free. And yet, all it takes to set my hand shaking like a leaf, fifteen years later, thousands of miles away, at the other end of another continent, is a chance remark by a waiter in a restaurant. (*TSL*, 247)

The events revolves around Tha'mma, the grandmother's link with her ancestral city Dhaka and Mayadebi's family and their friendship, their sojourn with the English friends. The grandmother is presented as a sturdy and tough character, much feared but prized; she is also disdained as a chauvinist or, at best, a still-surviving representative of a fossilized nationalism. The grandmother is nostalgic of her birthplace, East Bengal, where she has spent her childhood. She shares all her experiences with her grandson. The story takes us to three generations of a Bengali family spread in three countries as a consequence of historical development. The grandmother, Jethmoshai, Mayadebi and Saheb belong to the first generation while the father and the mother represent second generation and Ila, Nick, Tridib, May and the narrator represent the third generation. However, the events are not presented sequentially and the narrative is not confined to the incidents taking place in the narrator's life.

The novel shifts easily from past to present and from present to past. Memory, time past and reality, time present have been masterly managed by the author. The novel is divided into two part "Going Away" and "Coming Home". On the sub-titles Anjan Kumar writes:

> ...one is constantly plagued by doubts in the novel as to whether the characters are going to Calcutta or coming to Calcutta or coming to London or going back to London. The two sections of the Novel clearly

> indicate this enigma of having to decide whether home is Calcutta or Dhaka [Bangladesh] or London. (32)

By the end of the first section, the narrator comes to know about Ila's indifference towards him. The second section ends with the narrator's regaining self-possession, he is able to get back his love, Ila, his union with May is established and he is able to accept the untimely death of Tridib. Thus, "Going Away" the first segment may mean "going away from self" and "Coming Home" the subsequent segment may mean "coming back into the self".

There is seldom any character that has been able to detach from the past. Their identities are marred by their pasts. The narrative advances and surpasses the rigid barrier of time, place and action with the action of each character leaving indelible impression on the rest of others. Memoirs of the narrator works as restructured family history and give a significant meaning. The novel moves forward with the help of the memory of the socio-political situation by the grandmother, Tha'mma. After retirement as a Headmistress, she begins her expedition on the paths of faded memories. She remembers her house in Dhaka, which was like a massive pyramid inhibited by so many members that even the most knowledgeable person failed to make out the exact relationship with others.

Quest for freedom has been the central theme of *The Shadow Lines*. It is clearly evident from the narrative that total freedom is impossible. Though everyone demonstrates an urge to be free, nobody is free until the end. In her essay "The Division of Experience in *The Shadow Lines*", Rajeswari Sunder Rajan affirms "There is...an explicit contrast between the cultural rootedness of the passive male protagonists and the migrancy of the women. Both Tridib and the narrator 'belong'—not just in their native Calcutta milieu but the 'world' itself." While Tridib represents the ideal mode of being-in-the-world the narrator aspires for it. The narrator, Robi and Ila crave for freedom from the memory that haunts them.

Amitav Ghosh is very autobiographical in approach in *The Shadow Lines*. He was born in Calcutta in postcolonial era on 11 July 1956 but was not confined to the limits of national boundaries. Besides India, he grew up in East Pakistan (Bangladesh), Sri Lanka and Iran. He was brought up on the stories of partition, the freedom struggle and the aftermath of World War II. He portrays the characters in the bildungsroman who are not confined to the borderlines of nations, rather they are multicultural and multinational in attitude and approach. Postcolonial literature seeks to assert the richness and strength of indigenous cultures for restoration of traditions gradually degraded during colonization. Tha'mma's concept of freedom is the mouthpiece of restoring the lost Indian glory. For her, political freedom that leads to intellectual as well as social freedom is necessary. She is nostalgic about the turbulent days of her youth of the Swadeshi movement days in Bengal. She asserts to prefer to be killed for the cause of freedom, if given a chance. During her student days, she had wanted to earn some glory by assisting the terrorist organizations fighting for the country's liberation by means of running errands for them—cooking for them and washing their clothes. She donated the gold chain with a ruby pendant, presented to her by her husband, to the war fund. It was all for the sake of freedom. However, the same group of people coming from India in embassy car and the nation become the cause of her sorrow in 1964. After Tridib's tragic untimely murder, she realized that these political boundaries are mere superficial lines to divide people and places. The struggle against the British rule has aroused nationalism in her. Her fearlessness and anti-imperialist patriotism is appreciated by her grandson.

Symbolism is the device used by the novelist in the references to houses, maps and mirrors, and finally the borders. Anjan Kumar states:

> All these symbols in one way or the other deal with the theme of man's search for identity, his search for roots. This is not a story of the grandmother but it is a story of the eternal suffering of every man torn between the past and the present. (32)

The bildungsroman based on partition and immigration is man's eternal quest for freedom. If we keenly observe the fictional work, it is revealed that it is not possible to be completely free. Almost all the characters in the novel demonstrate a yearning for freedom but at the end, none is completely free. The novelist affirms this lesson in the voice of Robi:

> You know, if you look at the pictures on the front pages of the newspapers at home now, all those pictures of dead people—in Assam, the north-east, Punjab, Sri Lanka, Tripura—people shot by terrorists and separatists and the army and the police, you'll find somewhere behind it all, that single word; everyone's doing it to be free. (*TSL*, 246)

However, Ila's concept of freedom was different; it was purely individualistic. Unlike Tridib and the narrator, she lived intensely in the present. For her, there is no natural home, she must make or discover her own place in the world. She tried to get rid of her Indianness and left for London. She marries an Englishman, buys a house, and finds a job, but all in vain. Once, she goes to the nightclub of the Calcutta Grand Hotel for drinks. After his companions disapprove her proposal to dance, she wished to dance with a strange businessman. Coming out of the dance bar, Robi tries to convince her that it was none the business of Indian girls. Ila replies, "What the fuck do you mean? She spat at him. 'What do you mean girls'? I'll do what I bloody well want when I want and where" (*TSL*, 88).

Sitting in the taxi back to home she shouted:

> Do you see now why I've chosen to live in London? Do you see? It is only because I want to be free. [ ] Free of your bloody culture.... (*TSL*, 88-89)

She thought that her living abroad makes her superior to the narrator. Despite the narrator's love for her, she marries Nick Price, though he did not love her and was unfaithful to her and a wastrel. It was a mere show off of upper middle class values of Ila. Though she hated small children, she starts working for an organization meant for children. Both the grandmother and Ila are unrooted characters, typifying two of the characteristic forms of twentieth-century diaspora. While Ila is the post-colonial cosmopolitan, her great-aunt is a refugee.

Tha'mma realizes that borders have a tenuous existence. Even a history of bloodshed cannot make them real and inflexible. Borderlines on maps are merely the handwork of the administrators and cartographers. In 1964, while she plans to fly to Dhaka, she wonders if "she would be able to see the border between India and East Pakistan from the plane". To the question of her son as to if "the border was a long black line with green on the side and scarlet on the other, like it was in a school atlas", she replies "Of course not. But surely there's something—trenches perhaps, or soldiers, or guns pointing at each other, or even just barren strips of land. Don't they call it no-man's land?" She is confused if there aren't any trenches or anything, how could people make out the differences?

Tridib, though a student of archaeology, has a deep interest in history. "He can perceive not only 'the permanent pastness of the past' but also live in pastness in the present. His 'imaginative eye' can see the permanent in the transient and explode all the artificial barriers of time and space. It escapes the bondage that limits ordinary human consciousness". For him, freedom can be achieved only through imagination. His preoccupation with 'invention' is essentially a desperate nonetheless fruitless endeavor to cut through the net of discursive formations. He asserts that we should attempt properly, for "we could not see without inventing what we saw...if we didn't try ourselves, we would never be free of other people's inventions". Suvir Kaul in his essay "Separate Anxiety: Growing Up Inter/National in *The Shadow Lines*" writes:

> As the repository and archivist of family stories, stories told by his grandmother Tha'mma, by Tridib, by Ila, and finally by Robi and May, the unnamed narrator of *The Shadow Lines* is constantly engaged in the imaginative renewal of times, places, events and people past. This remembering is often tinted with the sepia-tones of nostalgia, often darkened by the dull shades of grief, but in each case it is fundamentally a search for meaning, for explanations and reasons,

> for the elusive formal and causal logic that will allow the narrator's autobiography (and equally, the national biography that is interwoven with it in the novel) to cohere, to make sense. (267)

Amitav Ghosh portrays two types of postcolonial characters, the ones like Mayadebi and Shaheb, who belong to the elite class and the others live in close contact with the west like Ila. They want to be a part of colonizer's world. Above all the novelist has chosen the language of the colonizers in writing the novel.

In spite of the long and intolerable oppression by the colonizers, the postcolonial writers insist the equality of cultures. Amitav Ghosh conforms to this norm as a postcolonialist in *The Shadow Lines* by making the protagonist Tridib fall in love with Maya and Ila, an Indian marries an Englishman, Nick Price, and finally towards the end of the novel, the relation of the narrator and May has been able to bridge the cross-cultural gap successfully. The characters of Indian origin dwell in both the worlds and have their own respectable positions in both. However, Ila, being brought up outside India, is a perplexed character torn between the two worlds. She only strives for English recognition.

Jethmoshai, the Ukil-babu's relatives went to bring back their elderly relative from Dhaka to Calcutta with the pretext that it was 'not safe for him here anymore.' He was very old "seemed childlike—shrunken, tiny, with spit hanging in threads from the corners of his mouth." However, he refuses to go back to India and even refuses to acknowledge its existence:

> I don't believe in this India-Shindia. It's all very well, you're going away now, but suppose when you get there they decide to draw another line somewhere? What will you do then? Where will you move to? No one will have you anywhere. (*TSL*, 215)

Continuing the legacy of his first novel *The Circle and Reason,* Amitav Ghosh has successfully written that revolves around the diaspora of East Pakistan after independence. The narrator's family belongs to Hindu religion that moved to

Dhaka and Calcutta after the formation of East Pakistan. At a crucial juncture, when Europe was completely devastated due to World War II, they developed friendship with the Price family of England. Their relationship has been able to establish a bridge between the cultural differences between the two families and finally the two nations, by the able craftsmanship of Amitav Ghosh. The narrative begins shortly after the narrator's arrival from England. They all had been to Dhaka because of the grandmother's origin there and unfortunately Tridib, the narrator's uncle turns victim in Old Dhaka by the irate mob. The riots that broke out both in India and Bangladesh were due to the stealing of *Mui-i-Mubarak*, the relic of Prophet Mohammed in Kashmir. The narrator argues that as one incident of a country has its impact in two different countries sharing borders, the border seems redundant and superfluous. The narrator wonders:

> when they discovered that they had created not a separation, but yet undiscovered irony—the irony that killed Tridib: the simple facts that there had never been a moment in the four-thousand-year-old history of that map, when the places we know as Dhaka and Calcutta were more closely bound to each other than after they had drawn their lines—so closely that I, in Calcutta had only to look into the mirror to be in Dhaka; a moment when each city was inverted image of the other locked into an irreversible symmetry by the line that was to set us free—our looking-glass border. (*TSL*, 233)

The novel entirely deals with bridging the cultural gap between the East and the West through the metaphor of travel. Before independence, the father of Mrs. Price, by living in India, ignited the close affinity between the Price family and that of the narrator. He was a sort of traveling Englishman. He left home in Cornwall to undertake travel in Malaysia, Fiji, Ceylon and finally India, particularly, in Calcutta. Tridib, during war period, went to London and lived with the Prices. Finally, the narrator also dwells in travel.

The Shadow Lines divulges the fragility of partition. Borderlines between countries and the cartographical lines which are supposed to be the dividing lines separating people cannot be the ones bringing fundamental changes in the identity of the people on either sides of the border 'the truth of the precepts that were available' to them. Ghosh utters in the voice of the narrator:

> I believe that distance separates, that it is a corporeal substance; I believe in the reality of nations and borders; I believed that across the border there existed another reality. The only relationship my vocabulary permitted between those separate realities was war or friendship. (*TSL*, 219)

However, in spite of the geographical separation the identical history and cultures of the subcontinent bring the inhabitants closer to each other and keep them bound. The narrator makes different circles with the help of 'a rusty old compasses' on the map and takes different landscapes, irrespective of states and continents, and finally concludes that "within the circles there were only states and citizens; there were no people at all" (*TSL*, 233). He does not blame the people who draw the borders between India and Pakistan rather terms them 'sensible people of good intention'. He refers to the catastrophic days of bloodshed that displaced many people from both the sides and made them refugees.

> They had drawn their borders believing in that pattern, in the enchantment of lines, hoping perhaps that once they had etched their borders upon the map, the two bits of land would sail away from each other like the shifting tectonic plates of the prehistoric Gondwanaland. (*TSL*, 233)

The novelist has been very successful in bridging the cultural gap between the two nations at the end of the bildungsroman with the sexual union between May Price and the narrator on his last night, in London, which gives him "the glimpse of...a final redemptive mystery" (*TSL*, 252).

In spite of being separated by national borders, the people of Calcutta and Dhaka follow and observe the same culture. Though both of these cities are geographically separated as parts of different countries, they are bound in the narrator's consciousness through common suffering. Thus, *The Shadow Lines* becomes one of the notable creations of postcolonial literature and finds its place among *Train to Pakistan* of Khushwant Singh and *Final Solutions* of Mahesh Dattani.

Works Cited

Ghosh, Amitav. *The Shadow Lines*. New Delhi: Oxford University Press. 1995. Print.

Ghosh, Tapan Kumar, Bhattacharya, Prasanta. Ed. *The Pursuits of Amitav Ghosh: Some Recent Readings*. New Delhi: Orient BlackSwan. 2013. Print.

Kumar, Anjan. *The Novels of Amitav Ghosh: Major Themes*. New Delhi: Adhyayan Publishers & Distributors. 2013. Print.

https://www.outlookindia.com/website/story/the-ghosts-of-mrs-gandhi/282817

http://www.mcser.org/journal/index.php/mjss/article/viewFile/7285/6974

http://shodhganga.inflibnet.ac.in/bitstream/10603/7898/9/09_chapter%203.pdf

14

Amitav Ghosh's *The Hungry Tide*: A Subaltern Narrative

Palakurthy Dinakar

The subaltern narratives speak of the oppressed sections of the society. Sub (under) alter (other) has the Latin origin, *subaltern* means one group will be under the influence of other group in rather a large group. The subalterns may be any section of the society which is under the pressure, humiliation, rejection and suppression of other group. The oppressed may be women, dalit in Indian context or others who are the sufferers of gender or victims of racial discrimination, caste, colour and orthodox social norms at the global context. The word 'subaltern' is first used by Italian Marxist Antonio Gramsci and popularized by Ranajit Guha and Gayatri Chakravarti Spivak. Ranajit Guha feels that the subaltern studies is the name for the general attribute of subordination in South Asian Society whether this is expressed in terms of class, caste, age, gender and office or in any other. Gayatri Spivak expresses her opinion in her popular essay "Can the Subaltern Speak?" used the term subaltern for the colonized and the oppressed sections of the society.

Amitav Ghosh's creativity can be divided into two main streams—fictional and non-fictional. His fictional works are *The Circle of Reason* (1986), *The Shadow Lines* (1988), *In an Antique Land* (1992), *The Calcutta Chromosome* (1996), *The Glass Palace* (2000), *The Hungry Tide* (2004), *Sea of Poppies* (2008) and non-fictional works are *Dancing in Cambodia, At Large in Burma* (1998), *Countdown* (1999), *Imam and the Indian* (2002). His works cover multi-layered complexity with different angles. His works in many ways experiment with time and mystery. They try to map the cultural spaces and travels across geographical terrains. They question different roles, freedom extended to the marginalized and the subalterns. They enquire into the identity of subalterns in the hegemonic society.

Many of the protagonists in the works of Amitav Ghosh are the representatives of subalterns, as they suffer because of their insignificant position in the society. They are ill-treated and humiliated in the hegemonic society. The characters like Alu, the orphan in *The Circle* of *Reason,* Rajkumar, the orphan street boy, and the servant maids in *The Glass Palace,* the slave Bomma in *In an Antique Land,* Nirmal and Piyali in *The Hungry Tide,* Murugan, Mangala and Latchman in *The Calcutta Chromosome*. Amitav not only describes the realistic picture of certain section of the society but he also narrates their struggle to overcome their pathetic situation in order to overcome their humiliation. He focuses on the fight of the subalterns for their cultural and social identity and their tussle to move them from margin to the centre.

Ghosh is a highly intellectual writer, whose preoccupations largely overlapped with this new generation of critics, and whose innovative textual experiments offered new insights and openings into the cluster of conceptual and theoretical concepts that had been developed to describe, analyse and interpret the complex of colonial and postcolonial relations (Mondal, 164).

The paper tries to highlight the pitiable conditions of the neglected strata of the society in the Sundarbans region in *The Hungry Tide*. Amitav questions and blames the State for their lethargic attitude in providing basic amenities to the sufferers of the region through the characters Nirmal and Kusum. Amitav was successful in projecting the troubles and tribulations of the refugees of the Sundarbans whose status is considered to be subalterns by the natives. They are affected by animals, serpents, creatures, famine and even the nature is also against them. They are supposed to be in danger around the clock and suffer a lot because of the climatic conditions which are unfit for human inhabitation. “There are no borders here to divide fresh water from salt, river from sea. The tides reach as far as three hundred kilometers inland and every day thousands of acres of forest disappear under water only to re-emerge hours later” (7).

The plot of the novel *The Hungry Tide* was in the mind of Amitav from his childhood because as a young boy he stayed in the Sundarbans in the house of his uncle Chandra Ghosh, headmaster of a local primary school. He visited the same place again during his teens because of his interest in the people and atmosphere in the tide country. Amitav had the opportunity to understand the problems of the refugees of the 'tide community' at a very young age. Amitav's likening for the region and the community is reflected through the character Fokir. Amitav was very much moved with the article of Annu Jalais, a historian which is published under the title "Dwelling in Morichjhapi". The article explains the indifferent attitude of the West Bengal Government towards the refugees belong to the tide community in providing rehabilitation as it was in the manifesto in the Left Front's elections. Jalais also explains the dreadful experience of the refugees at the hands of the police and their fight against the atrocities of the people.

Thirty police launches circled the island, thereby depriving the settlers of food and water, they were also tear-gassed, their huts razed, their boats sunk, their fish and tube wells destroyed, those who tried to cross the river were shot at... several hundred men and women and children were believed to have died during that time and their bodies thrown in river (Jalais, 15).

The refugees can be considered as subalterns not only for the adverse climatic conditions but also for the humiliation of the natives and the police. The refugees try to bribe the police and if it is not possible they resort to physical violence "they tried to break their collective strength by offering bribes. But when it failed, they resorted to threats of physical violence as their next strategy" (223). The story of the novel *The Hungry Tide* centres on two principal characters named Kanai Dutt, a businessman from Delhi and Piyali Roy, an Indo-American scientist and their encounter with the people of 'tide community'. Kanai visits his aunt Nilima, an activist in a non-government organization. Nilima maintains a hospital in the island. Piyali Roy comes to the same place to study the life of dolphins. Both Kanai and Piyali were of the common interest to study the life of oppressed sections of the society. They meet an illiterate inhabitant of the region, Fokir who was ready to be their guide during their stay.

Another principal character in the novel is Nirmal, a retired local school headmaster, who is unifying force of the refugees in order to fight for their rights. He fights for the cause of the subalterns without caring the police violence and the threats from the natives. His untiring spirit brings the refugees to a common platform but they were punished by the police as they have "burnt the settlers huts and sank their boats and land waste to their fields" (279). Nirmal has progressive ideas and strongly believes in the maxim 'revolution and transformation' is the only solution for the problems of the refugees of the region. His fight for the welfare of the refugees is the quest for his identity which is identified with the refugees. He was moved by the heinous act of the police, who resort to killing of the settlers and raping of women and throwing them into the rivers mercilessly. He was one of the victims of Marichjhapi massacre but he was let off when his identity was revealed as the retired headmaster, "He was put on, in a bus with other refugees. They were to be sent back to the place they had come from—in Madhya Pradesh, or wherever it was. But at some point they must have let him off because he found his way back to Canning" (279).

Amitav, being a Marxist, tries to identify himself with Nirmal in the struggle for the cause of the subaltern refugees. Later, Nirmal dies due to the physical and psychological torture of the police. Nirmal like Amitav has the Eastern concern outlook with Western education and knowledge. The unsuccessful attempt of Nirmal is an indication for the failure of translating idealism into reality and it is the example for the high handedness of the hegemonic society. Nirmal's fight for the homeless for the cause of a 'home' which is a place of love, peace, harmony and rehabilitation, that can be considered as a dream for the people of the tide community. Nirmal puts a question to everyone about the ownership of the land as, "Whose is the land, nature's or man's, is a question that cannot be easily answered. The questions like "who, indeed are we?" and "where do we belong"?... Who was I? Where did I belong? In Kolkata or in the tide country? In India or across the border? In prose or in poetry" (254).

Amitav also portrays the agonized story of Piya, who has a soft corner for Fokir but his wife Moyna suspects their suspicious relationship. Moyna has some financial transactions with Piya who pays huge amount to Moyna towards "the rent of the boat, the provisions and all that and she would also pay Fokir a salary plus a per diem. On top of that, if all went well there'd be a bonus at the end...he would stand to make about three hundred US dollars" (210). She was happy with the financial support of Piya but suspects her and asks in her native language, "Why a highly educated scientist like you needs the help of my husband—someone who doesn't even knows how to read and write" (211). Piya could not understand her question, so Kanai translates it to Piya, who was "frowned, puzzling over this. Could Moyna really be as dismissive of her husband as her question seemed to imply? Or was she trying to suggest that Piya should hire someone else?" (211). But Piya finally decides that "there was no one else she wanted to work with and tries to pacify Moyna by saying, through Kanai, that Fokir "knows the river well. His knowledge can be of help to a scientist like myself" (211). It is a clear indication that the people who are oppressed will be in a state of doubt to believe anyone who comes across in their life.

Amitav focuses on the state of 'homelessness' as a source of willpower. He also concentrates on the cultural status of subalterns in an alien land. When Nilima arrives at Lusibari, she notices that a large number of women in the region are dressed as widows:

> Making inquires, she learnt that in the tide country, girls were brought up on the assumption that if they married, they would be widowed in their twenties-thirties if they were lucky. This assumption was woven, like a skin of dark wool, into the fabric of their lives: When the men folk went fishing, it was the custom for their wives to change into the garments of

> widowhood. They will put away their marital reds... wash the vermilion from their heads. (80)

Nilima was moved with the bad practice prevailed in the region and decided to enlighten them. Through the character of Nilima, Amitav wanted to convey the message that the elite and educated sections of the society should work for the upliftment of the poor, weak, oppressed subalterns. He wanted to uphold the values and convey the message that when Nilima was ready to sacrifice her life, can't we join our hands and voice for the rights of the subalterns. "I am not capable of dealing with the whole world's problem. For me a challenge of making a few little things a little better in one small place is enough. That place for me is Lusibari" (387). Some critics are of the opinion that Nilima is the fictitious counterpart of Amitav, whose feelings are expressed deliberately. He tries to fight for the rights of the subalterns through characters like Nilima and Nirmal.

Amitav through his works provides enough material to read subaltern history as a counter discourse to national identity. He challenges the social stigma, hegemonic society and fight for the rights of the subaltern people. His ideas try to dethrone the considerations of the canonised opinion foisted by colonial rules. He considers migration and dislocation are the results of the colonials and a curse to the oppressed people, who can be named as subalterns. Amitav asks the validity of borders on the earth which divide the people into two groups, native and subalterns through his works. He raises his voice in support of the subalterns, who are often pushed forcibly to the margin and made them marginalized sections of the society. His concern for the subaltern is noteworthy in the novel. He represented the plight of the Sundarban's refugees as the representative for the dislocated people across the globe. He described the native and the police as 'the hungry tide' which are ready to devour the small creatures on the shore.

Ghosh's musing on language, on translatability, on the forgotten massacre of Marichjhapi, in which dominant cultures forcibly wipe out movements from below, are deftly woven into the interactions between the characters. Yet the most dominate theme is of a great sweep away by water, the flood on land, the revolution in the mind. As the reigning deity of the tide country Bon Bibi, in Ghosh's vision a local cult, presides over this flood; she is goddess of hoe but also of vengeance (Ghose, 6).

Works Cited

Ghose, Sagarika. "The Shadow Links." Rev. of *The Hungry Tide* by Amitav Ghosh. *The Indian Express*. 27 June 2004: B: 1. Print.

Ghosh, Amitav. *The Hungry Tide*. 2004. New Delhi: Harper Collins, 2006. Print.

Jalais, Annu. "Dwelling on Morichjapi." EPN Special Article. Web. 23. Nov. 2006. Print.

Mondal, A. Anshuman. *Amitav Ghosh—Contemporary World Writers*. New Delhi: Viva Books, 2010. Print.

15

Sea of Poppies: Introspective Narrative

Anju S. Nair

Abstract

Metafiction sheds light on fundamental issues in connection with fictional creation in general. The writers of metafiction focus on questions of primary importance not only to novelists, but to man in general. For writers of metafiction, the most fundamental assumption is that composing a novel is basically so different from composing or constructing one's 'reality'. Writing itself other than consciousness becomes the main object of attention. Metafiction questions not only the role of the novelist but also the authority of authority of consciousness of the mind. The characteristic features of metafiction can be traced in *Sea of Poppies* by Amitav Ghosh. The novel shares not only the content of a typical postmodern novel but also its strategies.

The dialectic of fiction and fact in Amitav Ghosh's novels as distinguished from the traditional mix of fiction and fact is postmodern in its spirit. What is interesting is that the novels are made to be aware of this kind of mix and this self-awareness of the novels makes the author doubly conscious of his fiction making; both the novelist and the novel are introspective. In other words, the novelist wears a metafictional mask in narrating his story/history. Hence, his novels not only contain stories/histories but also stories/histories of stories and histories. They problematize the telling of story/history. This metafictional claim of the novel makes it postmodern.

Metafiction is defined variously but one can notice the same spirit underlying the definition. According to Linda

Hutcheon, "metafiction...is fiction about fiction—that is, fiction that includes within itself a commentary on its own narrative and/or linguistic identity" (Hutcheon, 1). Patricia Waugh says that:

> Metafiction is a term given to fictional writing which self-consciously and systematically draws attention to its status as an artifact in order to pose questions about the relationship between fiction and reality. In providing a critique of their own methods of construction, such writings not only examine the fundamental structures of narrative fiction, they also explore the possible fictionality of the world outside the literary fictional text. (Waugh, 2)

The common quality whereby a writer can be identified as 'metafictional' "is that they all explore a theory of fiction, through the practice of writing fiction" (Waugh, 2). Metafiction poses the question whether anything can be described at all. The metafictionist feels that the world cannot be 'represented'. Waugh says that "in literary fiction it is, in fact, possible only to 'represent' the discourse of that world" (Waugh, 3).

In his article "Metafiction", Robert Scholes "tries to explain the nature of contemporary experimental fiction by four directions in literary criticism, which he classifies as formal, structural, behavioural and philosophical" (quoted in Christensen, 10). Scholes link the various manifestations of metafiction to these critical schools, finding Barth's fiction mainly formal; Barthelme's behavioural, etc. Scholes is one of the first to employ the term metafiction but he does not give any explicit definition of it. In a later article, Scholes describes metafiction, or 'self-reflective fiction' as he calls it, as: "a fiction which, if it is 'about' the possibilities and impossibilities of fiction itself... (quoted in Christensen, 10).

Metafiction deals with questions essential to the novelist, the narrator's conception to the novelist, the narrator's conception of his own role and art, and of the reader. Writers are to a great and lesser extent, conscious of these relations, but the metafictionist differs by making these questions the subject of his work. Thus, metafiction sheds light on fundamental issues in connection with fictional creation in general. Further, writers of metafiction focus on questions of primary importance not only to novelists, but to man in general. The metafictionist also deals with "the fundamental issues of communication by directing attention to the narrator, the narrative and the narratee in his work" (Christensen, 14). However, one fact is made explicit in metafiction, that is, while he reads, the reader lives in a world which he is forced to acknowledge as fictional. However, paradoxically the text also demands that he participate, that he engages himself imaginatively, intellectually and effectively in its co-creation. This two-way pull is the paradox of the reader. The text's own paradox is that it is both narcissistically self-reflexive and yet focused outward, oriented toward the reader.

The distinction between self-reflexive (or meta-) fiction and a celebratory form of postmodernism is echoed by certain critics. James Mellard says that "in the event that myth, archetype and language are subverted...the novelist may then turn for subject and authority or validation to the act of writing itself" (Bertens and Fokkema, 38). According to another critic Raymond Federman, "There is.... Behind the new fiction's project an effort of sincerity. A search for a new truth. A genuine effort to reinstate things, the world and man in their proper places—in a purer state" (Bertens and Fokkema, 39). This urge leads postmodern literature in two directions. The first is the direction of metafiction. Knowledge about the world traditionally claimed by fiction, must be replaced by the act of searching-researching within the fiction itself for the meaning of what it means to write fiction. It is an act of self-reflection.

For writers of metafiction, the most fundamental assumption is that composing a novel is basically so different from composing or constructing one's 'reality'. Writing itself other than consciousness becomes the main object of attention. Metafiction questions not only the role of the novelist but also the authority of consciousness of the mind. The traits of metafiction can be traced in the writings of Amitav Ghosh.

A frame is a construction, constitution...established order, etc. Both modernism and postmodernism begin with the view that both the historical world and works of art are organized and perceived through such structures or frames. Waugh says "when applied to fiction frames involve the formal organization of the novels" (Waugh, 28). However, metafiction foregrounds 'framing' as a problem. It asks: "What is the 'frame' that separated reality from 'fiction'?" (Waugh, 28). Metafiction draws attention to the fact that it is finally impossible to know where one frame ends and another begins. Framing devices in metafictional novels include incorporation of dreams, visions, hallucinatory states and pictorial representations which are finally indistinct from the apparently real. It also poses the question whether the ending of the events begins the writing, or the ending of the writing begins the events.

Amitav Ghosh's *Sea of Poppies* begins with Deeti's apparition of a ship. The beginning of the novel subtly opens the issue of the bonded labourers in the ship Ibis: "the vision of a tall-masted ship, at sail on the ocean, came to Deeti on an otherwise ordinary day, but she knew instantly that the apparition was a sign of destiny for she had never seen such a vessel before, not even in a dream: how could she have, living as she did in northern Bihar, four hundred miles from the coast?" (*SOP*, 3).

Deeti, a simple, pious lady, caring mother and an efficient housewife, who lives in a village in Bihar, draws her vision and preserves it in the *pooja* room. Her daughter is puzzled by her action. (and the readers too!) As revealed in her vision she has a sensation that she would be meet the people in the near future. "I don't know, said Deeti, for she too was puzzled by the sureness of her intuition: I just know that it must be there; and not just the ship, but also many of those who are in it; they too must be in the walls of the *pooja* room" (*SOP*, 9). Sarju, the midwife, on the Ibis taken as *girmitiyas* along with the rest, falls sick and shows no sign of recovery. As she lay dying she gives a pouch of poppy seeds to Deeti and tells her to use it when needed. She also requests Deeti to remember her in the shrine: "Sarju raised a trembling hand to point to the images on the beam above Deeti's head. Because I want to be there too, she said. I want to be remembered in your shrine" (*SOP*, 451).

At the end of the novel, Zachary Reid, the second mate, the son of an American slave, experiences a feeling of warmth when he sees Deeti for the first time on the Ibis. It is a reminder that the apparition of Deeti at the beginning of the novel has become a reality. Reid recognizes her, though he was seeing her for the first time, "Now, in the fading glow of the clouds, she turned to look at him and he saw that she had piercing, grey eyes. Although it was the first time he had seen her face, he knew he had glimpsed her somewhere, standing much as was now, in a wet sari, hair dripping, looking at him with startled eyes" (*SOP*, 512).

Baboo Nob Kissin Pander, a *gomusta*, is a character who is in a hallucinatory state throughout the novel. After the death of Ma Taramony, his spiritual Guru ma, Baboo Kissin's heart was filled with 'premonitory foreboding' (*SOP*, 145). He is an ardent devotee of Lord Krishna and whenever he heard the sound of flute he would kneel down and close his eyes in fear. When Zachary Reid enters at the opening of the door, Baboo believes it is Lord Krishna himself: "Could it be then, that this ivory tinted rupa was exactly what Ma Taramony had warned him of: a Guise, wrapped in veils of illusion by the Divine Prankster, so as to test the quality of his devotee's faith? But even then, surely there would be some additional sign, some other mark...?" (*SOP*, 146). As the novel proceeds, Baboo who strongly believes that Zachary Reid is Lord Krishna provides some comical instances for the readers, particularly through the conversations between Reid and Baboo, like the following conversation, one in a state of illusion and the other in reality:

> "I regret to inform that his place is not apt."
> "apt for what?"
> Leaning towards Zachary ear, the gomusta hissed: "For mischiefs with cowgirls."

> "What the hell you talking about, Pander?" cried Zacharian exasperation. "I was just helping the woman to pick up her stuff."
> "Better to leave ladies alone," said the gomusta. "Flute also better not show"
> "They may get too excited."
> "Show my flute?"..., Zachary wondered whether the gomusta was not merely eccentric but actually mad. (*SOP*, 364)

The ending of the novel is marked with a touch of absurdity. The five characters on the Ibis, Serang Ali, Jodu, Neel, Ah Fatt and Kalua escape in a boat leaving the others behind. The first mate and the subedar are dead and only the key figures are dead and only Deeti, Paulette, Baboo Nob Kissin and Zachary are left. From the deck of the ship, they watch the long boat disappearing. The indentured labourers are at a loss because they do not know where the Ibis is heading to. Similarly, the five people who escaped in a boat are unsure of their destination. Hence, the novelist ends the novel on a dramatic note of suspense and excitement. Amitav Ghosh leaves the readers speculating about the fate of those left in the ship and those who had left in the boat. It is a deliberate and ambiguous ending. In fact, the novel does not have an end. On the other hand, the ending of the novel/writing begins the events. In metafiction, it is precisely the fulfillment as well as the non-fulfillment of generic expectations that provides both familiarity and the starting point for innovation. Metafictional writers assert that although literary fiction is only a verbal reality, it constructs through language an imaginative world that has, within its own terms a full referential status as an alternative to the world we live in.

Sea of Poppies is self-conscious text and according to Hutcheon this "self-awareness has been more and more structurally internalized moving from the preface into the structure of the novel itself" (Hutcheon, 45).

Works Cited

Bertans, Hans and Fokkema, Douwe W. *Approaching Postmodernism: Papers Presented in a Workshop on Postmodernism*. Philadelphia: John Benjamins Publishing Company, 1986. Print.

Chirstensen, Inger. *The Meaning of Metafiction: A Critical Study of Sterne, Nabakov, Barth and Beckett*. New York: Columbia University Press, 1981. Print.

Ghosh, Amitav. *Sea of Poppies*. New Delhi. Penguin Books. 2009. Print.

Hutcheon, Linda. *The Poetics of Postmodernism: History, Theory, Fiction*. London: Routledge. 1988. Print.

Waugh, Patricia. *Metafiction: The Theory and Practice of Self-conscious Fiction*. London: Metheun. 1984. Print.

16

In an Antique Land: A Transcultural Travel Narrative

Lingaraj Patra

Travel writing is an interdisciplinary genre. Though it has a long history, it has been the subject of relatively little scholarly research. The origin of it can be dated far back to the second century A.D., when Pausanias undertook his ambitious ten volume *Description of Greece*, combining a firsthand observation of Greece's topography with an insightful study of its culture and politics. It is a genre that has engaged the interest of the readers across time and cultures.

In recent times, travel writing has occupied a special niche in the area of study and can boast of being categorized as a special genre in the realm of literature. The various areas of study include issues of imperialism, diaspora, multiculturalism, nationalism, identity, gender, globalization, colonialism, post-colonialism, transculturalism, cross-culturalism, hybridity location and displacement, etc. Some important aspects of travel writing, that we may derive after being overtly exposed to the various definitions propounded by many a writer, may be recorded as follows:

Temporal and spatial progress
Bewildering diversity
Refractory to definition
Heterogenous
Generic indeterminacy
Not easily demarcated
Raffish open house

Thus, travel writing as a genre, by and large, evokes the ideas and nuances of the above-mentioned points. However, in the past few centuries, the crux of travel literature—the nature of travel itself—has changed radically. With ease of transportation, the world has become a global village and travel writing can no longer remain connected with a fascination to the 'exotic'. The contemporary travel literature is an open genre that blends elements of history, anthropology, journalism and sometimes employing fictional devices in an essentially non-fictional category. The study of Amitav Ghosh's *In an Antique Land* is definitely a glaring example of it. This novel probably takes its title from the first line of Shelley's poem "Ozymandias" which reads "I met a traveler from an antique land".

A transcultural work of fiction is a work that transcends the boundaries of a local culture in its choice of topic, vision and scope and contributes, to feeding the need for a wider global literary perspectives. Amitav Ghosh's *In An Antique land* deals with the postcolonial themes of alienation, dislocation, traveling, migration, quest for identity, transculturalism, economic insecurities, colonial power structures, etc. which influence the human conditions under the impact of transnational movements.

John Hawley's remark in this regard is highly noteworthy. He very rightly observes:

> The book is not recognizable as a novel, nor is it simply a historical investigation. It is a new genre something that blends an anthropological record with a travelogue, a diary and perhaps some imagined sections. The effect that this has on the reader is to force us to question whether particular events and characters are literally factual. (Ghosh, 89)

A popular and highly acclaimed author, Ghosh draws heavily upon the characters, traditions and dichotomies of his native land, yet his protagonists and themes often extend beyond India's actual boundaries, exposing the cross-cultural ties between India and the alien countries. Ghosh has been hailed by critics as one of the new generation of cosmopolitan Indian intellectuals writing in English, forging a contemporary literary métier. The majority of Ghosh's writings focus on exploring geographical and social boundaries.

One of the most famous and widely appreciated works, *In an Antique Land* is based on the historical and anthropological research that he conducted in Egypt during the 1980s. Set in Egypt, the book tells us quite an absorbing story of two Indians and a Jew, removed from each other by more than 800 years. The book tells two narratives: first, Ghosh's stay as a doctoral research scholar in Lataifa, a small hamlet near Alexandria, in the early 80s: second, life of a 12th century Tunisian Jewish merchant, Abraham Ben Yiju and his Indian slaves, Bomma and Ashu whom he acquired during his 18 years stay in Mangalore. In the form of the two narratives, the book deals with the many deviance of history, and how it inflicts upon ordinary people. So, the book is a refreshing study of civilizations, their so-called progress and the irreversible change of times.

Ghosh, as a writer is unpredictable and unconventional. In an interview with Ranjan Banerjee, he once remarked about this book. "No this time I am not writing a novel. Not even sociology, history or Belles-lettres based on historical research. My new book cannot be described as any one of these. It's a strange sort of a work. Within the parameters of history, I have tried to capture a story, a narrative without attempting to write a historical novel. You may say, as a writer, I have ventured on a technical innovation (*Ananda Bazar Patrika*).

Thus, this book can be termed as a braided narrative and has triggered many eyebrows while making a categorization of its genre.

In an Antique Land is a book unique of its kind where one can find a synthesis of varied branches of knowledge like History, Anthropology, Philosophy, Sociology and Religion. There is an aspect of multiculturalism spreading across continents and centuries in the novel. The book primarily points out at the tragic turn of events in history of Asia and Middle East. It is a solemn assertion to the writer's deep sense of understanding and intense desire as an uncompromising, genuine researcher covering the fieldwork as a socio-anthropologist and historian over decades.

In an Antique Land can be attributed as an experimental work and the writer does a kind of "muddy the boundaries" of fact and fiction at one end and on the other dissolves the boundaries of different nation and continents. In an essay, Arnab Babul rightly comments on this novel—"The writer here acts as a dodger—now narrating the authenticated history in guise of a fiction, in the next moment presenting fiction in factual terms, teasing readers to involve themselves in the play of construction and deconstruction showing in true postmodern fashion, an aversion to distinction and resisting the ideas of boundary and closure" (Negotiating Postmodernism, Ideas of the West/the other in *In an Antique Land*, 83). The novel presents two parallel narratives, one revolving around Ghosh's stay in the villages of the Nile Delta while doing field work for his doctoral thesis and a later revisiting of the same places in order to meet the community of his friends; and the other depicting imaginative reconstruction of the travels of a twelfth century Jewish Merchant Abraham Ben Yiju, the knowledge Ghosh gleaned from the documents of the Cairo Geniza, an ancient archive.

Though on the surface of it, quite apparently, the book can be termed as a factual account of two seemingly different civilizations widely separated in course of time, but Ghosh has the uncanny touch of narrative style with a very intelligent and imaginative approach dealt with the transcultural aspects relating to fact, fiction, autobiography, history, anthropology and travel. The two narratives that are separated by such a wide time-gap are seemingly casting a shade on each other and more importantly one informing the other. In her study on this novel, Upasana Dutta points out, "Throughout Ghosh's oeuvre there is a tendency to find connections between apparently vastly diverse subjects—nations, cultures, individuals, families find unprecedented connections tying them together in spite of being separated by time and space."

The novel is journey based and the story moves around the narrator's research being conducted in Egypt. The subject of discussion begins in the 12th century and ends with the commencement of operation desert storm in the year 1991. Ghosh, being an astute researcher, has very precisely interlaced the post-colonial themes of alienation and dislocation which takes place due to travel and migration.

The theme of transculturalism is first portrayed with the character Ben Yiju. He was a Jewish trader, left Aden possibly because of debt or financial irregularities and settled on the Malabar coast in the early 12th century. In the Prologue of the book, Ben Yiju is described as, "a Jewish merchant, originally of Tunisia, who had gone to India by way of Egypt, as a trader, and had spent seventeen years there. A man of many accomplishments, a distinguished calligrapher, scholar and Poet, Ben Yiju had returned to Egypt having amassed great wealth in India" (8).

Ben Yiju married a Nair lady, Ashu, from Malabar, and acquired and then befriended a low caste slave, Bomma. They were not in the usual kind of master-slave relationship as he trusted Bomma and made him his business agent. Yiju is more like a patron and Bomma a client. Regarding their meeting, the narrator writes "The Geniza documents provide no indication at all about and Bomma's path came to cross Ben Yiju's. From certain references in Ben Yiju's papers, it seems likely that he took Bomma into his service as a business agent and helper soon after he had established himself as a trader in Mangalore". He further writes, "their arrangement was probably more that of Patron and client than master and slave, as that relationship is now understood" (212).

Though the very presence of the slave, brings home the idea of subaltern figure, yet, the presence of it with a similar diasporic experience like his master's gives "a right to be there, a sense of entitlement". It is quite an interesting relationship that the writer notices between a slave and his master. Although there has been a wide socio-cultural differences, the relationship between the two culturally diverse sections were not as noxious by the cultural and political barriers as they unfold before us now.

Language and cultural differences often create a wide unbridgeable divides. While portraying the issues of cross-culturalism Ghosh is confronted with the barriers of language.

Language is a problem in travelling. One has to acquire or learn a new language in an alien set up. The writer, when locates Yiju's documents, is first struck by the unusual hybridity of language. Ghosh writes, "Ben Yiju's documents were mostly written in an Unusual, hybrid language: one that has such an arcane sound to it that it might well be an entry in a book of Amazing facts. It is known today as Judaeo-Arabic; it was a colloquial dialect of medieval Arabic, written in the Hebrew Script" (78). Since most of the documents are written in a colloquial dialect of medieval Arabic, it poses a seemingly impassable barrier before the writer to verify the authenticity of it. In his own words, Ghosh writes:

> When I first read about it, Judaeo-Arabic sounded bafflingly esoteric: it is not easy, after all, to see oneself sitting down to leaf through a collection of eight hundred year old documents, written in a colloquial dialect of medieval Arabic, transcribed in the Hebrew script and literary strewn with Hebrew and Aramaic. At its easiest, Arabic is very difficult for a foreigner. (79-80)

Though Ghosh has learnt Arabic in Tunisia and somehow managed to decipher the language in the manuscripts, he is often trapped by language while encountering cross-cultural dialogues, with the *Fellaheen*. He feels awkward and is never in a comfortable position to counter the *Fellaheen's* repeated questions about the Indian's cultural practices. It is Nabeel who comes to his rescue and says "they were only asking questions... just like you do. They didn't mean any harm. Why do you let this talk of cows, and burning and circumcision worry you so much? These are just customs; it's natural that people should be curious. These are not things to be upset about" (166).

Leaving homeland for better opportunities and financial prospects have been significant traits since time immemorial. Characters travel and travel to cross the boundaries of their homeland and suffer alienation in this novel. Ben Yiju and Bomma suffer a kind of loneliness and desperation to return to their roots in 12th century. In the same way, both Nabeel and Ismail, allured by the prospects of easy money, leave their home and become money producing machines in the hand of their family members. Their emotional happiness is pitted against their market value. Both of them suffer alienation in the land of their dreams. Though Ismail returned to his roots, for not being able to cope with the unfavourable situation, Nabeel stays back to fulfill his dream of earning some more money.

Ghosh returns to Egypt after a gap of seven years. The growing trend of consumerism has brought some eye-catching changes in the once familiar villages of Lataifa and Nashawy. The youngmen of these villages have gone to gulf countries and have brought huge sums of money. When Ghosh visits Abu Ali in Lataifa with Seikh Musa, he notices a lot of changes in less than a mere decade. He finds "a T.V. set, a food Processor, a handful of calculators a Transistor radio, a couple of cassette players, a Pen that was also a flash light, a watch that could play tunes, a key-ring that answered to a handclap and several other such objects" (246). Even the old-dilapidated house of Abu Ali has vanished and a new three-storeyed mansion has been built there. Old moped gives way to a new Pick-up Toyota Truck. The narrator feels, "I was assaulted by a sudden sensation of dislocation as though I had vaulted between different epochs" (247). Here, not only the physicality of things but also the inner socio-cultural bearings have been "upturned and rearranged".

Thus, to conclude, travelling is a predominant theme in the novels of Amitav Ghosh. His characters keep on moving and crossing the boundaries in order to explore new possibilities of truth and fulfillment in an alien land. In the novel *In an Antique Land*, Ben Yiju and Bomma travel during the medieval period. Nabeel and Ismail travel from Egypt to other Arab countries to seek better financial stability in the modern times. The writer himself is a traveller in the novel and travels to Egypt in 1980, 1988 and 1990 for his field work of doctoral research. Travel in the novel is a symbol of quest and discovery and the narrator having an extraordinary sense of history and place has shown his deep interest in exploring the transcultural diversities in a socio-cultural backdrop of the societies of two centuries separated from one another by eight hundred years.

Commenting on this James Clifford has rightly pointed out, "It is less a matter of localized dwelling and more a series of travel encounters. Everyone's on the move and has been for centuries dwelling-in-travel...a view of human locations as constituted by displacement as much as by stasis practices of displacement might emerge as constitutive of cultural meanings rather than as their simpler transfer of extension" (Routes: *Travel and Translation in the Late Twentieth Century,* 2-3).

Works Cited

Bhattacharji, Sobhana. "Amitav Ghosh's Travel Writing: *In an Antique Land*, Dancing in Cambodia and The Imam and the Indian". *Indian Literature*, Vol. 47, No. 6 (218) (Nov.-Dec., 2003).

Chambers, Claire. "Anthropology as Cultural Translation: Amitav Ghosh's *In an Antique Land.*" *Postcolonial Text*, 2.3, 2006.

Dutta, Upasana. "Modern Directions in Travel writing: Amitav Ghosh's *In an Antique Land* and William Dalrymple's *Nine Lives:* In Search of a Sacred in Modern India" *International Journal of Travel Writing*, 2.3 (2013): 69-78. Print.

Ghosh, Amitav. *In an Antique Land*, New Delhi: Ravi Dayal Publisher, 1992.

Kiteley, Brian. "Trapped by Language: On Amitav Ghosh's *In an Antique Land*". Shelly: Ozymandias.

Michael, Mewshaw. "Travel, Travel Writing and the Literature of Travel", *South Central Review*, Vol. 22.

Smith, Eric D. "Caught straddling a Border: A Novelistic Reading of Amitav Ghosh's *In an Antique Land.*" *Journal of Narrative Theory*, 2007: 447-72.

17

Trans-cultural Communication in Amitav Ghosh's *The Hungry Tide*

S. Jayalakshmi

Amitav Ghosh's *The Hungry Tide* is marked with journeys, visits and human movements across time and space. It also captures the problems and concern regarding borders such as nationality and gender. Further, the novel emphasizes not only crossing the land but also crossing of water bodies at different places. The present paper ties to analyze *The Hungry Tide* as a migratory discourse in the form of journeys, visits and mobility.

Ghosh's narrative here, rather than encompassing rust swathes of south-east Asia, prays then to focus a magnifying lens on what might be called a micro-culture within the region namely, the Sundarbans or 'tide country', the islets of the Ganges delta that lie south of Kolkata and just east of the West Bengal/Bangladesh frontier.

The story centres on two visitors to the Sundarban Community, Kanaidult and Piyali Roy (Priya), and their interaction with that community and with each other. Kanai, a Delhi businessman in his forties, is a semi-outsider, paying a rate visit to his aunt Nilima, an NGO activist who runs a hospital on one of the islands; Piya, an Indo-American Scientist from Seattle in her twenties, interrupts into the Sundarban world as despite her Bengali origins less a diasporic Indian than an outsider pure and simple. "The American" Kanai is there to pick up and read a journal left him by his late uncle Nirmal, an idealistic Marxist intellectual in the Bengali tradition, whose contents will oblige him to delve deep into his family history. Piya's journey to the tide country is part of ongoing research on dolphins, Piya Knows Bengali you Know no Bengali?... I was so little when I left India that I never had a chance to learn... (*THT*, 12). Her ignorance of her own language heritage induces her to take Kanai on board as interpreter between her and Fokir, the illiterate fisherman and protégé of Kanai's aunt, who serves as her guide.

Ghosh's novel takes as its task the exploration of a vast field human communication, testing both its possibilities and its limits as the characters seek to cross multiple barriers of language, religion and social class, those between human beings and nature, between traditional and cosmopolitan India, between urban and local is articulated through the characters, with far most of the novel. Globalization embodied by the Americanized Piya with her hi-tech GPS device, local identity symbolized by Fakir and Kanai, the Delhi-resident, partly-globalized modern entrepreneur, shifting uncertainly somewhere in between.

The Hungry Tide is a unique combination of fiction and cultural-anthropological research. The tidal land is the destination for two travelers in the novel, Piyali Roy and Kanai Dutt with one aim: to research into the mysteries of the Sundarbans while Piya intends to study Irrawaddy dolphins, Kanai through the journal of his uncle Nirmal researchers into the shifting ghettos of a group of refugees. I attempt to explore the idea of "Ecopoetics" through an analysis of *The Hungry Tide* with the Concept of Chronotopes and chronotopic molifs proposed by Mikhail Bakhtin in "Forms of Time and of the Chronotope in the Novel".

We try to understand the novel in terms of the "Folkloric" and "Idyllic" chronotopes, and also examine "places" and "non-places" as related to each other especially the chronotope of "non-places" related to the terrains of the mind. "Bakhin has studied chromos and topes as inseparable from each other". There is a constant interplay of time-space aspects when we look at ecological and human perspectives narratives. In contemporary critical debates, chronotopes have been useful in understanding the delicate balance between temporality and spatiality in the novelistic form.

In *The Hungry Tide,* Ghosh moves tentatively towards an admission of the possibility. After all, of communication across cultural barriers, at least within certain limits and subject to a rational effect of will. At the end, both Piya and Kanai voluntarily undertake a reconstruction of their experiences in the Sundarbans; each has lost the textual evidence but each is willing to piece the text back together from memory. Beyond this both actual, and surprisingly return to the Sundarbans Kanai shift his residence from Delhi to Kolkata to be near the tide country and visit often, thus moving at least halfway, towards a neo-Gandhian renunciation of cosmopolitan and metropolitan India in favor of the more demotic claims of what some call the "real India".

The Hungry Tide, in contrast to other novels of Amitav Ghosh, is geographically very narrow. It is confined to Sundarbans Island in the Bay of Bengal. Though the novel presents limited border-crossing as far as the geographical locations are concerned, it moves across a wide range of conceptual questions related to human beings and their of sharing of a complex and delicate ecosystem with animals.

Characters also use thoughts to effect mental migration in *The Hungry Tide*. Piya, though travels physically across Bengal, goes back to America mentally Memories and sensations bring continents together in her thoughts. Looking over her shoulder, Piya spotted a tea-seller patrolling the platform. Reaching through the bass, she summoned him with a wave. She had never cared for the kind of chai on offer in Seattle, her hometown, but somehow in the ten days she had spent in India, she had developed an unexpected affinity for milky over boiled tea served in earthenware cups. There were no spices in it for one thing and this was more to her taste than the chai at home. Kanai's profession is also a kind of journey. He moves through languages and communities. Ghosh explains the transnational significance of Kanai's job.

> He ran a bureau of translators and interpreters that specialized in serving the expatriate communities of New Delhi; foreign diplomats, aid workers charitable

organizations, multinational companies and the like. (*THT*, 20)

The Hungry Tide is made up of interwoven stands Kanai's narrative and Piya's the present lived by the characters and the past of Nirmal's journal the variously alternate, converge, diverge and reconverge. As the novel comes to an utopian possibility opens up a coming together of the book's narrative and conceptual strands, global and local, urban and rural linguistic and scientific, and Anglophone and Bengali-speaking even it may by male and female.

It is concerned with issues of migration such as geographical enigma, travel, exploration, encounter and memory. Memory in Ghosh's novel has a cartographic significance and it is a novel-making device. In gradual sedimentation of memory, place emerge like a photograph from a dark place.

The novel offers many subtle and symbolic modus of migration for the readers. Memory is a prime mode of mobility in the novel. Ghosh projects Sundarbans as a borderless locale where in the identify of the constantly shifts. Amitav Ghosh's works not only explain how the personal experience overlap with historical details, but also imply how his fiction in *The Hungry Tide* is a blend of autobiography and symbolic. It has at least two layers of meaning manifest and latent.

The excellence of Ghosh, "a champion of post modern cultural weightlessness" lies in the fact that beneath the explicitly revealed primary meaning, there is sufficient hidden or metaphorical meaning in the title of the novel. That is why the novel has been extensively admired by the scholars for instance, Amardeep Singh calls it "the work of novelist at the peak of his powers".

The novel touches upon the conservation issues of dolphins and tigers along with its interest in the history of human settlement in the Sundarbans. Amitav Ghosh indicates that with some amount of will and planning, both the tigers and human beings can be protected. This vision also indicates that the boundaries of lives between species have to be overlooked to develop healthy ecosystem.

Works Cited

Primary Sources

Ghosh, Amitav. *The Hungry Tide*. London: Harper Collins, 2004. Print.

Secondary Sources

Choudhury, Bibhash. *Amitav Ghosh Critical Essays*. New Delhi: PH Learning Limited, 2009. Print.

Dwivedi, O.P. The Fiction of Amitav Ghosh. India: Book Enclave Publishers, 2010. Print.

Manandhar Kumar, Vijay. *Amitav Ghosh's The Shadow Lines*. Delhi: Signature Books Publishers, 2011. Print.

Pandey, A.P. *New Horizons in Indian English Fiction*. Kanpur: Bhasker Publishers, 2010. Print.

18

Nature vs. Nurture: An Eco Critical Reading of Amitav Ghosh's *The Hungry Tide*

S. Karthik Kumar

In Indian English literature, the versatile writers like R.K. Narayan, Raja Rao, Arundhati Roy, Anita Desai, and Kiran Desai have upheld the importance of nature in the world especially for human life. They have established a tradition of novel writing in which natural environment like landscape plays a vital role. In the tradition of Indian English novel, Amitav Ghosh is distinct because he is one of the earliest writers who write with an environmental consciousness and concern.

Amitav Ghosh is an eminent contemporary Indian English writer with many bestsellers to his credit. He is known for his fiction and non-fiction. He is a writer endowed with postcolonial temperament. He does not believe in "boundaries", hence the settings of his novels often overlap national boundaries. In his works, we also find the blurring of borders between genres. In his novels, one can find the blend of autobiography, history, and fiction.

Ghosh is a remarkable contemporary Indian writer whose most of the novels project the author's environmental concern. He is also unique because he weaves legends, myths and individual and national histories in order to build the environment for his fictional works. In his writings, nature is not just a background, rather it forms a "foreground." His narratives also provide us with authentic pen-picture of environmental calamity caused by man—nature interaction. His writings prove his sense of responsibility as a tinge of ecological consciousness and environmental alarm pervades his writings.

Ghosh's novel *The Hungry Tide* is situated on the Sundarbans, where land and sea constantly yield to each other in a daily elemental cycle. *The Hungry Tide* is a work with an environmental orientation which suggests that the human history is caught up in the natural history. In his novel *The Hungry Tide*, Ghosh has dealt with some of the contemporary environmental issues by using myth, history and legends of the Sundarbans, the islets of the Ganges delta that lie at south of Kolkata and east of West Bengal—Bangladesh frontier. The vast, intermittently submerged archipelago, largely covered by mangrove forests forms the delta of the Ganges and spreads over an area of 250 kms between the Hugli river in West Bengal and the *Meghna* river in Bangladesh. This delta is the largest mangrove forest in the world at the mouth of Ganges and is spread across areas of Bangladesh and West Bengal. Two-thirds of the Sundarbans are in Bangladesh, and only one-third is in India.

The region derives its name from the "sundari" (beautiful) tree, as the mangrove trees are locally called, which are able to tolerate the environmental conditions of salt water, and they constitute the flora of the area. Thus, "Sundarbans" means "beautiful forest." It is intersected by a complex network of tidal waterways, mudflats and small islands of salt-tolerant mangrove forests. It is a place in which the sea, the river, the land, humans and animals all co-exist. However, the region is not only beautiful, the co-existence is sometimes in harmony, but often in competition. The inhabitants of the region lead precarious lives as attacks by deadly tigers are common and at any time, tidal floods rise and surge over the land without any warning. The title of the novel foreshadows the realities of surviving in such a desolate area, which is prone to the destroying effects of rogue tidal waves and tropical cyclones. In this place of vengeful beauty, the inhabitants, mostly the fishing folk, transgress the man-made boundaries of nation. For them, the children of nature, there are no boundaries. Thus in the very choice of his setting for his novel, Ghosh sets forth his objective that nature has no boundaries or divisions and that it is humanity which has to depend on nature for its survival. Galuzzi depicts the setting of the Sundarbans as a place of both ecologically and politically authentic nature:

> On the southern tip of West Bengal in eastern India, just south of Calcutta, the great river Ganges fans out into many tributaries over a vast delta before ending a journey that began in the distant Himalayan north with a plunge into the Bay of Bengal. The mouth of this delta is made up of about three hundred small islands, spread over an area of about ten thousand square kilometres and straddling India's border with Bangladesh. It is one of those areas of the world where the lie of the land mocks the absurdity of international treaties, because it is virtually impossible to enforce border laws on a territory that constantly shifts. (25)

In the Sundarbans, the contours of the land constantly change with the ebb and flow of water. The channels of the rivers are spread across the land like a fine-mesh net. Some of these channels are mighty waterways and are so wide that one shore is invisible from other. Everyday thousands of mangrove forests merge and re-emerge as the tides engulf several islands. The powerful currents of tides reach as far as 300 kms inland, which results in the disappearance of thousands of acres of forests. There are no borders to divide fresh water from salt and river from sea. This tide country offers no visible borders between land and water. Ghosh majestically focuses a magnifying lens on the micro-culture within the Sundarbans or the tide country. The novel presents a pen picture of wildlife versus human suffering. The novel explores the plight of human beings and their survival in an endangered ecosystem, where the humans have to struggle with animals and tides. As an ecological conscious writer, Ghosh examines and offers his critique of human perception of environmental nature, and how it has changed throughout history. Ghosh describes his setting for the novel, the Sundarbans, in the following words:

> A mangrove forest is a universe into itself...Mangrove leaves are tough and leathery, the branches gnarled and the foliage often impassable dense. Visibility is short and the air still and fetid. At no moments can human beings have any doubt of the terrain's utter hostility to their presence, of its cunning and

resourcefulness, of its determination to destroy and expel them. Every year dozens of people perish in the embrace of that dense foliage, killed by tigers, snakes and crocodiles. (8)

Ghosh also delineates the human intercommunication with nature through the experiences of main characters like Piyali Roy—a young marine biologist of American-born Indian who comes to the Sundarbans for the research of Gangetic dolphins; Kanai Dutt—a businessman from Delhi who arrives at the islet of Lusibari to collect and translate the journal of his uncle; Nirmal, in which he has described the strong relation between the nature and human world; and Fokir a young, illiterate local fisherman. The lives of these three people from different social and geographical settings collide in the Sundarbans. Piya and Kanai happen to meet on the train to Kolkata. Piya's journey to the Sundarbans begins with a disaster just as she is thrown from a boat into waters infested with crocodiles. It is then Fokir comes to her rescue. Piya decides to engage Fokir to help in her research and to accompany her as a guide in the canals, creeks and rows of the area, and requests Kanai Dutt to be a translator between her and Fokir.

The Hungry Tide begins with the juxtaposition between a map of the Sundarbans and a scene of travelers orienting themselves to the area. It centers on two visitors to the Sundarbans, Kanai and Piyali (Piya), and their interaction with the community of tidal country people and with each other. Kanai, a Delhi-based businessman, comes there to pay a visit to his aunt, Nilima, an NGO activist who runs a charity, a hospital, a guest house and educational services in the name of Badabon Trust on one of the islands, Lusibari. Nilima's work revolves around the welfare of women, education for children and basic health care amenities for the citizens of the tidal land. Kanai comes to collect a parcel that his late uncle, Nirmal, has left him. The parcel appears to contain a diary, excerpts from which are sprinkled throughout the novel. The package he discovers is an account of his uncle's last days, which revolves around Kusum and her son Fokir, who are portrayed as the victims of eviction from the island of Marichjhapi. Through this package, Ghosh reveals the story of the Sundarbans, its geography, origin, landscape, waterscape, skyscape and the story of human beings whose life is entwined with the ecology of the Sundarbans.

Kanai is a businessman who quits his initial interest in Bengali poetry to found an interpretation agency in New Delhi, specialising in the field of accent modification for call-centre employees. He is proud of India being globalized and he says "there's a lot going on in India right now, and it's exciting to be part of it" (72). Only at the behest of an aunt, Kanai returns to the Sundarbans, bumps into Piya, the dolphin specialist, on a train. Having grown in Seattle, Piya remembers Bengali simply as the language her parents argued in. As a child, she shunned the sounds of Bengali. To her, language is just a means for communication and it should be free of emotions. Ghosh writes: "She [Piya] wanted...sounds that had been boiled clean, like a surgeon's instruments, tools with nothing attached except meanings that could be looked up in a dictionary-empty of pain and memory and inwardness" (21).

Though Piya and Kanai are temperamentally opposite to each other, they are also drawn towards each other. The Sundarbans has a magical spell on them. Once they tread the territory of the region, they are oblivious of the modern culture which they have ingrained. As they are cut off from the busy, materialistic, urbane and artificial modern world and encounter world of primitive nature in its nakedness, their ego melts and disappears. It seems as though it is for the first time that they realize their true selves. Thus, Ghosh exposes the falsity and façade of the sophisticated modern life that is remote from nature. Kanai's businesslike self-assurance crumbles when he is suddenly cut off from his party in the jungle and he enters a realm in which "his mind emptied itself of language.... The sounds and signs that had served, in combination, as the sluices between his mind and his senses, had collapsed: his mind was swamped by a flood of pure sensation" (98). Piya undergoes a similar experience when Fokir recites the legend of Bon Bibi-mythical tiger goddess of the tide country. "Suddenly the language and the music were all around her, flowing like a river, and all of it made sense.... Although the sound of the voice was Fokir's, the meaning was Kanai's, and in the depths of her heart she knew she would always be torn between the one and the other" (108).

Ghosh presents Nirmal as a person having knowledge of history, geography and geology. It is the result of the fact that Ghosh's writing has never had a strict demarcation between fiction and non-fiction. He has always combined the roles of a novelist, a journalist, a scholar and a historian. Lawrence Buell in *The Future of Environmental Criticism*, argues that ecocritics explore literary texts as, "refractions of physical environments and human interactions with those environments, notwithstanding the artifactual properties of textual representation and their mediation by ideological and other socio-historical factors" (30). Ghosh presents nature as main protagonist by giving a detailed description of human-nature interactions.

Ghosh in *The Hungry Tide* presents landscape not just a scenery or a flimsy stage set, but as an energizing medium from which human lives emerge and by which those lives are bound and measured. Piya, an Indo-American scientist from Seattle comes to the Sundarbans as an American despite her Bengali origins. Though she is born in Kolkata, she is brought up in Seattle, USA, from a very early age. Her professional interest in water mammals brings her back to India. Her journey to the tide country is a part of her ongoing research on dolphins. She is aware of the fact that the species of river dolphins, *Orcaella Brevirostris,* commonly known as the Irrawady dolphin, inhabit the Bay of Bengal near the Sundarbans. She is armed with a rangefinder, a depth sounder, clip charts, pens and a monitor that is connected with the satellite through the GPS (Global Positioning System), and the sketches of the dolphins. Ghosh brings about the fact of a research that shows that there are more species of fish in the Sundarbans than could be found in the whole continent of Europe. He maintains:

> This proliferation of aquatic life was thought to be the result of the unusually varied composition of the water itself. The waters of river and sea did not

> intermingle evenly in this part of the delta; rather, they interpenetrated each other, creating hundreds of different ecological niches, with streams of fresh water running along the floors of some channels, creating variations of salinity and turbidity. These micro-environments were like balloons suspended in the water, and they had their own patterns of flow.... Each balloon was a floating biodome, filled with endemic fauna and flora. (125)

The novel clarifies that it is the proliferation of the mingled environment which is responsible for creating and sustaining a dazzling variety of aquatic life forms in this micro part of the world. Fokir brings her to Garjontola, a place where she finds a whole shoal of dolphins. Ghosh empowers Fokir on many levels, in his familiarity with the tide country and its creatures. His mother, Kusum choking with pride says, "see saar: the river is in his veins" (245). Even Piya, an outsider praises his power while being out in water. It seems as if he is always watching the water even without being aware of it. She says that she has worked with many experienced fishermen before but has never met anyone with such an incredible instinct.

Piya's American vanity crumbles before Fokir's innocence and sense of nature. It brings about a complete transformation in her character and she openly acknowledges: "Very few people can adapt themselves to that kind of rhythm—one in a million, I'd say. That is why it was so amazing to come across someone lie Fokir" (267). She exclaims to Kanai, "You saw how he spotted that dolphin there, didn't you? It's like he's always watching the water—even without being aware of it. I have worked with many experienced fishermen before but I've never met anyone with such an incredible instinct: it's as if he can see right into the river's heart" (267). She adds, "Fokir's abilities as an observer are really extraordinary. I wish I could tell you what it was like to be with him these last few days—it was one of the most exciting experiences of my life" (268).

Ghosh portrays Fokir in full spirits in water and not the sullen, resentful creature he evidently seems to be on land. Piya recognizes and values Fokir's knowledge. His embodied knowledge of the river becomes a map on Piya's GPS monitor. Her quest for *Orcella* is enabled by Fokir's knowledge and courage throughout the novel. The judgment runs counter to the evaluation of Fokir's wife, Moyna and Kanai who see his knowledge as a relic lacking value in the modern economy. Providing different perspectives on Fokir, Ghosh allows readers to understand and comprehend that this sort of dismissal of knowledge by dominant epistemologies forms a part of current environmental crisis as it weakens local knowledge of places. In her famous essay, "Home Is Where the Orcella Are," Dutta Sharma points out that Fokir, "lives in idealized harmony with the rhythms of the tide country" (135). He belongs to a community who is marginalized by the state to live in the environmentally challenging area. He loses his life and becomes a victim of seasonal cyclones in the process of steering Piya safely through the forests. He fits the archetype of the hapless and illiterate native, exposed to the man-eating tigers, sharks, crocodiles, snakes, tides and cyclones inhabiting the tide country. Wind and water prove to be a lethal combination in the violent storm during which Fokir is killed.

The Hungry Tide depicts the fact that it is not easy to make human and non-human world co-exist in an ecologically challenging environment. The novel puts forth the dilemmas involved in conserving endangered ecosystems and animals when the livelihoods and life of local inhabitants are simultaneously put at risk. The novel brings to light the adverse impact western environmental activism on local ethical understanding. Ghosh refers to the disaster in 1970 of refugee settlers on the island of Marichjhapi and skillfully brings in a post-colonial political conflict between demands of wildlife conservation and needs of the Sundarban inhabitants. He highlights that the people of the Sundarbans are an integral part of the local. However, the model the westerners pursue to conserve wildlife i.e. tiger in the land in accordance with their political activism, causes untold sufferings to the local inhabitants. Kusum says in the novel:

> ...the worst part was not the hunger or the thirst. It was to sit here, helpless, and listen to the policemen making their announcements, hearing them say that our lives, our existence, was worth less than dirt or

> dust. 'This island has to be saved for its trees, it has to be saved for its animals, it is a part of a reserve forest, it belongs to a project to save tigers, which is paid for by people from all around the world.' Every day, sitting here, with hunger gnawing at our bellies, we would listen to these words, over and over again. Who are these people, I wondered, who love animals so much that they are willing to kill us for them? Do they know what is being done in their names? Where do they live, these people, do they have children, do they have mothers, fathers?....our fault, our crime was that we were just human beings, trying to live as human beings always have, from the water and the soil. (263)

The Hungry Tide is discussed under the realm of ecocide, deep ecology, social ecology, environmental racism and environmental justice issues. Ghosh portrays the pathetic condition of both the land and its people in the Sundarbans. It is a location where locals and outsiders meet together, share and feel that the ecological degradation is the global concern. The objective of Ghosh is to bring to light the environmental decline in the Sundarbans and to create an awareness to help prepare action plans for the safety of the settlers. *The Hungry Tide* can be considered a survey on an endangered ecosystem—the Sundarbans in the Bay of Bengal.

Works Cited

Buell, Laurence. *The Future of Environmental Criticism: Environmental Crisis and the Literary Imagination*. Oxford: Blackwell, 2005. Print.

Dutta Sharma, Brahma. "Environmentalism Versus Humanism in Amitav Ghosh's *The Hungry Tide*". *The Journal of Contemporary Literature* IV (2): 15-22. 2012. Web. 6 May 2013. Print.

Galuzzi, Fausto. "The Theme of Translation in Amitav Ghosh's *The Hungry Tide*." *Perspectives on English Studies*, edited by R.A. Henderson. Torino: Trauben. 2009. Print.

Ghosh, Amitav. *The Hungry Tide*. Delhi: Ravi Dayal, 2004. Print.

Nayar, Pramod K. "The Postcolonial Uncanny: The Politics of Dispossession in Amitav Ghosh's *The Hungry Tide*." *College Literature* 37 (4): 88-119. 2010. Web. 15 May 2012. Print.

19

Maximalism in Amitav Ghosh's *The Glass Palace*

D. Geraldin

Abstract

The article explores the postmodern theory, Maximalism, in Amitav Ghosh's novel, *The Glass Palace*. The main ideology of postmodernism highlights the social realities in a different way than modernity. Contrary to the modernist quest for meaning in a chaotic world, the postmodern author avoids, playfully, the possibility of meaning; and it is a parody of this quest. In postmodernism, this playfulness becomes central and the achievement of order and meaning becomes unlikely. The main concentration of postmodernism is on the destructured, decentered and dehumanized subject. Maximalism, which is against minimalism, exhibits everything in a gross manner. The author takes pleasure to show off minute details of less important things to the plot with excessive attention. This article studies Amitav Ghosh's novel *The Glass Palace* which is postmodern in style to analyse the concept of maximalism.

Postmodernism is a late twentieth century movement in arts, architecture, and criticism; and is a departure from modernism. It is a skeptical interpretation of culture, literature, art, philosophy, history, economics, architecture, and literary criticism. Although postmodern thought came after or developed from modernistic thought, it is in opposition to the ideologies of modernism, introducing traditional or classical elements; or simply a return to tradition.

Postmodern writing challenges the reader as an active co-creator of meaning than a passive consumer. It believes that human knowledge is fragmentary and limited and there can never be objective knowledge because the structures that enable knowing are derived from subjective conditions like human emotions.

There are various themes and techniques of postmodernism which are often used together: fragmentation, paradox, questionable narrators, contradiction, permutation, discontinuity, randomness, excess, short circuit, maximalism, minimalism, etc. which manifest chaotic condition of the world in equally chaotic technique and form. Thus, postmodern fiction presents its readers with a challenge, instead of enjoying it, they have to work to understand it and question their own responses and examine their views about what fiction is. Accepting this challenge makes postmodern writing pleasurable to read.

The term maximalism refers to digression, reference, and elaboration of detail which occupy a great fraction of the text. It is associated with writers like David Foster Wallace and Thomas Pynchon, whose works are bulky. Maximalism refers to anything which is excessive, overtly complex, showy, and grossness in quality and quantity. Critics like B.R. Myers attack the maximalist novel as being disorganized, sterile and filled with language play and empty of emotional commitment.

The maximalists attempt to include in their fiction everything belonging to that age-authentic and inauthentic things as they are; their work intends to contain the maximum of the age, in other words, to be the age itself, and because of this their novels are often encyclopedic. Where minimalism is all about making things neat, tidy, and brief, maximalism goes against the grain by embracing excess.

Along with other postmodern characteristics, maximalism gives the author the chance to experiment. In an age in which the line between authentic and inauthentic has become blurred, the postmodern writer just throws everything into the mix rather than getting bogged down with what's real/false or certain/uncertain.

Amitav Ghosh's *The Glass Palace*, a postmodern text, gives a record of the British invasion of Burma in 1885, their consequent victory, the exile of the last King of Burma with his family to India, World War II, Japanese invasion of Burma and Malaya, Indian National Army, the Burma Nationalist movement, military rule in Myanmar; and also the life and culture of the people of Burma, and Malaysia. The novel portrays the freedom struggle, and the pitiable condition of innocent people who are indirectly hit by the violent attitudes of the British for territorial power. The characters, plot, events, settings and regions open the readers' eyes to acts of forced displacement.

The Glass Palace is filled with various techniques, one among which is maximalism. Postmodernism's love of intertextuality and metafiction adds to its maximalist character. Maximalism includes heaps of outside information and references. The novel brings out the livelihood of the people of Burma and Malaya. The chief business products in those countries during pre-independence period are teak, rubber and petroleum. The author dives into the products and gives a detailed note on them which is extravagant. Apart from that, the novel also details on various places and daily life of that era.

The chief characters, Saya John and Rajkumar, get themselves busy when the rivers rise with their teak business. They start their journey from Irrawaddy to transport teak from Mandalay to Rangoon. It is described in a very elaborative manner which is though not necessary for the fictional stream.

Saya John and Rajkumar reach the desired place to start their business but as usual they don't find elephants to carry their loads and they hire porters to do the job along with them. During their travel along the mountain, they had to cross from one bank to another with more caution as the stream carried along logs of wood. The travel of teak wood is described with interesting details which goes to many paragraphs.

> Often the logs came not singly but in groups, dozens of tons of hardwood caroming down the stream together: when they hit each other the impact would be felt all the way up the banks.... One after another logs would go cannoning into one another, adding to the weight of the accumulated hard-wood.... With a

> great detonation the dam would capsize and a tidal wave of wood and water would wash down the slopes of the mountain. (*TGP,* 68)

The transportation of teak is continued from the stream to that of Rangoon in chapter 10. As postmodernism doesn't stick to any hard and fast rules, its texts can be any length and Postmodernists, as well, like to describe stuff:

> The streams' confluences were guarded by retrievers specialized in the capture of river-borne logs: for the sum of three annas per log....
>
> Once brought to the banks, the logs were anchored and moored. When enough had accumulated, skilled raftsmen bound them together into river-worthy craft.... The rafts travelled only between dawn and dusk, covering some ten to fifteen miles a day, powered solely by the flow of the river, and guided only by oars. (*TGP,* 121)

Apart from transportation of teak, the text also gives elaborate note on their cutting, and drying which goes to pages:

> In the dry season, when the earth cracked and the forests wilted, the streams would dwindle into dribbles upon the slope,... The trees, once picked, had to be killed and left to dry, for the density of teak is such that it will not remain afloat while its heartwood is moist....
>
> Dead though they were, the trees would sound great tocsins of protest as they fell, unloosing thunderclap explosions that could be heard miles away, bringing down everything in their path, rafts of sapling, looped nets of rattan. (*TGP,* 69)

The author takes pleasure to give the science behind teak: "Teak is a relative of mint, *tectona grandis*, born of the same genus of flowering plant, but of a distaff branch, presided over by that most soothing of herbs, verbena. It counts among its close kin many other fragrant and familiar herbs" (*TGP,* 70).

Elephants play an important role in the transportation of teak along with man power. Great number of people relied on elephants for their livelihood. Different skilled people were employed to handle the elephants. The novel uses specific terms used for people and things in Burma and Malaya during that period. The handlers are named as "oo-sis and pe-sis", persons specialized in the tying of chains are called as "pa-kyeiks". Throughout the text, Amitav Ghosh uses various specific names used for various persons, places, and things.

During the course of the story, a hint on "anthrax" is given. Rajkumar learns from Doh Say, his friend, that lives of the oo-sis are endangered; and one such is anthrax, the most deadly animal diseases. The author begins and goes on as: "Anthrax was common in the forests of central Burma and epidemics were hard to prevent.... Few were the insurers who would gamble against a disease such as this" (*TGP*, 92).

The text also gives details on the origin of the term "anthrax" and talks about the proceedings of the disease in the human and elephant's body: "The word anthrax comes from the same root as anthracite, a variety of coal. When anthrax strikes human beings it shows itself first in small pimple-like inflammations.... When anthrax erupts on an elephant's hide the lesions develop a volcanic energy" (*TGP*, 92).

The novel then gives insight into the history behind petroleum. "To the people of the area this ooze was known as earth-oil: it was a dark, shimmering green, the colour of bluebottles' wings" (*TGP*, 122). The text details on origin, texture, uses, and properties of petroleum.

> Long before the discovery of the internal-combustion engine there was already a good market for this oil: it was widely used as an ointment, for the treatment of certain skin conditions. Merchants came to Yenangyaung from as far away as China to avail themselves of this substance. The gathering of the oil was the work of a community endemic to those burning hills, a group of people known as twin-zas, a tight-knit, secretive bunch of outcasts, runaways and foreigners. (*TGP*, 122)

The author gets out of the main stream of the story to tell about things that seem to divert the readers from the plot. On the one hand, it is interesting to know about many things, authentic or inauthentic; on the other hand, it takes time to return to the string of the story and characters. It is well known that the postmodern text, unlike other texts, takes the readers mind, heart and soul to understand the story in a three dimensional aspect. Thus, the postmodern text gives a holistic stature to the fiction, which is not a mere fiction.

Works Cited

Bhardwaj, Kundan. *Post-modern Literary Theory*. New Delhi: Sonali Publications, 2012. Print.

Chenniappan R. and R. Saravana Suresh. "Postmodern Traits in the Novels of Amitav Ghosh." *The Criterion: An International Journal in English*. 2.2 (2011): 1-4. Print.

Ghosh, Amitav. *The Glass Palace*. India: Harper Collins, 2013. Print.

20

Shifting Contours/Marring Boundaries: A Cultural Reading of Amitav Ghosh's *Sea of Poppies*

Vidya Merlin Varghese

Abstract

Cultural differences or cultural divides have augmented the disparity among mankind. Cultural diversity is the salient feature of the Indian subcontinent. Regions are divided or differentiated by the variant cultural patterns. Pre-independent India was known for its distinct cultural divide. Amitav Ghosh's *Sea of Poppies* narrates the historical events of the nineteenth century Calcutta, in the form of an entertaining story mixed with ample ingredients of love, intrigue, colonialism, violence, murder and adventure. The bulk of events occur upon the ship Ibis that is en route to Mauritius. The novel is the first amongst the Ibis trilogy penned by the author. What makes the novel enthralling is that the writer has artfully charted out the cultural divide and differences of the inmates aboard the ship. The Opium trade of the late nineteenth century also provides the backdrop of the tale. The paper "Shifting Contours/ Marring Boundaries: A Cultural Reading of Amitav Ghosh's *Sea of Poppies*" proposes to chalk out the cultural elements within the text. The cultural reading is an attempt to portray, in the light of Cultural Studies, how boundaries that lead to cultural distinction and distances on land tend to be marred or shifted while on sea.

Cultural differences or cultural divides have augmented the disparity among mankind. Cultural diversity is the salient feature of the Indian subcontinent. Regions are divided or differentiated by their variant cultural patterns. Pre-independent

India was known for its distinct cultural divide. Amitav Ghosh's *Sea of Poppies* narrates the historical events of the nineteenth century Calcutta, in the form of an entertaining story mixed with ample ingredients of love, intrigue, colonialism, violence, murder and adventure. The bulk of events occur upon the ship Ibis that is en route to Mauritius. The novel is the first amongst the Ibis trilogy penned by the author. What makes the novel enthralling is that the writer has artfully charted out the cultural divide and differences of the inmates aboard the ship. The Opium trade of the late nineteenth century also provides the backdrop of the tale.

In his book *On Literature* Umberto Eco makes a profound statement on textual readings when he says that "literary works...offer us a discourse that has many layers of reading and place before us the ambiguities of language and of real life" (4). The researcher uses this statement as the guiding force to examine Ghosh's text. The paper entitled "Shifting Contours/ Marring Boundaries: A Cultural Reading of Amitav Ghosh's *Sea of Poppies*" proposes to chalk out the cultural elements within the text. The cultural reading is an attempt to portray, in the light of Cultural Studies, how boundaries that lead to cultural distinction and distances on land tend to be marred or shifted while on sea. Culture Studies evolved as an intellectual field of analysis by the late twentieth century. Theorists strived to define and view culture from a broader point of view. Early influences on culture studies as a genre are structuralism and Marxist ideology. As an academic discipline, it examines borders, power barriers—political, social or cultural, cultural clashes, identities, etc. The reach and extent of Cultural Studies is unimaginable. Any object of everyday life can be the focal point for the culture studies scholar's perusal.

The text chosen for study is Amitav Ghosh's *Sea of Poppies*. The novel abounds in a number of signifiers that make the cultural study of the work all the more enticing. The novel elaborates the events that occur on a ship named Ibis. The ship is charted for Mauritius and the inmates are a potpourri of sailors, convicts, labourers, and officials. The journey is marked by upheavals, celebrations, treachery, debauchery and romance.

These elements serve as signifiers that help in mapping the cultural blueprint of the text. When a text is analysed or read from the cultural perspective, it unveils multiple facets of latent activities of what is commonly included within the ambit of culture. Pramod Nayar has stated in *An Introduction to Cultural Studies* that "culture is produced through everyday living: the food people eat, the fashions they adopt, the entertainment they prefer or the festivals they celebrate" (29). It is a general understanding that culture is derived from one's environment. These activities serve as cultural markers or signposts that reveal the cultural quintessence of the text.

Culture is manifested at different levels; hence the researcher has chosen language, religion, rituals, clothes, name, and food cum eating habits and body as the cultural objects that help interpret the cultural markings of the text. The work has a number of cultural signifiers but the researcher has pinned only upon a select few in order to discern the cultural landscape of the text. Culture marks the lived space of humans. It is generally group specific but not uniformly distributed within a group. The inmates of the ship make up a group that happens to follow a different and distinct way of life while on board. One must not forget that they have come from variant cultural and social backgrounds and what they valued or imbibed on land, alters categorically while they are off shore. Each cultural marker selected for scrutiny, clearly presents this sea change. There are instances in the story where cultural disparity on shore affects attitudes and decisions on board.

The novel is divided into three sections: land, river, and sea. The cultural vantage points are spread over the first two sections. The off shore and on shore cultural distinctions come to plain view by the third section. Amitav Ghosh researched immensely before chalking out this novel. The novel has the Opium trade of the nineteenth century as the backcloth. The East India Company had benefitted largely from this trade which adversely affected the fortunes and future of the rajas. Bengal or specifically Calcutta, serves as the major port city from where the human cargo-comprising of lascars, castaways, migrants, sailors, sepoys—boards the ship, Ibis. Calcutta was the most important centre for the opium trade of the British Empire. The Opium Trade with China helped them establish an empire in India. In course of time, Calcutta becomes the centre spot for governance. Opium was grown in India and it was valued as a medicine that relieved pain, assisted in sleep and reduce stress. Indian princes pledged their estates and fortunes to the company as part of the trade. The early years of trade were beneficial for the princes but when millions of Chinese died of opium addiction, the Chinese emperors took steps to check its sale. The British force took up arms against them and this resulted in the Opium Wars (British Library: Opium and the expanse of trade).

By the nineteenth century, the British trading company had become a power spot in Bengal, which paved way for the British empire to colonise India. When Ghosh states that "opium was the exclusive monopoly of the British..." (85), he is pointing towards opium being a significant reason for triggering a cultural shift in the text. The "Sudder Opium Factory" was "among the most precious jewels in Queen Victoria's crown" (91). In the sea section of the tale, Deeti realizes the significance of the poppy seed when she refers to it as "the star that took us from our homes and put us on this ship" (452). Before the onset of the trade, the farmers at Ghazipur, Bihar, used to grow "main winter crops" like "wheat", "dal" and "vegetables", but now they "were shrinking in acreage" (29). "The 'English sahibs' would allow little else to be planted..." (30). The new owner of the Ibis, Benjamin Burnham, acquired the ship to use it for "the export of opium" (11). He burgeons into a "merchant-nabob" (77) because of opium business.

Deeti has to strain all alone to improve the poppy yield on her land (154). Her husband, Hukum Singh, became an opium addict after he was wounded in the war (34). He gets "a much coveted job in the opium factory" through the influence his uncle, who served as "subedar in the East India Company's army" (31). Deeti's life was designed by the poppy seed right from her wedding night. She mixes the drug in her mother-in-law's drink and soon becomes the "fond new daughter-in-law" (38). She recognizes the potency of the drug to tame men to work as dazed slaves in the Opium factory (95-97). The decline in the sale of opium affects the financial foundation of Neel, a Raja (87). The Raja had become the company's creditor so much so that he gets an official letter from the Company stating that "his debts to Burnham Bros, had already far exceeded the value of the entire zamindary…" (88). Opium trade thus improves the prospects of the settlers but it disturbs the balance in the lives of the inhabitants of the land.

Language is a significant cultural marker of the text. Language is an integral part of culture chiefly because transmissions of thoughts and messages is always done through the means of language. "Since the beginning of human civilization, language has played a crucial (perhaps the most crucial) role in making of identity, whether that identity is of the individual, the community, the race or the nation," quotes Nayar in his essay "Language, Culture and Identity" (22). Cultural contexts construct our identities. Language serves as a significant tool to identify the class distinctions, social activities, intellectual caliber and much more. "An understanding of human language and communication presupposes an understanding of culture" (Everett 47). While on land, the characters spoke many tongues—Bhojpuri (Ghosh 71), Laskari (104), Bengali (119), Latin, Sanskrit and French (131). English, the language of the colonizers, becomes the prestige language, but when the natives mastered it, the sahibs found it difficult to consider them as equals, in fact, they regarded native gentlemen "with a dislike that bordered on contempt" (88). The old Raja did not know the foreign tongue but he got on well with the foreigners (87).

When Paulette is given shelter at Burnham's residence, Burnham sees to it that he would "personally instruct her" chiefly because "her command of English" was "far from perfect" (130). She learns that the servants at the Burnham household regarded her as a European "memsahib" and "they would often ignore her if she spoke to them in "Bengali" because "kitchen Hindusthani" was considered as "the language of command in the house" (123). When the Ibis arrives at Hooghly Point, the ship's pilot, Mr Doughty warns Zachary to master "the zubben" or "the flash lingo of the East" and to see to it that his "Oordoo and Hindee" should not be too good that he should happen to turn into a "native" (49). Thus, language—be it mother tongue or foreign tongue—has its own distinct role in establishing the power positions of the characters.

Language, a cultural instrument, is best manifested through songs, stories and names. What is learned on shore is latent while on land because each individual was busy with their day to day events but when the Ibis halts at the Ganga-Sagar Island, the migrants realize that "this was the last they would see of their homeland..." (397). Thoughts of leaving land make the men uneasy but the women shared their memories of life on land through songs. The songs in the text revive the cultural history of the people. The songs mellowed the disturbed men folk. Most of them are in Bhojpuri, which according to Neel was the "speech of those who bore the yoke" (399). Neel's father forced him to abandon the rustic tongue as "it would ruin his accent when it came time for him to learn Hindusthani and Persian.... The language had wilted in his head but when on board he happens to hear Deeti singing in his long forgotten tongue, he is nourished by its rhythm and marvels at the grandeur of the language in expressing the nuances of love, longing and separation..." (399).

The songs thus establish the cultural grounding of the inmates while they are on sea. Parting from land is indeed painful but the songs are followed by stories or myths associated with the Ganga-Sagar Island. The migrants and the "qaidi" become united by a common language—Bhojpuri (400). The captain reminds the people on board that "the laws of the land have no hold on the water" (404). The inmates huddle together and refer to themselves as "ship siblings" (356). They leave the land due to different reasons but the ship turns out to become the "adoptive ancestor and parent of dynasties yet to come..." (357). The ship thus becomes a place or a territory with its own new founded unstable, fragile boundary. In the work *Cultural Studies in the Future Tense*, Lawrence Grossberg defines "places" as "contexts constituted by transits and translations, always defined by their relations to other places" (35). The ship is defined or transformed into a lived space when life on shore is remembered by the inmates (Ghosh 405).

The body is the next significant cultural marker. "The body is the expressive space by which we experience the world" (Westley 12). It turns out to be a significant cultural object in the text. The body either naked, fully or partially covered has its own cultural implications. In her article "Dress Needs: Reflections on the Clothed Body, Self hood and Consumption", Kate Soper says that "clothes have been extensively used to assert the cultural status of human beings, to police the border between humans and animals, to deny or cover our animality and thereby preserve a seemly distance from the beast" (17). The clothes worn by the principal characters undergo a categorical shift when they are on board. While on land, what one adorns and how one adorns it reflect his/her caste, social status, taste, and power position. On land, Neel Ratan is a raja hence he wears "fine shanbaff dhotis and abrawan-muslin kurtas" (Ghosh 106) but while on the Ibis, he is dressed in plain convict clothes which consisted of "one gamcha, two vests two dhotis of dungri weave" (290). Paulette was forced to wear Mrs Burnham's ill fitting gowns (126) while she shifts into saree to conceal her identity on board (359). Similarly Zachary, the second mate wore "workaday clothes, canvas trowsers and the usual sailor's banyan" (18) but he changes into "pukka sahib" (20) when he slips into "a white linen shirt, riding breeches and a double breasted summer paletot" (19).

Roland Barthes has stated in his *The Language of Fashion* that "The wearing of an item of clothing is fundamentally an act of meaning that goes beyond modesty, ornamentation and protection. It is an act of signification and therefore a profoundly social act right at the very heart of the dialectic of society" (90-91). The text proves this by revealing that clothes also indicate a transformation of persona, in addition to a concealment or revelation of identity. Baboo Nob Kissin, Mr Burnham's gomusta wore "kurta and dhoti", moreover he tied his hair into "a long priestly tikki" (132). After his spiritual transformation he puts on "a saffron coloured" loose gown and "undid the bindings of his tikki" so that his hair fell loose on his shoulders (167). Jodu roamed around on land in "a torn lungi and banyan" (101) but when he wears "a blue sailor's banyan and a pair of old canvas trousers", Paulette, his childhood friend, notices how much he had become a "stranger" (150). Bhyro Singh, the subedar wears his "old regimental uniform" while administering his whip upon the miscreant (486). The whole ceremony of flogging gets intensified with the ceremonial attire of Bhyro Singh. The clothed body thus augments fear, power positions, enchantment and much more.

The body can also be indicative of physical might and weakness. Kalua earns a stronghold on the sea by "virtue of his prodigious strength" (240) but on the land his "physical prowess" was used by the thakurs to "earn a good profit" (54). Neel was labeled to have been "sickly since birth" (326) but he marvels at his own transformation while on the ship. Old bonds are temporarily broken but he attains new friends and well wishers on the ship (497). Bodily features emerge in the memory of the characters. Deeti's shrine includes the prominent physical attributes of all the other characters. She etched Zachary's eyes (10), Paulette's long arms (126), the disfigured mark on Jodu's forehead (62), Baboo Nob Kissin's "fernlike ears" (134) and Kabutri's "pigtails" (394) to mention a few. "To take away a person's clothing is to put him or her 'out on the heath', to snatch away the clutched straw of human dignity" (Soper 21). The body becomes an object of discrimination in the novel. Deeti silently witnesses the inhuman act of the landowners humiliating Kalua (57) and she cannot but help remembering how she had gone through the same shameful experience (36). Their similar experience of physical humiliation, unites them (179). The body becomes an object of entertainment. Dance and singing was part of celebrations on land (105) and it is carried on board too (460).

The next significant cultural marker in the text under consideration is the rituals. "Rituals are episodes of repeated and simplified cultural communication in which the direct partners to a social interaction, and those observing it, share a mutual belief in the prescriptive and descriptive validity of the communication's symbolic contents and accept the authenticity of one another's intentions" (Alexander, 29). There are rituals pertaining to variant day to activities like death, marriage, prayer, cleanliness, etc. in the text. These rituals are intertwined with the religious practices of the people. In her book, *Religion: The Basics,* Malory Nye is of the view that any ritual act has a "meaning" (130) and the study of rituals will open up the cultural meanings, symbolisms and societal structuring inherent in the actions. Marriage ritual on board (460) and off board (32) are distinct both in their manner of celebration and method of execution. Songs become an integral part of the ceremony in both the places. However a notable change is that while on the land, marriage alliances were always made with equals (30) but while on board, differences were not accounted for because "the sea had washed away their past" (431).

Each character performs and reveals his own individual religious ritual background either by reading the *Bible* (24) or through rote recital of the *Quran* (104). Each performance was mechanically performed while on the land but as the ship heads on its journey through the waters, instinct or fear urges each one to pray in their own way. The lascars murmured the "fatiha" (369), Steward Pinto kneels down and chants "Hail Mary" (371), Neel joins the migrants in uttering the "Gayatri Mantra" (372). The body cleansing rituals reveal the cultural disparity of the inmates. On board Neel had to wash his body "with a few mugfuls of water" (383). Neel, who was fastidious about making himself unclean by merely touching another person (107) was moved by the power of touch or intimacy (384) while he was on the ship. Baboo Nob Kissin being a celibate would "look askance upon a woman's touch" (133) while he was a gomusta on the land, but towards the end of the novel, Zachary notices him standing on the main deck with his arms intertwined with that of Paulette and Deeti (512).

Dining, eating and analogous activities have a cultural tint in them. It serves as a significant marker of the social taboos, tastes, power significations, etc. Food serves as an instrument of cultural differences. Before they board the ship, the migrants are fed well because they had to "grow strong" to work as labourers in Mauritius (204) but while on board, food and water was rationed (401). Neel asks his servants to prepare an elaborate non vegetarian menu to treat the English men (118), but he had to sit at the table "without ever touching any of the food" (106). He is served homely food in the first few days of his stay at the jail (218) but the practice was stopped abruptly that Neel, driven by hunger, eats food "prepared by hands of unknown caste" (267). This helps him bear the limited supply of food on board. The text also gives an account of foods deemed to be forbidden and what would happen if they refused to consume them (246). The elaborate Indian dinner serving routine (108) is contrasted with the English dinner party (251). Food habits are solely imbibed by training. Paulette, a French woman was looked after by an Indian lady, hence "the first solid food that she ate was rice-and-dal khichri" (67) but at the Burnham residence she had to accustom herself to new dinner customs (127). Zachary who was a sailor in the first part of the story, was used to the menu of "lobscouse, dandyfunk and chokedog" and he switched to "unfamiliar flavours" (23).

Names have been an integral part of culture. Names function as a label indicating social status and cultural background of the characters. Each of the lead figures in the story alter their names while on board. This name shifting indicates a conscious cultural shift of identity. On shore, "just to hear someone's name would reveal their religion, their caste, their village" (110). These identity indicators change while they are on board. Deeti becomes Aditi, Zachary-Zikri Malum, Jodu-Azad, Kalua-Madhoo, Paulette-Pugli, Lei Long Fatt becomes Ahfat, Neel Ratan Halder becomes forgerer 1838 only to assume new identities. The ship becomes their vessel, their "mai-bap", and they become a new family (356).

The cultural standpoints chosen by the researcher thus presents a cultural perspective of the text. The text is a cultural product and the paper attempts to discern how culture is manifested through the different perspectives. The cultural reading turns out to be an examination and exploration of the many discourses inherent in the text.

Works Cited

Alexander, C Jeffrey. Bernhard Giesen and Jasen L Mast, ed. *Social Performance: Symbolic Action, Cultural Pragmatics and Ritual* United Kingdom: CUP, 2006. Print.

Barthes, Roland. *The Language of Fashion*. London: Bloomsbury, 2004. Print.

Eco, Umberto. *On Literature*. London: Vintage Books, 2002. Print.

Everett, Daniel. *Language: The Cultural Tool*. London: Profile Books Ltd., 2013. Print.

Ghosh, Amitav. *Sea of Poppies*. India: Penguin Random House, 2015. Print.

Grossberg, Lawrence. *Cultural Studies in the Future Tense*. New Delhi: Orient Blackswan Pvt Ltd., 2012. Print.

Nayar, Pramod. *An Introduction to Cultural Studies*. New Delhi: Viva Books, 2008. Print.

———. "Language, Culture and Identity". *The Humanities: Methodology and Perspective*. Abhijit Kundu, Pramod K. Nayar and Shweta. India: Pearson Education, 2009. Print.

Nye, Malory. *Religion: The Basics*. London: Routledge, 2003. Print.

"Opium and the Expansion of Trade". British Library, www.bl.uk/learning/index.html.

Soper, Kate. "Dress Needs: Reflections on the Clothed Body, Self hood and Consumption". *Body Dressing*. Ed. Joanne Entwistle and Elizabeth Wilson. Oxford: Berg. 2001. Print.

Westley Hannah. *The Body as Medium and Metaphor*. Amsterdam: Rodopi, 2008. Print.

21

A Paradoxical Reading of *The Shadow Lines* with Reference to Tha'mma

G. Srilatha

Abstract

Amitav Ghosh, a contemporary Indian novelist, is primarily obsessed with history. His writings focus on issues related to politics and history. He is mostly influenced by the stories of his father which deal with the World War and British Indian Army. The silences of his father's generations and the writer's memories were crystallized into the form of novels. His best novel *The Shadow Lines* is based on the theme of partition. Three generations of a family are weaved in the story. The narrator journeys from Calcutta to Bangladesh and onto England. Through the journeys, the writer explores the impact of violence on human life.

The story illustrates the growth of Calcutta as a city and India as a nation over a period of three decades or more. Tha'mma, the grandmother of the narrator talks on the issue of the partition of Bengal and the whole idea of Nation, Nationalism and Nationhood. Tha'mma lived in Dhaka before partition; she was married to an Engineer posted in Burma. She loses her husband very early and had to raise her only son. She worked as a school teacher to meet her ends and after her retirement she becomes nostalgic of the past.

Tha'mma fails to consider herself as a migrant. She has no sympathy for her refugee relatives living in a state of utter penury. The grandmother hardly realizes the after effects of partition until she plans to visit her sister in Dhaka. Only when she has to undergo the usual procedure of compiling her immigration papers, she understands the reality of the Partition of her state. Her visit to her home in Dhaka also turns out to be poignant in ways more than one. As a child, she makes stories about the disputed upside down house. She wonders how the place of her birth has come to be messily at odds with her nationality.

Tha'mma's memories of Dhaka are narrated in the form of vivid stories to the narrator. Though the Dhaka of the grandmother's youth has changed, the memory of her house becomes an image in her mind. Most of the grandmother's vision is nostalgic. Grandmother finds herself a foreigner in her own birthplace. She feels resentful that she should be a foreigner in her own city. She finds it hard to get reconciled to the mechanical rules of rationality. She has to 'invent' her country anew. This paper is an attempt to make a paradoxical reading of *The Shadow Lines* with reference to Tha'mma.

The Shadow Lines (1988) is acclaimed as a masterpiece as it evokes post-colonial situations, cultural dislocations, and anxieties in the period from 1962 to 1979. Travelling is a very important part in the works of Ghosh. In *The Shadow Lines* the narrator journeys from Calcutta to Bangladesh and into England. The narrator in the novel has not moved outside of Calcutta till he is an adult, crosses borders easily with the help of imagination.

Traversing borders becomes almost an obsession with Ghosh. His cousin Tridib, who is both his hero and teacher, constantly relates experiences. Three quarters of the novel's fictional life is Tridib's story, as seen through the narrator's eyes. Ghosh shows that men and countries set up borders to exclude people and create differences based on nationalities, race, culture, and religion. The borders set up by men are not geographical, but mental constructs and the lives on the maps are mere shadow lines.

The novel is divided into two sections: the first section is titled "Going Away" and the second section is titled "Coming Home". The narrative structure is multilayered. The narrator travels to and fro from London to Calcutta to collect material for his Ph.D thesis. Multiple stories of the narrator's grandmother and her sister, of his uncles, Tridib and Robi of his cousin, Ila and of May Price, contribute to the structure of the novel. However, the narrator has inherited the central story from Tridib. The narrator appears as a mirrored image of Tridib and tries to reflect time past and time present, places and people.

The narrator's mind is disturbed by the event which took place in 1960s when his uncle and childhood hero, Tridib was killed in a Hindu-Muslim riot in Dhaka. During the event, the narrator was 12 years old. The narrator's name is unknown. The manner of Tridib's death is very effective as it represents the timeless moment in the tortured consciousness of the family. The story is weaved in layers and each layer is a fusion of private lives and private events. The narrator interacts with his grandmother, who recalls her East Bengal background and memories of her childhood days in Dhaka in a sprawling house with its idiosyncratic occupants. Through Tridib, the narrator views the life of Calcutta.

Tridib was eight years old when he stayed with his parents, with Mrs. Price, a family friend in London in 1939. Tridib's narration had been so vivid that even after 40 years, the narrator while on a visit to London, went to explore these places. In the second part of the novel, the Grandmother Tha'mma's journey to Dhaka becomes a symbolic search for a point of fixity. The paradox of the novel is the manner in which the child narrator and as an adult learns about the two versions of the violence that led to Tridib's death.

The novel is not narrated in a sequential manner, instead the experience of the hero-narrator is shown. Memory is one of the narrative techniques. Tridib teaches the narrator to see with passion and to see with imagination. The culture of Calcutta and London are revealed through the narrator's memory. The narrator recalls his past associations to shape his visions under the influence of Tridib. The historical events from 1962 to 1979 illustrate the cultural dislocations and anxieties and interpret the issues of fractured consciousness in close encounters. The young narrator hears the story of Tridib's journey to England in instalments. The impact of politics on the lives of ordinary people and on human relationships is shown.

In the second section of the novel "Coming Home", Ghosh returns to Calcutta and Dhaka. The division of Bengal and suffering caused by partition is mainly portrayed through the grandmother's story. After the grandmother's retirement in 1962 as a headmistress, the narration focuses on how the grandmother becomes nostalgic of the past. Tha'mma's retirement from the public sphere brews trouble at home. Her lack of activity affects her mentally and she starts losing her zest for living. She becomes obsessed of the past and recollects her house in Dhaka. She possess a bachelor's degree is history which enables her to obtain a job in Calcutta. Thus, she remained in Calcutta for years and never visited Dhaka, her home town. She recollects her ancestral home in Dhaka:

> It was very odd house. It had evolved slowly, growing like a honeycomb, with every generation of Boses adding layers and extensions, until it was like a huge, lop-sided step-pyramid, inhabited by so many branches of the family that even the most knowledgeable amongst them had become a little confused about their relationships....Theirs was a big joint family then, with everyone living and eating together: her grandparents, her parents, she and Mayadebi, her Jethamoshai—her father's elder brother—and his family, which included three cousins of roughly her own age, as well as a couple of spinster aunts. (121)

People suffered intensely due to the partition of the country. The impact of the partition in Bengal is portrayed in the novel. As a result of partition, numerous Hindu families had to leave their ancestral home in East Pakistan and settle in Calcutta. Similarly, many Muslim families were also uprooted from Bihar, Bengal and Assam and had to migrate to newly formed Pakistan.

The dichotomy in the situation gave rise to confusion in the minds of people.

The narrator's grandmother desires to visit Dhaka is to see her old house. Her vision of the ancestral home is very nostalgic. Tha'mma is invited by Shaheb to Dhaka, for Tha'mma it is coming home to Dhaka. Before Tha'mma departs to Dhaka she receives a letter from her sister, Mayadebi in which the discovery of Jethamoshai is mentioned. They wish to bring their uncle Jethamoshai back to India. Tha'mma, Tridib and May depart for Dhaka and are received by Mayadebi and Robi. There they find Jethamoshai being taken care by a rickshaw puller, Khalil. The senile condition of Jethamoshai mind prevents him from recognizing them as his relatives; they plan to escort him in Khalil's rickshaw in the pretext of going to the court and later hand over him to his relatives.

Later Mayadebi, Tridib, May Price and Robi, grandmother sets out in the Mercedes car with the driver and a security guard of the High Commission. To their surprise, the big mansion is replaced by a crumbling building occupied by a large number of people. Their uncle Jethamoshai is called as Ukilbabu is taken care of Khalil, a cycle-rickshaw driver. To their surprise the old uncle fails to recognize them and refuses to move to India. While Tha'mma says they have come all the way to take him to India, the old man refuses to move. In his words,

> I don't believe in this India-Shindia. It's all very well, you're going away now, but suppose when you get there they decide to draw another line somewhere? What will you do then? Where will you move to? No one will have you anywhere. As for me, I was born here, and I'll die here. (215)

Jethamoshai feels safe in Dhaka, but in reality it is not so. The old man questions the whole ideology of nationalism, which creates boundaries and causes separation. He also raises pertinent questions on the concept of freedom. While the old Jethamoshai is at peace in his ancestral home the narrator's grandmother has confused loyalties. The old Jethamoshai feels secured by giving muslims a place to stay in his mansion. He achieves a form of communal harmony and peace of mind, which is denied to others.

However, Mayadebi and Tha'mma with the help of Khalil move Jethamoshai from the house. While all were travelling in Mercedes car, and Jethamoshai in Khalil's rickshaw, the mob surrounded them. The security man fires a shot, the mob attacks the rickshaw. Tridib and May Price get out of the car. The mob in frenzy kills Khalil, oldman and Tridib. Thus, the violence takes place leaving memories of fear and guilt in Robi and May Price.

The novel ends with an unveiling of the mystery of Tridib's violent death. May Price, for years has been guilty that her reckless act of rushing out of the car to save Jethamoshai and Khalil had caused Tridib's death. She says,

> For years I was arrogant enough to think I owned him his life. But I know now I didn't kill him; I couldn't have, if I'd wanted. He gave himself up; it was a sacrifice. I know I can't understand it, I know I mustn't try, for any real sacrifice is a mystery. (251)

So, May Price tells the narrator that Tridib's death remains a real sacrifice, a mystery which cannot be comprehended rationally.

The novel weaves together personal lives and Bangladesh. The grandmother is a displaced person and had to leave her ancestral home Dhaka and settle in Calcutta after partition. She returns to Dhaka and her homeland in 1964. Dhaka is a different city in her mind. Her memories of Dhaka are narrated in the form of vivid stories to the narrator. The grandmother's vision is nostalgic. The communal riots in 1964, in both India and Pakistan, lead to the untimely death of Tridib, by an impassioned mob, in old Dhaka. The death of her nephew changes her perception. She talks now of fighting for freedom.

Precise details of the death of Tridib are conveyed by May to the narrator, years later at a dinner in London. May narrates the story to exercise her feeling of guilt, that she was responsible for Tridib's untimely death. "Going Away" narrates the narrator's relation to Tridib, and Tridib leaving for England in 1939. The second part "Coming Home" begins on a note of reminiscence and is characterized by a collection on the part of the narrator.

Seventeen years later, the truth of Tridib's death is revealed to the narrator by Robi, an eyewitness of the murder. The grandmother's memories have been passed on to the narrator as lively, animated stories. Though the Dhaka of the grandmother's youth has changed, the memory of her house becomes an image in her mind, important enough to live for. The communal outbreak in 1964, in both India and Pakistan, leads to the untimely death of Tridib, an incident which changes the grandmother's perception. Her home in Dhaka, filled with memories of lively experiences, now becomes a reminder of death and communal violence.

The novel illustrates Mayadebi's "Going Away" from India to England with her family. The narrator moves from India to England from one real space to another, perhaps in a quest for freedom—cultural, emotional and intellectual. Ghosh explicates the lives of many people older generations of the subcontinent: of people who have lost their spaces—literal, emotional and spiritual, because of the partition. The grandmother's fascination for terrorist heroism during her youth, highlights her yearning for freedom. She recalls her desire to work for terrorists, who she believed, were fighting for freedom of their land.

This yearning for freedom continues well into her declining days because, paradoxically, though in a free country, as far as she is concerned, she is not free. She has been uprooted by the violent ruptures and dislocations caused by historical accidents, along with the indefinitely great number of individuals. The grandmother's memories of Dhaka, her homeland before partition, are passed on as colorful stories to the narrator, with a lucidity that makes him imaginative vision very clear (194). The best part of the grandmother's life is spent in Dhaka, an emotionally happy and fulfilling space—space that is real, yet filled with the make-believe of a child.

She moves to Calcutta to work as a teacher upon the death of her husband, initially living in a one-room tenement, and later in a small flat where she had always been careful to maintain a titular control over the household. India becomes her "Invented Country" only because of the partition, a historical accident which has dislocated her geographically, emotionally and spiritually. She continues to stick to her mental space, Dhaka, though decades later "the only worthwhile thing" left for her to do is "rescuing her uncle from his enemies and bringing him back where he belonged to her invented country" (136-37).

The grandmother is brought up in an environment of police raids in the University of Dhaka during the British rule, and the terrorist movement in Bengal during the first few decades of this century. Her need to be free, to have a space of her own, are reasons enough to motivate her. But she has "nothing but contempt" (89). The grandmother's strong sense of belonging to a space is brought out with her attitude that everyone who lives in a country should have earned his right to be there. Ila, she says, has no right to be in England because she doesn't belong there. It took those people a long time to build that country... (77-78). Identity relates to a sense of identification with a specific territory. It expresses a sense of belonging to a space and of individual identity. Ghosh shows that the force of nationalism in the quest for freedom, can be a source of violence, a violence that kills Tridib.

After moving into a larger house, which seems immense after the cramped little flat, the narrator notices that the grandmother no longer cares for control over the household. The vastness of the new house brings back memories of her huge childhood home in Dhaka. The past becomes very important to the narrator's grandmother. Imagination and memory make possible for her the recollection of the concrete reality of her ancestral home and the region. Decades have elapsed and she has stayed away in Calcutta, yet in her mind, the place of her childhood remains as real as ever.

It is a memory, a thought that sustains, soothes and provides a sense of belonging. She feels the need to go back to her childhood space, ostensibly to bring her old uncle back with her. In truth, there is a deep desire to go back to that space which once was real and now remains only in memory to see for herself, if the geographical space she still considers her home, is so emotionally too. Yet, grandmother experiences a fear within, at going back to a familiar and loved space: a fear of anticipation, of not finding that space which has been enshrined in her mind. "I feel scared. Do you think I will be wise after all these years? It won't be like home anymore" (149). There is in the grandmother a passionate eagerness to retain her old space, and therefore she is not ready to face the reality that may come her way.

The grandmother is unable to understand the concept of boundaries. The idea of boundaries carries a very particular significance and the grandmother wonders if she would be able to see the border between India and East Pakistan from the plane; if

There's something

Don't they call it no man's land?

The grandmother could hardly realize that the boundary demarcating the two countries is only a 'shadow line'—that the border isn't on the frontier but in "all those cards" she has to fill. The irony hits her hard. Her birth place is Dhaka, which is no longer a part of her country, a place she no longer belongs to and her nationality is 'Indian'. She is unable to comprehend how her birthplace is at odds with her nationality.

"In any case her Dhaka had long since vanished into the past.... The Dhaka she was thinking of was the city that had surrounded their old house" (193-94). Ghosh shows the pathetic situation of grandmother's lost dream. The grandmother has an idea of real space—a space she thinks she belongs to, but in Dhaka when she looks for her determined space-culturally and linguistically determined space. She finds it no longer there. "Where's Dhaka?...this isn't Dhaka" (195). She finds the new hotels, race courses, and the cinema hall, all wonderful, but where's Dhaka?" There are changes, both culturally and linguistically. Her "home" has been occupied by Muslim migrants from across the border and the grandmother instantly realizes that in real life, there are no determined spaces. There are objectives for a person being in a particular place.

To the grandmother and Mayadebi, the house holds an idyllic vision of "balconies and terraces, rising in steps out of the ground; the garden where they had once spent their evenings making up stories about their uncle's part of the house" (217). But to Saifuddin, the mechanic, the place has to be put to practical use "the old portico had sprouted a tin shed," which served as an automobile workshop. It was all changed, but now my grandmother didn't care any longer. It wasn't the house she remembers, the house she had built for me in Calcutta, but it was near enough (208).

Saifuddin plans to send the old man with them, so he can claim for the whole house. Hospitality and invitation to one's territory is subject to one's control, or ownership of that territory. The grandmother is worried about Tridib's death and not about the Muslim refugees who have occupied her home. She develops hatred for Pakistan and talks of fighting for freedom.

She sells her most precious piece of jewellery to help fund the war. "For your freedom, we have to kill them before they kill us; we have to wipe them out" (237) India becomes her real space. The grandmother effectively dramatizes the trauma of partition; the lack of emotional, politics, and literal space to those who are uprooted by this separation, only "a yet undiscovered ivory the mob that killed Tridib" (233).

It is in England that the narrator realizes the truth, when he emerges from the shadows of Ila and Tridib. He returns to India because he is aware of what Ila has lost and learns what his real home is. "Home" is not a geographical entity, but an emotional, moral and intellectual entity, which can be identified in the shadows of one's own inner being. The paradoxical element is that, although the grandmother is in Dhaka, she finds herself a foreigner in her own birthplace. Grandfather feels resentful that she should be a foreigner in her own city. She finds it hard to get reconciled to the mechanical rules of nationality. She has to 'invent' her country anew. In her childhood, grandmother had seen partition walls coming up in her own parental house and she felt nervous wherever people said "we're like brothers" (123).

Tha'mma was 32 when her husband passed away. As she was a graduate in history by Dhaka University, she got a job in a school in Calcutta, where she worked for 27 years. She did not have time to go back to Dhaka. In 1947 after partition, Dhaka became the capital of East Pakistan. From then on, she never heard of Jethamoshai and her aunt. After partition, except Jethamoshai, everyone left the house in Dhaka. The old house was occupied by Muslim refugees from India, especially from Bihar and U.P. He was taken care by a family. But Tha'mma was unhappy, "Imagine what it must be like to die in another country, abandoned and alone in your old age" (135).

Grandmother was excited about going to Dhaka by airplane wonders how the borders will look like. She was curious to see the border between India and East Pakistan from the plane. In her words,

> But if there aren't any trenches or anything, how are people to know? I mean, where's the difference then? And if there's no difference both sides will be the same; it'll be just like it used to be before, when we used to catch a train in Dhaka and get off in Calcutta the next day without anybody stopping us. What was it all for then—partition and all the killing and everything—if there isn't something in between? (151)

The narrator's father explains what border means, "It's not as though you're flying over the Himalayas into China. This is the modern world. The border isn't on the frontier: it's right inside the airport. You'll see. You'll cross it when you have to fill in all those disembarkation cards and things.... They want your nationality, your date of birth, place of birth, that kind of thing" (152).

Tha'mma recollects how formerly she would travel without any forms from Burma to Dhaka. In the words of the narrator, "You see, in our family we don't know whether we're coming or going—it's entirely my grandmother's fault. But of course, the fault wasn't hers at all: it lay in language. Every language assumes a centrality, a fixed and settled point, to go away for was a word for a journey which was not a coming or a going at all; a journey which was not a coming or a going at all; a journey that was a search for precisely that fixed point which permits the proper use of verbs of movement" (153).

According to the narrator, the people like his grandmother have no home but in memory, learn to be very skilled in the art of recollection. The irony is that the grandmother is in Dhaka, still she is in search of Dhaka. They say "But you are a foreigner now, you're as foreign here as May" (195). Everything in Dhaka appeared strange for the grandmother. "We could not recognize the streets we were careering through. We did not know whether we were going home or not. The streets had turned themselves inside out: our city had turned against us" (203).

People cried and that fear has a texture of a fear of the victims of an earthquake, of people who have lost faith in the stillness of the earth.

> It is a fear that comes of the knowledge that normalcy is utterly contingent, that the spaces that surround one, the streets that one inhabits, can become, suddenly and without warning, as hostile as a desert in a flash flood. It is this that sets apart the thousand million people who inhabit the sub continent from the rest of the world—not language, not food, not music—it is special quality of loneliness that grows out of the fear of the war between oneself and one's image in the mirror. (204)

The old man refuses to move with his relatives, in fact he did not move with his sons during partition. Though he is advised by the relatives that it is not safe for him to stay there, he refuses to move. According to him, "I understand very well, the old man muttered. I know everything. I understand everything. Once you start moving you never stop. That's what I told my sons when they took the trains" (215).

To conclude, Amitav Ghosh has made an attempt to show the displacement of people during partition and their emotional longingness towards the places. Although the events in the novel are not narrated in a chronological manner, Ghosh moves from the present to the past and back to the present. The image of the journey is central to the novel. Here, borders are meant to be crossed. Through the life of Tha'mma, the writer has illustrated how a generation was affected during partition and had lead a nostalgic life of the past. Most of the grandmother's vision is nostalgic. Her ancestral home in Dhaka has been occupied by Muslims after the partition. Therefore, when she visits Dhaka after partition, she sees that her birth place has changed completely. Paradoxically, she becomes a foreigner in her birth place.

Works Cited

Ghosh, Amitav. *The Shadow Lines*. Ravi Dayal Publishers, Delhi: 1988. Print.

Kirpal, Vinay, ed. *The New Indian Novel in English: A Study of the 1980s*. Delhi: Allied, 1990. Print.

Kapadia, Novy. *Amitav Ghosh's The Shadow Lines: Critical Perspectives*. Delhi: Asia Book Club, 2001. Print.

———. "Imagination and Politics in Amitav Ghosh's *Shadow Lines*," *The New Indian Novel in English: A Study of the 1980s*, ed. Vinay Kirpal. New Delhi: Allied, 1990. Print.

Sudrann, Jean. "Goings and Comings," *Yale Review*, 79 (1990), 414-38.

Kaul, Suvir. "Separation Anxiety: Growing Up Inter/National in Amitav Ghosh's *The Shadow Lines*. Delhi: Oxford University Press, 1995. 268-86.

Hawley, John C. ed. *Amitav Ghosh: Contemporary Indian Writers in English*. Delhi: Foundation Books. 2005. Print.

22

Ecological Degradation in Amitav Ghosh's *The Great Derangement: Climate Change and the Unthinkable*

Candy D'Cunha

Abstract

The present century has been witnessing the environmental degradation and destruction in the ecosystem throughout the world. The lack of seriousness in dealing with the contemporary ecological crisis is prototypical of the approach of mainstream society. Responding to environmental crisis requires a complete rethinking and reorienting in our way of being and behaving. Fundamentally, a renewed approach of the imagination and looking for other possible ways of being and interacting with human and non-human can, to a certain extent, contribute to the solution of the environmental crisis.

Amitav Ghosh is one of the greatest writers of the present era. He is well known for his grandeur and style of narrative technique, coupled with thematic adaptability, knowledge, education and an acute anthropologist's sagacity, which captures all through the reader's interest. His work, *The Great Derangement: Climate Change and the Unthinkable* is an informative work, which enthrals the minds of the readers to understand the destiny of human, if he doesn't change for the better. He tries to draw the minds of the readers to heed to the cry of the earth. Ghosh shares his personal experience about his ancestors, who were ecological refugees. His personal experience tries to sketch out the various situation and hazards of climate changes he had been observing from years.

Ghosh affirms that it is a strong challenge placed on every individual to respond with great commitment and mature responsibility to the cause of achieving harmony in the universe. The present paper is an attempt to trace various ecological concerns in the works of Amitav Ghosh's *The Great Derangement: Climate Change and the Unthinkable* which will help in the creation of a better world.

The concept of imagination both in the East and the West about the environmental catastrophe has been planted in many parts of the world. Many themes concerning environmental degradation have been debated upon to explore the causes of the environmental disaster and arrive at a relevant solution.

His popular works like *The Glass Palace*, and *The Hungry Tide*, have strong roots in ecological issues. Researching Ghosh's novels can be enlightening to the groups that are working for the improvement of the ecological harmony.

Ghosh's work, *The Great Derangement* is an enlightening work as it captivates the minds of the readers to understand the destiny of human if he doesn't change for the better. He tries to draw the minds of the readers to heed to the cry of the earth. Ghosh has mastered the technique of storytelling, making use of his own insights and experiences which are thought provoking for the human to understand the state of the environmental disaster.

At the outset of his storytelling, Ghosh asks the readers: "Are we Deranged?" The brilliant platform which Ghosh lays, elucidates his concern to save the world by preparing the minds of the readers to self-examine the situation in and around them. He suggests, "Politics, much like literature has become a matter of personal moral reckoning than an arena of collective action." This concept can realistically authenticate the elusive splendour of Indian belief and flexibility to survive against various cultural, political, scientific and intellectual assaults on India today and tomorrow, which runs quickly and relentlessly in the man-nature relationship.

Ghosh shares his personal experience about his ancestors who were ecological refugees. The nostalgic family trip in a stream boat unfolded the story of Padma river. The story was woven around the great storm which washed away their dwelling and surrounding. Ghosh recollects:

> I imagined a great storm, with coconut palms bending over backward until their fronds lashed the grounds; I envisioned women and children racing through howling winds as the waters rose behind them. I thought of my ancestors sitting huddled on an outcrop, looking on as their dwelling were washed away. (5)

The impact of such a disaster on that dark stormy night made an indelible mark on his mind. His past seems to have looked into his eyes as if to ask, "Do you recognize me, wherever you are?" (5).

Ghosh recollects his college days at Delhi University. Working as a part-time journalist, he remembered an incident of a hailstorm which gradually changed into an unseasonal weather. The weather became so harsh to such an extreme extent that people on the roads were washed away. The whirlwind was so robust that it hit the Yamuna river and raised waves as high as 20 or 30 feet. The report in the newspaper quoted a witness:

> I saw my own scooter, which I had abandoned on the road, during those terrifying moments, being carried away in the wind like a kite. We saw all this happening around but were dumbfounded. We saw people dying.... (18)

Even today in Delhi, Ghosh tries to educate the readers of the weather condition. He tries to send alert signals of warning to humanity. He says that we are now in the era of normality, with high, improbable, flash floods, hundred-year storms, persistence drought, spell of unprecedented heat, sudden landslide, breached glacial lakes, etc.

Humanity is at the crossroads due to the tremendous fear of terrorism and wars of various kinds which disturb the harmony and peace in the environment. The Delhi Peace Summit conducted by some of the prominent thinkers of the world, along with A.P.J. Abdul Kalam, the former President of

India; Manmohan Singh, the former Prime Minister of India; and six Nobel Laureates for Peace and three Nobel Laureates for Science, touched upon some of the ecological concerns and the urgent need for environmental justice.

This summit brought out several insights into exploring a variety of topics and themes on environment and to build bridges between cultures and nations. Special references were made on Science, Religion and Spirituality and on promoting world peace. The dangers of a nuclear war were also strongly addressed in the meeting. The Nobel Laureate in Chemistry and Peace, Linus Pauling said:

> Nuclear war or war in general, is very much a matter of science. All weaponry stuff is a misuse of science. Individual scientists have been tempted into working for the government, working on weapons either directly or indirectly. It would be better if most of them were working for the welfare of human beings in one way or another. (T.D. Singh, 2005: 134)

Looking back at the bygone ages, we notice that the ecological instability began with the industrial revolution. The eighteenth century witnessed the gradual change of climatic conditions as it succumbed to the new phenomenon of setting up of many factories and industries. As a consequence, human's relationship with nature changed forever.

Ghosh ties to quote the ghost stories of Charles Dickens, Henry James and Rabindranath Tagore. He tries to read and interpret the environmental concerns through those ghost stories of literary fiction. He draws his conclusion from the stories that they certainly represented as projection of humans, who were once alive. Connecting these stories to the Delhi tornado, he says that animals like Sundarban tiger, and freakish weather, have no human reference at all, as he writes:

> All of this makes climate change events peculiarly resistant to the customary frames that literature has applied to 'Nature': they are too powerful, too grotesque, too dangerous, and too accusatory to be written about in lyrical, or elegiac, or romantic. (43)

Ghosh tries to highlight the novel of Mary Shelley, *Frankenstein* or *The Modern Prometheus*, that created a sensation in the literary world after it had been published in 1818. He says that even the reviews for such a novel came out of literary mainstream. Ghosh questions: "How science fiction came to be demarcated from the literary mainstream" and he put forward another question: "What is it in the nature of modernity that has led to this separation?" (92).

The attitude of human towards the sacred nature deteriorated slowly and led him to falsely imagine that he is the supreme ruler of the earth. Many Western countries tried to use industrialization solely for unplanned growth. Many societies adopted the idea of uncontrolled progress which aimed at a healthier, happier and prosperous life. In the bargain, environment became the victim of human's progress.

Natural resources like minerals and coal were used in factories. Smoke caused heavy pollution and it led to the damage of the environment. As wood was used in a wrong manner, instead of being recycled, it gradually changed into non-renewable fossil fuels.

Ghosh elaborates that the nineteenth and twentieth centuries have witnessed several scientific discoveries and new technologies, which led to rapid industrialization in many Western countries. This brought about an unimaginable exploitation of natural resources. With the invention of the engine and the automobile, the consumption of fossil fuel in industries and for transportation increased rapidly. Huge machines which were made for sawing and felling trees, were used in forests for converting them into industrial wood.

Thousands of dams were constructed with the invention of concrete, and river water was diverted for agriculture and power production. Food production was increased with the help of chemical fertilizers and pesticides, but they also polluted water and degraded the soil. Ground water was extracted in huge amounts with the help of pumps for irrigation. Many species became extinct. Millions of birds, whales, fish, and animals were hunted down and destroyed by using powerful guns and big ships.

As the ecosystem is severely degraded in many ways, the question remains, "will nature restore the ecological balance over time?" The earth has existed for over five billion years, and human generations for about three to five million years and civilizations for about 10000 years. Many of these generations have often contributed to the degradation of the environment but still mother earth survived these crises and cataclysm.

The last third of the twentieth century witnessed several problems of ecological backlash that mounted feverishly. Undoubtedly, science has brought about wonders to the world in helping humanity in many ways. Humans also need to understand the darker side of science, as it has the potential to wipe out human from the face of the earth. The products of science like the nuclear, biological, chemical weapons can destroy the human race for ever. The former Prime Minister of India, Manmohan Singh, in his article on Science, Religion, and Spirituality states:

> Concern for the environment has followed hard on the heels of the concern about the destructive potential of the weapons of mass destruction that twentieth century technology has gifted to the people of the world. (T.D. Singh, 2005: 158)

Manmohan Singh touched upon many aspects of advancement of science and its contribution to humanity. He questioned the implications of these developments for the future of India. He expressed that the purposeful use of modern science and technology can improve the human condition, chronic poverty, ignorance and diseases which affect millions of people in our country. He said that science and technology should make the environment sound and sustainable and bring comfort for the livelihood of India's vast population.

Manmohan Singh pointed out that the use of science and technology should bring in a new spiritual awakening. He reminded that one should not take seriously the lines of Rudyard Kipling that: "East is East and West is West, and never the Twain shall meet"—to support the notion that Eastern and Western Cultures are so alien to one another that any attempt to reconcile them is fruitless. Instead, Singh suggested that one should strive to promote inter-faith dialogue and evolve a universal value system which can suit the increasing inter-dependence of the world in which we live in and hope for enduring peace and harmony in the world.

Ghosh quotes the science fiction and speculative fiction of Margaret Atwood. The very dystopian element in the novel speaks of suffering and destruction of nature. It is the duty of human to self-realize. He continues to express that the novels of Atwood have opened a doorway into what we might call a 'spirit world'—a universe animated by non-human voice (97). This non-human voice creates the very notion of awakening. Erach Bharucha says:

> Each of us creates waves around us in our environment that spread outwards like the ripples generated by dropping a stone in a quiet pond. Every one of us is doing something to our environment and it is frequently the result of an act that we can hardly ever reverse as after once the stone hits the water, one cannot stop the ripple effect from disturbing the pond. (Erach Bharucha, 2005)

We need a paradigm shift in understanding and dealing with the ecological crisis that our common home is facing. We need to rediscover the earth as our home, our dwelling place, as more than our simple environment. It is only when we start caring for our common home, we will be able to listen attentively to the groaning of the earth and understand the pain that she is going through. Ghosh elaborates:

> Climate change poses a powerful challenge to what is perhaps the single most important political conception of the modern era: the idea of freedom, which is central not only to contemporary politics but also to the humanities, the arts and literature. (159)

Joshtrom Kureethadam, in his book on *Creation in Crisis: Science, Ethics, Theology,* highlights three important concerns of environmental ethics as a triple cry, namely:

- Cry of the Earth
- Cry of the Poor

- Cry of the Creator

Cry of the Earth recalls to one's mind the groaning of the earth which in fact is suffering from aches and anguish. The climate change is the main reason for the earth to be torn to pieces and why it sheds tears. The other reason for the earth to mourn is the global warming associated with biodiversity. Another reason lies in the anthropogenic activities that disturb the earth and cause confusion in it. These concerns are also powerfully presented, directly or indirectly by other environmentalists in their works. The need of the hour is to pay heed to the stark reality of mother earth which is badly wounded with bruises.

Cry of the Creator is the other element connected to mother earth. The earth was carefully fashioned and created by the Creator of the universe. He took utmost care to see that each and every element in nature was made special and with a purpose. The Creator is pained to see the distorted face of the earth which is the outcome of the evil desires and selfish motives of human. The Creator is certainly offended by the commercialisation of the earth and the harm that is caused to it. The spiritual facet of the earth is broken and the Creator weeps for the huge loss of his creation. The earth which was supposed to be a happy dwelling place for producing peace and harmony has been converted into a place of violence and crime.

The last cry is the *Cry of the Poor* and of the marginalized, made victims by the rich and powerful, who exploit and use nature for making themselves even richer. The poor have very little role to play in restoring the distorted face of nature. The fruits of science and technology are enjoyed mainly by the rich. The abuse of technology makes the poor people homeless, helpless and vulnerable. They are the ones who suffer and bear the consequences of natural calamities, disasters and other human atrocities. For all these reasons, often the poor pour out their pain, suffering and helplessness upon the environment (K. Joshtrom, 221).

Ghosh makes a reference in the concluding pages to Pope Francis' Encyclical letter entitled, *Laudato Si'—On Care for*

Our Common Home, which suggests that the theological and philosophical reflections on the situation of humanity and the world can sound tiresome and abstract, unless they are strongly grounded in a fresh analysis of our present situation, which in many ways is unprecedented in the history of humanity.

Pope Francis uses the term 'rapidification' for the several changes which are really affecting the rhythm of the planet, with a more intensified pace of life. He urges human to translate the cultural and ecological crisis into a new habit wherein an "ecological citizenship" may be formed. He further says that sound virtues are to be instilled into the minds of people to help them to make selfless ecological commitments. Caring for the daily little actions is essential to promote harmony and peace. The Pope suggests that human should be educated to be responsible in taking care of the environment as he says:

> Education in environment responsibility can encourage ways of acting which directly and significantly affect the world around us; such as avoiding the use of plastic and paper, reducing water consumption, separating refuse, cooking only what can reasonably be consumed, showing care for other living beings, using public transport or carpooling, planting trees, turning off unnecessary lights, or any number of other practices. (*Laudato Si'*, 2015: 164)

On the other hand, Ghosh mentions that the concluding part of *Laudato Si'* is the urge for change and for a better world. The Pope strongly hopes that such ecological awareness takes place at various levels such as in families, schools, media, social and public conversations. Humans should plant seeds when they are young, and later, continue to bear the fruits of their labour. Ghosh mentions:

> The prayers with which the *Laudato Si'* concludes, on the other hand, are an appeal for help and guidance. As such, they are also acknowledgements of how profoundly humanity has lost its way and of the limits that circumscribe human agency… Pope Francis' critiques of the era that he describes as 'a period of

irrational confidence in progress and human abilities'. (212)

Ghosh reveals that if the religious groups around the world can join hands with popular movement, they may be able to provide the momentum that is needed for the change (215). It is a strong challenge placed on every individual to respond with greater commitment and mature responsibility to the cause of achieving harmony in the universe. The paper is an attempt to trace various ecological concerns in the works of Amitav Ghosh's, *The Great Derangement: Climate Change and the Unthinkable* and to hope for a better world.

Works Cited

Abreu, Suren. *Befriending the Earth*. Mumbai: St Paul Press, 2008. Print.

Arun, Neerja and Rakesh Saraswat. *Ecology and Literature Global Perspective*. New Delhi: Creative Books, 2009. Print.

Bharucha, Erach. *Textbook of Environmental Studies for Undergraduate Courses*. New Delhi: Rajeev Book Binding House, 2005. 12. Print.

Francis, Pope. *Encyclical Letter Laudato Si (On Care for Our Common Home)*. Kerala: Carmel International Publishing House, 2015. 164. Print.

Ghosh, Amitav. *The Great Derangement: Climate Change and the Unthinkable*. Haryana: Allen Lane. Penguin Random House India, 2016. Print.

Kureethadam, Joshtrom. *Creation in Crisis: Science, Ethics, Theology*. New York: Orbis Books, 2014. Print.

Singh, T.D. *Towards a Culture of Harmony and Peace*. Delhi Peace Summit, New Delhi: Anderson Printing House, 2005. Print.

23

Multiple Narratives in Amitav Ghosh's Travel Writings: A Reading of *In an Antique Land*

K.V. Raghupathi

What is travel writing? Travel writing has existed for centuries, though in different forms. It has served different purposes for different people. Historians have derived their own version of history and ordinary people have rejoiced in it. It is both entertaining and informative and has emerged as an important genre within fiction. Within this genre, there are umpteen sub-genres such as nature travel writings, mountain travel writings, jungle travel writings, pilgrimage travel writings, political travel writings, secular travel writings such as, Stephen Alter's (2001) journey from *Amritsar to Lahore* (a personal travelogue that covers the longest short distance between two marquee cities of Punjab, Amritsar the city of golden temple and Lahore the quintessential capital of Punjab); his another book, *Sacred Waters: A Pilgrimage to the Many Sources of the Ganga* (2001) which combines myth, history and actual experience (134); or Pankaj Mishra's through smaller town of India (*Butter Chicken in Ludhiana: Travels in Small Town in India,* Penguin, 1995); or Bill Aitken's *Seven Sacred Rivers* (1992) which recounts his visits to several Hindu and Sikh temples in Afghanistan and so on. Others include, Manoj Das, Kaka Kalekar, Balaji Sahni, Raghubir Singh (photographer), Shashi Tharoor, Iqbal Ali Shah, Dilip D'Souza and Vikram Seth.

Can travel writing be treated as a part of literature? The answer is yes, though some critics contend it. R. Balachandran (10), for instance, separates travel writing from writing of literary worth. He argues that there is not much stylistic and formal experimentation in it. Though his argument carries a pinch of merit, travel writing has emerged as important non-fiction writing and on that account of lacking stylistic experimentation, it cannot be berated. Travel writing is mostly autobiographical since the writer narrates his/her own experiences of journey. Tim Macknitosh Smith (97) says travel writing is the most egocentric form of literature after autobiography.

What happens in travel writing? The writer discovers his/her self. While rediscovering his/her own self, the writer may also discover history. In both the cases, the writer looks for adventure and exploration. Travel writing blended with history is most important one. Writers belonging to this sub-genre consciously bring in history, the actual. To this group belongs Amitav Ghosh. His first non-fiction travel book, *In an Antique Land,* about the travel in the East was published in 1992. Six years later came the slim and riveting *Dancing in Cambodia* (1998).

What kind of travel writer is Amitav Ghosh? He cannot be bracketed with ordinary travel writers. Research is the backbone of all his books. Not just for his historical novels, but also for his travelogues and essays, even if he's actually experienced the things he writes about. "Writing about personal experience does not make research unnecessary", explains Ghosh. "Suppose, for example, that I were writing about the years I spent in Delhi. Even though my memories of that time are quite vivid, I would almost certainly need to look at street maps, newspapers, etc. if I were to write about them" (https//hindustantimes.com, "What Makes India's Greatest Writer Amitav Ghosh so darned angry?" updated Jan. 29, 2017).

In an Antique Land has three narratives: anthropological, historical and personal (travel memoir)—all blended into each other. The first anthropological narrative revolves around two visits made by Ghosh to two villages in the Nile delta while he was writing his doctoral dissertation (1980-81) and again a few years later (1988). In the second narrative, presented parallel to the first narrative (anthropological), Ghosh reconstructs the history of a 12th century Jewish merchant Abraham Ben Yiju, and his slaves Ashu and Bomma, using documents from the Cairo Geniza. The clear cut marking between anthropological and historical is blurring; both narratives blend and complement to each other in the book. The background is: while at Oxford in 1978, going through the twelfth century manuscripts of Egypt in Oxford library, Amitav Ghosh read about Abraham Ben Yiju, a Tunisian Jewish merchant, who came to India via Egypt around 1130 A.D. and Ben Yiju's slave is from Tululand of ancient India. He was granted a scholarship that allowed him to travel to a small Egyptian village in 1980, Lataifa, a couple of hours journey to the south-east of Alexandria to further his research. With a view to verifying the authenticity of the available material, Amitav Ghosh had gone to Tunisia and learnt Arabic and later journeyed to Egypt in 1980. The village was located in the delta of the Nile river and Ghosh lived among the *fellaheen*, or Egyptian peasants. In 1988 and 1990, Ghosh returned to the Egyptian village he visited previously to continue his research. The result of his visit and revisit of Egyptian village is his third book, *In an Antique Land* in 1992. It resulted from Ghosh's continuing interest in 12th century Egyptian culture. The cover proclaims IAAL "History in the guise of a traveller's tale". It shows that "he is not a mere fictionist but an indefatigable researcher, a social anthropologist and a keen traveller as well. It bears testimony to Ghosh's interaction with at least four languages and cultures spread over three continents and across several countries. Unlike of some other contemporary writers, his canvas keeps on conquering new lineages, giving expression to new ideas and themes" (Dhawan, 24).

Further, Ghosh discovers records pertaining to the Jewish settlers in and around Cairo while he was at Oxford. In the 12th century, Jewish settlers, in an around Cairo, were reluctant to discard written documents for fear that the name of God might be contained within and they would therefore be desecrated if the paper was soiled. The synagogue created a Geniza, or cellar, where people could dispose of written materials without fear of desecration. For seven centuries, local Jews deposited everything from shopping tits, letters, religious texts and legal documents into the Cairo Geniza. At the end of the nineteenth century, Western scholars discovered the Geniza, appropriated its contents, and its wealth of history was divided among the Western scholarly communities. While studying at Oxford, Ghosh discovered records of these documents and noticed a reference to a slave named Bomma. Ghosh traveled to Egypt in an effort to uncover more information about the slave and the time period in which he lived.

This book is the story of Amitav Ghosh's decade of intimacy with the village community. As a parallel to the story of his research, goes his personal narrative. Mixing conversation and research, imagination and scholarship, it is an eccentric history of the special relationship between two countries, Egypt and India, through nearly ten centuries of parochialism and sympathy, bigotry and affection. In the 1980s, Amitav Ghosh moved into a converted chicken coop. It was on the roof of a house in Lataifa, a tiny village in Egypt. During the day, he poured over medieval letters sent to India from Cairo by Arab merchants. In the evenings, he shut out the bellowing of his fat landlord by turning up the volume of his transistor radio and wrote stories based on what he had seen in the village—the story of Khamees the Rat, the notorious impotent (already married twice); of Zaghloul, the weaver determined to travel to India on a donkey; of one-eyed Mohammad, so obsessed with a girl that he spent nights kneeling outside her window to listen to the sound of her breathing; of Amm 'Taha, part-time witch, always ready to cast a spell for a little extra money; and, of course, the story of Amitav Ghosh himself, known in the village as the Indian doctor, the uncircumcised, cow-worshipping kaffir, who would not convert to Islam.

Besides other mini-narrative of the stories, include the story of Abraham Ben Yiju, a Jewish merchant who travelled between the Middle East and India during the twelfth century, and of his Indian slave, Bomma. Ben Yiju's "origin lay in a region that was known as Ifriya in the Arabic-speaking world Middle Ages—an area centred around what is now Tunisia." Imitating the migration of traders to Egypt, Ben Yiju also migrated to Egypt, joined the "Synagogue of the Palestinians," the building designed to last until a good seven hundred years after Ben Yiju's lifetime. "A man of many accomplishments, a distinguished calligrapher, scholar and poet," Ben Yiju, a born trader, migrated from Egypt to Aden. His paper shows that his acquaintance with a wealthy and powerful trader, Madmun ibn ai-Hasan ibn Bundar, proves to be a turning point in his life. It is possible that Ben Yiju was introduced to Madmun, by letters of introduction by his friends and relatives. After Ben Yiju settled as a trader, in the Malabar before 1132, there was a continuous exchange of letters between Madmun, Yusuf ibn Abraham and Khalaf Ibn Ishaq from Aden, and Ben Yiju from India. What is more interesting is the fact that, unlike other traders cum travellers, Abu Said Halfon and Abu ZikriSijlmasi, Yiju "does not seem to have travelled back to Aden or Egypt even once in the nineteen or twenty years that he was in India." Once he had settled in Mangalore, according to a document available, he married Ashu, a slave girl. She is not anywhere in the entire corpus of Ben Yiju's except in a set of accounts scribbled on the back of one of Madmun's letters. "It links her to the matrilineal community of Nairs, who still form a substantial section of the population of the southern part of the Malabar Coast." The document reveals that in India "concubine is permitted between everyone, so long as it is not with married woman." Ghosh relates anecdotes and musings about his life in a poor Egyptian village where he improves his colloquial Arabic necessary for deciphering old scripts and generally gets a better of what the Middle East is all about. Fortunately, this makes up the bulk of the book and the academic bits can be skipped without missing much.

He was in a trail of the story of the slave of MS.H.6, a story "miraculously preserved in the footnotes of history." It is a strange, colourful world—at once medieval and modern—presented in the garb of a traveller's tale. It is here, in the Egyptian backwater, that Amitav Ghosh sought to retrieve the remnants of the antique civilization of the twelfth century. His guides in both the villages were his neighbours: Abu Ali, his obese, gargantuan landlord; Shaikh Musa, the gentle and good-humoured village elder; Jabir, the son of Ali's cousin; Amm

'Taha, Ghosh's caretaker in Nashawy, who had a rare skill "in ferreting out...the most jealously guarded of household secrets" (34); the self-reliant and individualistic Busaina; Zaghloul, the superstitious weaver who was very fond of stories and "had a manner of telling them that was marvellously faithful to the metaphorical resonances of his chosen craft" (35); Ustaz Sabri, the well-educated and knowledgeable school teacher, battling, with the other young neighbourhood, against ignorance, poverty and exploitation and fashioning post-Revolution Egypt into the Islam; the college students, Ismail and Nabeel; the Rat, the beady-eyed local wit; and the village's Imam with whom Ghosh had a serious quarrel. Ghosh's journey into Egypt presents a pageant of characters before Indians.

Ghosh narrates from the viewpoint of a social anthropologist, the lives of these people—their dialects, manners, social and religious customs—and points out the commonalties and differences between Medieval Masr and the post-Revolution Egypt. "One such thread of commonality is between the dialects of the villages and the language of the manuscripts he studies: Over the next couple of years, as I followed the Slave's trail from library to library, there were times when the magnifying glass would drop out of my hand when I came upon certain words and turns of phrase for I would suddenly hear the voice of Shaikh Musa (one of the author's informants in his villages) speaking in the documents in front of me as clearly as though I had been walking past the canal, on my way between Lataifa and Nashwy" (36). Apart from the history of modern developing Egypt, there is an account of another Egypt, teeming with poverty, superstition, miracles, blood-feuds, and exorcism rituals world not far removed from the antique world inhabited by Ben Yiju and Bomma. Ghosh found their men like Ustaz Sabri, who were aware of the age-old and intimate ties between India and Egypt and of the similarity of the problems "that had been bequeathed to them by their trouble histories" (37). Most of the villagers had no clear idea about the country where Ben Yiju spent seventeen valuable years of his life. However, it was with these simple and largely unlettered *fellaheen*, who were devoutly religious but had no interests in politics, that

Amitav Ghosh felt at home since they seemed to belong to a "familiar world" (38).

Persistently, Ghosh's active and inquisitive mind searches for the relevance of Egypt-India relations over the time. Through Ustaz Sabri, Ghosh voices his own opinion: "Our countries were very similar, for India, like Egypt, was largely an agricultural nation. Our countries were poor, for they had been ransacked by imperialists and now both were trying in similar ways to cope with poverty...our two countries had always supported each other In the past: Mahatma Gandhi had come to Egypt to consult Sa'ad Zaghloul Pasha and later Nehru and Nasser had forged a close relation" (41).

"Going Back" (239-85) is the section which concentrates on the visit to Egypt in 1988. It registers socio-cultural change which has occurred in Egypt in recent years under the spell of the Western influence. People in villages are no longer ignorant about the city glamour. It is partly due to the Iraq-Iran war. In 1988, the people have refrigerators, washing machines, television sets, Toyota pick-up trucks, food processors, calculators, exotic pens and watches. It is no "surprise that Cairo absorbs outsiders." But ignorance, fanaticism, and superstition still prevailed. One example of modernity in Egypt is evident in the Imam. Recognizing that the Imam is a representative of 'Tradition,' Ghosh wishes to interview him about his role as a healer, but he is confounded to find that the Imam has totally lost faith in his profession which he now regards as the past. Instead, he shows him a glistering new biscuit tin: Half a dozen phials and a hypodermic syringe lay inside the box, nestling in a bed of' soiled cotton wool.... That is what he had been learning...the art of mixing and giving injections. There was a huge market for injections in the village; everybody wanted one. When the Imam realises that the fieldworker wants to ask about traditional medicine, he avoids the subject because the influence of the West has made it shameful: I knew then that he would never talk to me about the remedies he had learned from his father; not merely because he was suspicious of me and my motives, but also because those medicines were as discredited in his own eyes as they were in everyone else's.

In the narration, he is a bitter critic. He relates how an English academic came to Cairo to plunder a cache of ancient documents and who, in his letters home, complained of all the *baksheesh* he was obliged to pay to the natives.

He also exhibits his talent in his character descriptions. About Abu Ali he writes: "I first began to dream of Cairo in the evenings, as I sat in my room, listening, while Abu Ali berated his wife or shouted at some unfortunate custom who had happened to incur his displeasure while making purchases at his shop" (11).

Ali's voice always prevailed despite Ghosh's turning up the volume of his transistor radio. "...but Abu Ali's voice always prevailed despite the thick mud walls of his house and the squawking of the ducks and geese who lived around my room" (11).

"Nobody in Lataifa liked Abu Ali; neither his relatives, nor his neighbours nor anyone else in the hamlet—not even possibly, his wife and children. Some actively hated him; others merely tried to keep out of his way. It was hard to do otherwise; he was profoundly unlovable" (11).

"Still, dislike him as they might, Abu Ali's neighbours and kinsmen also held him in fear. The children of the hamlet were always careful to be discreet when they mimicked him: they would look up and down the lanes to make sure that neither he nor his burly eldest son, Ali were in sight, and then, screwing up their faces in imitation of the scowl, making imaginary sunglasses out of their fingers and thumbs, they would arch their backs and stagger down the lane, laboring under the weight of gigantic bellies" (11).

Further describing Ali's size, Ghosh writes humorously: "... once he had eaten lunch, he would roll on his back and doze, his eyes half-shut, like an engorged python stealing a rest after its monthly meal" (12). "For years he had eaten meat like other people ate beans, and eventually he had swollen up like one of the force fed geese his wife reared on their roof" (13).

From one of the elders of the hamlet Sheik Musa, Ghosh comes to know that Ali's has inherited his extraordinary size, right from his boyhood. "He had never been able to work in the fields because he had hurt his leg as a child, and had soon grown much heavier than others of his age" (12). At college in Damanhour as a son of an unlettered peasant, he had cultivated contact with students from influential families, and with bureaucrats and officials in Damanhour. The contacts had helped Ali "to set up a government-subsidized shop for retaining essential commodities at controlled prices" (12). This permit has helped Ali prosper in the village and it was the only shop of its kind in the village.

There are other people in the village that include Sheik Musa's son Ahmed, an earnest young man; cousin's son Jabir, "a boy in his late teens, with bright, malicious eyes and a tongue that bristled with bars" (13); his second son Hasan, serving his draft in the army. Unlike Ahmed, Hasan had not had education. He was taken out of a school at a fairly early age. Sheik Musa had brought him up as a *fellals*, so that at least one of his sons would profit from the land their ancestors had left them (27). Musa had special attachment to him. He often spoke about him before Ghosh. He had once shown a picture of Hasan. In the picture Hasan was "strikingly good-looking young man with a broad, strong face and clear-cut features" (27).

Ustaz Moustafa, Jabir's uncle, who studied Law at the University of Alexandria. He had spent several years in Alexandria as a student, specialized in civil and religious law and now practiced in a court in Damanhour.

The conversation between Ghosh and the people also becomes intimate, personal and special, the latter want to know more about India. Look at the following annoying conversation between Ustaz Mustafa and Ghosh:

> "I have read all about India" said Ustaz Mustafa, smiling serenely. "There is a lot of chilli in the food and when a man dies his wife is dragged away and burnt alive."
>
> "Not always," I protested, "my grandmother for example..."

> Jabir was drinking this in, wide-eyed.
> "And of course," Ustaz Mustafa continued, "you have Indira Gandhi, and her son Sanjay Gandhi, who used to sterilize the Muslims..."
> "No, no, he sterilized everyone," I said (30)
> Ghosh brings out the ignorance as well as false opinions and impression that people of Egypt had.
> "Tell me, are you Muslim?"
> "No," I said....
> "So then what are you?"
> "I was born a Hindu", I said reluctantly for if I had a religious identity at all it was largely by default.
> But the moment passed and in a troubled voice Ustaz Mustafa said: "What is this 'Hinduki' thing? I have heard of it before and I don't understand it. If it is not Christianity nor Judaism nor, Islam what can it be? Who are its prophets?"
> "It's not like that," I said, "there aren't any prophets..."
> "So you are like the Magi?" he said, bright-eyed. "You worship fire then?"
> I shook my head vaguely, but before I could answer, he tapped my arm with his fore finger. "No", he said, smiling coquettishly. "I know—its cows you worship—isn't that so?"

I cleared my throat; I knew a lot depended on my answers. "It's not like that," I said. "In my country some people don't eat beef because...because cows give milk and plough the fields and so on, and so they are useful."

Ustaz Mustafa was not to be bought off by this spurious ecological argument. "That can't be the reason", he began, but, then his eyes fell on his watch and a shadow of alarm descended on his face. He edged forward until he was balanced precariously on the rim of the bed.

"You still haven't told me about this 'Hinduki' business," he said. "What is your God like?"

I tried to stutter out an answer of some kind, but fortunately for me Ustaz Mustafa wasn't really paying attention to me anymore.

"Well thanks be to Allah!" he said quickly, eying his watch. "Now that you are here among us you can understand and learn about Islam, and then you can make up your mind whether you want to stay within that religion of yours" (32).

Questions such as "'tell me, are you a communist?'... 'All right then,' he said, 'if you are not a communist tell me this: who made the world, and who were the first man and woman if not Adam and Hawa?'" (34).

When Ghosh begins to protest and realizes that Ustaz Mustafa was no longer interested in the former's answers, the latter says, "Tomorrow I will take you with me to the graveyard, and you can watch me reciting the Quran over my father's grave. You will see then how much better Islam is than this 'Hinduki' of yours".

The funniest part of the narrative is that he is constantly pestered with questions. When Ghosh goes to a young teacher Ustaz Sabri's house in Nashawy where the latter is surrounded by half a dozen visitors, the former encounters an impatient small, wizened, prematurely aged man, Zaghloul, a self-taught weaver asks silly annoying question, "And in his country do they have ghosts like we do?" (107). In the presence of Shaik Musa and Khamees, Ghosh encounters similar annoying questions with Zaghloul: "The people in your country—do they have a Holy Book, like we do?", "...is it true what they say? That you are a Magusi, a Magian, and that in your country everybody worships cows?" (137), someone else in the group hurls a question: "In your country do you have military service, like we do in Egypt?" (137), another woman Busaina, married to a man from Nakhlatan, not far from Lataifa, later parted with her husband and returned to her father's house interrupts with a cry of despair, "Tell us, ya doctor: in your country do you at least have crops and fields and canals like we do?" (138), again she demands with amazement, "do you have night and day like we do?" (138), and finally she says with an earnest frown, "Stay here and become a Muslim and marry a girl from the village" (139). Zaghloul however bursts out, "But tell me, ya doctor, where is this country of yours? Can you go there in a day, like the people who go to Iraq and the Gulf?" (139).

Ghosh also records Egyptian culture in his description. Writing about their food, he says, 'once at a meal, set out on the tray was a very good one: arranged around a large pile of rice were dishes of fried potatoes, cheese presented in brine, salads of chopped tomatoes and fresh dill, plates of cooked vegetables, large discs of corn-meal bread, and bowls of young Nile perch baked with tomatoes and garlic' (28). The description is enticing and about the taste, he writes: "Everything was fresh and full of flavor, touched with that unnameable quality which makes anything grown in the soil of Egypt taste richer, more distinctively of itself, than it does anywhere else" (28). Another interesting feature of the time Ghosh spends in the Egyptian village is when he returns seven years later and sees the changes. The kids who used to pester him now have grown up, and many are working in Iraq to send money back home.

In an Antique Land, recounts both Ghosh's research and his experiences while living in a small Egyptian village. His descriptions of his adjustment to the rural Egyptian way of life, and the curiosity with which his neighbours viewed him, form a large portion of the work. His anthropological comparisons are interesting, well-researched, and thought provoking. His descriptions of his social interactions with the Egyptian villagers are known for their insight and wit. This shows that he has strong affinity for the people and places he writes about and has argued that his empathy adds a warm, almost protective personality of his work. Copious notes appended testify Ghosh's sincere and serious commitment to research. This again proves that Ghosh's travel writing cannot be sipped like a cup of tea, distinct from other forms of travel writing.

Works Cited

Balachandran, R. *The Cambridge Companion to Travel Writing*. Delhi: CUP. 2002. Print.

Bhattacharji, Shobana. "Indian Travel Writing", *The Routledge Companion to Travel Writing*. Ed. Carl Thompson. London & New York: Routledge Taylor & Francis Group, 2016. Print.

Dhawan, R.K. "Introduction," *The Novels of Amitav Ghosh*. ed. R.K. Dhawan. New Delhi: Prestige Books, 1999. Print.

Ghosh, Amitav. *In an Antique Land*. Ravi Dayal Publisher, Penguin, 2008. Print.

Ghosh, Amitav. *Dancing in Cambodia and Other Essays*. Ravi Dayal Publisher, Penguin, 2008. Print.

Smith, Tim Mackintosh. *Travel with Tangerine: A Journey in the Footnotes of Ibn Battutah*. London: John Murray, 2001; reprinted London: Picador, 2002. Print.